Simulation Theory

Theory of Mind (ToM) is the term used for our ability to predict and explain the behaviour of ourselves and others. Accounts of this theory have so far fallen into two competing types: Simulation Theory and 'Theory Theory'. In contrast with Theory Theory, Simulation Theory argues that we predict behaviour not by employing a model of people, but by replicating others' thoughts and feelings. This book presents a novel defence of Simulation Theory, reviewing the major challenges against it and positing the theory as the most effective method for exploring how we know each other and ourselves.

Drawing on key research in the field, chapters reopen the debates surrounding Theory of Mind and cover a variety of topics including schizophrenia with implications for experimental social psychology. In the past, one of the greatest criticisms against Simulation Theory is that it cannot explain systematic error in Theory of Mind. This book explores the rapidly developing heuristics and biases programme, pioneered by Kahneman and Tversky, to suggest that a novel bias mismatch defence available to Simulation Theory explains these systematic errors.

Simulation Theory: A psychological and philosophical consideration will appeal to a range of researchers and academics, including psychologists from the fields of cognitive, social and developmental psychology, as well as philosophers, psychotherapists and practitioners looking for further research on Theory of Mind. The book will also be of relevance to those interested in autism, since it offers a new approach to Theory of Mind which explains central symptoms in autistic subjects.

Tim Short is currently studying for his second PhD in Simulation Theory at University College London, UK. His first PhD was in particle physics, focusing on Monte Carlo simulation and computerised modelling of physics and electronics.

Explorations in Cognitive Psychology series

Perception Beyond Gestalt
Progress in vision research
Edited by Adam Geremek, Mark Greenlee and Svein Magnussen

Fine Art and Perceptual Neuroscience
Field of vision and the painted grid
Paul M.W. Hackett

Simulation Theory
A psychological and philosophical consideration
Tim Short

Simulation Theory

A psychological and philosophical consideration

Tim Short

Routledge
Taylor & Francis Group
LONDON AND NEW YORK

First published 2015
by Psychology Press

Published 2016 by Routledge
2 Park Square, Milton Park, Abingdon, Oxfordshire OX14 4RN
711 Third Avenue, New York, NY 10017

First issued in paperback 2016

Routledge is an imprint of the Taylor and Francis Group, an informa business

British Library Cataloguing in Publication Data
A catalogue record for this book is available from the British Library

Library of Congress Cataloging in Publication Data
1. Cognitive psychology—Mathematical models. 2. Human behavior —Mathematical models. 3. Philosophy of mind. I. Title.
BF201.S56 2015
128'.2—dc23 2014032193

ISBN 13: 978-1-138-29434-9 (pbk)
ISBN 13: 978-1-138-81605-3 (hbk)

Typeset in Galliard
by RefineCatch Limited, Bungay, Suffolk

Contents

Figures

Tables

Acknowledgements

Thanks to Ian Phillips, Lucy O'Brien, Maarten Steenhagen, Mark Lancaster, Kevin Riggs and Kathrine Cuccuru. It will be apparent to all readers that although I have never met Rebecca Saxe, I am very much in her debt. I am also grateful to Jane Madeley, Clare Ashworth and Emily Bedford at Routledge for a smooth and helpful commissioning and production process.

1 Introduction

We seem to understand one another. How do we do it? When does it go wrong? These are the two questions I will explore in this book. Humans seem to be able to predict one another's behaviour and explain it. Indeed, we spend much of our time happily engaged in these activities. The label for this way in which we predict and explain each other is 'Theory of Mind'. This term is perhaps slightly unfortunate; as Dennett (2007, p. 396) comments, it conjures up too much 'theorem-deriving' and 'proposition-testing'. I will be arguing in this book for less theoretical and more imaginative answers to the questions as to how we know each other and ourselves. I will be arguing for an account whereby we understand others by putting ourselves in their shoes.

The term Theory of Mind (ToM) is generally agreed to originate in the seminal paper by Premack and Woodruff (1978) which asked 'Does the chimpanzee have a theory of mind?'. The question there was whether the chimpanzee has the ability to predict or explain the actions of others on the basis of beliefs or perhaps quasi-beliefs about the mental states of those others. It was taken as read that humans have those abilities: we can in fact so predict and explain. Humans do have, then, a Theory of Mind, or at least Theory of Mind abilities. We know each other because of it, or we think we do.

Theory of Mind abilities have also been known as 'mind reading' or 'mentalising', because on some views, we predict behaviour by first ascribing mental states such as beliefs and desires to others and then working out what people with those beliefs and desires would do. Accounts of Theory of Mind that explain how we predict each other's behaviour have fallen into two competing types: Simulation Theory (ST) and Theory Theory (TT). This book will defend Simulation Theory of Mind against Theory Theory of Mind. These terms are often shortened to 'Simulation Theory' and 'Theory Theory'. Something should be said at the outset about these terms, since at least the latter one looks somewhat odd.

The oddity of the term 'Theory Theory' derives from its repeating the word 'theory'. This is intended to drive home the two domains of theory involved. First there is the theory in Theory of Mind which is just the label for whatever mechanism I use to predict your behaviour from the theoretical knowledge that you have a mind which, presumably, means you have beliefs and desires as well.

The second usage of the word 'theory' serves to underline that on the Theory Theory view, how I predict your behaviour – how I can use my Theory of Mind – is that I employ a theory to do so. The contrast is with Simulation Theory, which says that I predict your behaviour not by employing a theory of people, but by simulating you. My Theory of Mind on the simulationist account would be more like 'that's what I would do if that were me' and less like 'as a rule, people in situation X do action Y'. It would be more human and less scientific in construction.

The theory or simulation providing our Theory of Mind should not imply flawless performance. We need to explain the observed performance of Theory of Mind, which varies from good under some circumstances to poor under others. For example, I believe that if I see you going into a coffee shop, I have a good picture of some of your desires and beliefs: viz. you desire coffee and you believe that you will be able to get some in the coffee shop. So I can explain your behaviour when you go in. On the other hand, you may well be involved in more complex scenarios that defy my Theory of Mind abilities. I may be mistaken about your reason for going into the coffee shop; perhaps you do not desire coffee but you believe you will meet a friend. Indeed, there are many errors in Theory of Mind, and it is consideration of these errors that will form a major part of this book. That is because there is a serious challenge from Saxe (2005a) as to how one explains the systematic nature of these errors. She says that the inability of Simulation Theory to explain the systematic errors combined with the ease with which Theory Theory can explain the errors is a major reason to prefer the latter over the former. I agree with her that this is a serious challenge, but I disagree that Simulation Theory cannot explain the systematic errors. I will argue that not only can Simulation Theory explain the systematic nature of these errors, but it can do so better than Theory Theory, because it is more parsimonious and more plausibly ascribed to children who have a serviceable Theory of Mind by the age of five at the latest, among other reasons. Moreover, Simulation Theory alone is clearly more parsimonious than the current consensus position which is a poorly specified hybrid of simulation and theory.

Theory of Mind is part of 'folk psychology'. This is distinct to scientific psychology, which is the sort of activity conducted in university research laboratories. Both sorts of knowledge aim at understanding people, but the first one is conducted by everyone more-or-less all the time, while the second one is a specialised academic discipline. I will be aiming in this book to make a contribution to the second by providing a new approach to the first. Or more precisely, to provide a previous approach to understanding the first, Simulation Theory, with the resources to defeat its most serious challenge.

The motivation for this book derives from the importance of responding to the systematic error challenge from Saxe (2005a). Although for the sake of specificity, I will generally use Saxe's position as the one which I oppose, her view is a mainstream one which is widely defended. For example, Apperly (2008, p. 268) writes, 'many authors now argue for a hybrid account in which both Simulation and Theory play a role'. Saxe is within the mainstream as a hybrid theorist who sees roles for both simulation and theory in Theory of Mind. It is this entire mainstream consensus that I challenge.

The central argument for this consensus, as Saxe (2005a, p. 175) notes, is that there is 'occasional systematic error' in ToM. The sort of case she means may be exemplified by the notorious Milgram (1963) experiments in which subjects believed that they were giving severe electric shocks to others. The Theory of Mind error is that no-one predicts that the subjects will give the shocks. The errors are also systematic in that they seem to occur repeatedly: every time someone makes a prediction about how people will behave in the Milgram (1963) experiments, that prediction will be wrong. I will not dispute that these errors occur, nor that they are systematic in nature. I will instead seek to provide additional resources to Simulation Theory in a parsimonious fashion to allow it to explain the systematic nature of the errors.

Saxe holds that the systematic nature of these errors is easily explained on Theory Theory and not at all explicable on a Simulation Theory basis. She is joined here by a large number of writers including Apperly (2008, p. 268) again, who goes on to observe that 'cases where people make systematic errors . . . are seen by many as good evidence' for Theory Theory. He gives only two citations in support of this claim, of which Saxe (2005a) is one. So responding to this charge that Simulation Theory cannot explain systematic error is of the first importance. However, as far as I can see, there has been no significant response at all to this challenge from the Simulation Theory side, although Saxe (2005a) is comprehensive, clear and widely cited. This lack of a response to Saxe (2005a) has driven the consensus in favour of hybrid views of Theory of Mind involving both simulation and theory. The absence of a comprehensive response from the Simulation Theory side lets the Theory Theory side win by default. In this book, I will supply this lack.

My main response is going to be that cognitive biases, to which we are all subject, explain the systematic errors. As an example of a cognitive bias, I mean such effects as confirmation bias. This is the tendency we all have to seek only information confirming what we already believe. Often, the application of these biases is caused by emotional reasons. For example, we all want to believe positive things about ourselves, and sometimes we do that by ignoring evidence to the contrary. If the person doing the simulation has different emotional responses to the person being simulated, they may well not apply the same biases. For instance, someone else might be emotionally involved in maintaining their own positive self-image, but I might not be. If that emotional involvement leads them to apply any cognitive biases, that bias may not feature in my simulation. Thus my simulation will exhibit systematic error. The major thrust of this book will consist of using this approach to explain a wide array of experimental data to which Saxe appeals to back her hybrid or Theory Theory-heavy consensus view. I term this defence the Bias Mismatch Defence because it relies on the simulator and the person being simulated applying different biases to explain the errors in theory of mind and their systematic nature.

The experimental data in question falls into four categories; all of it relates to systematic error in Theory of Mind. The first two categories are mirror images of each other. In the first one, exemplified by the Milgram (1963) experiment, our Theory of Mind is systematically too 'rosy': we are too optimistic in our predictions about how people will behave. We expect them to be guided more by rationality or perhaps morality than they really are. The opposite second category involves our Theory of Mind being systematically too cynical. We are more pessimistic about the behaviour of others, and systematically so. For example, we seem to expect people to take much more credit for positive outcomes than they are really entitled to, while in reality they only do that to some extent. The third category involves the charge of 'suspicious congruency'. Saxe (2005a) claims that if people have incorrect views about how minds work, and their predictions of the behaviour of others are wrong in ways that reflect those incorrect views, this must mean that Theory Theory is correct. For example, scientific psychology includes cognitive dissonance theory, while folk psychology does not. Since cognitive dissonance theory seems to be true in that it makes correct predictions of some behaviour, then folk psychology will make systematic errors when people attempt to predict behaviour in situations where cognitive dissonance is a factor. Finally there is a category of developmental data: it relates to a systematic failure in prediction by children around the age of five. It appears that they confuse ignorance and error, so they think that if someone does not know about something, they must be wrong about it.

The arguments for Simulation Theory that rely on the discovery of 'mirror neurones', put forward for example by Gallese and Goldman (1998), lie outside the scope of this book. While convincing, the results are heavily disputed by Theory Theorists. I suspect that a full consideration of the current state of this evidence and the surrounding arguments could only be adequately done in a separate book-length treatment.[1]

I will proceed as follows. In Chapter 2 I discuss some key motivations for considering Simulation Theory: parsimony and simplicity. It is better on both counts to postulate that we use our own minds to simulate the minds of others; by contrast the Theory Theory postulates an array of theoretical machinery which children develop. I will give descriptions of the two main types of each of Simulation Theory and Theory Theory. I will give a list of objections to Theory Theory. I will show how the logical geography of Simulation Theory delineates the array of possible sorts of Simulation Theory. This brings out a major risk: the collapse of Simulation Theory back into Theory Theory. Such collapse would mean that it is not a separate defensible position. Ways of avoiding such collapse are outlined.

In Chapter 3 I outline the unanswered problem for Simulation Theory: the 'argument from error'. Saxe (2005a) argues that Simulation Theory cannot account for systematic errors in Theory of Mind in certain circumstances, because if we use our minds to simulate other minds, we should be accurate. This chapter gives Saxe her best case in four of the areas she considers: occasions when our Theory of Mind is too cynical, others when it is too rosy, circumstances when there is a 'suspicious congruency' between how we think minds work and the errors we make and finally some developmental data related to the False Belief Task.

In Chapter 4 I note that the consensus nowadays is for a hybrid position, which holds that both simulation and theory play a part in our Theory of Mind. There are two sets of problems for this view. One set relates to problems with pure Theory Theory, including its lack of parsimony, the need to solve the frame problem and the way all children seem to develop the same Theory of Mind. The second set of problems derives from the hybrid nature of the consensus, which means an account of interaction between theory and simulation is required. Will they answer separate questions, or somehow work together?

In Chapter 5 the question as to why we need a new defence is answered by agreeing with Saxe that the existing defences do not work. The Bias Mismatch Defence is introduced: simulation does not model bias is the central idea. A list of biases that will be employed, for example Confirmation Bias, is given and each is outlined. The reasons why biases may not be simulated are given. There are two main ways: Affect mismatch and system mismatch. In the first, the emotional impact on the target is not fully felt by the simulator. In the second, they use different reasoning systems.

Chapter 6 covers an array of 'too rosy' evidence introduced by Saxe (2005a), which arises in situations where we are systematically over-optimistic in our predictions of the rationality or morality of ourselves and others. For example, no-one predicts the way participants in the Milgram experiment are prepared to give out severe electric shocks to strangers for minor infractions. These data are explained by appealing to Conformity Bias, the tendency to do what one is told. A set of 12 experiments Saxe cites in support of her challenge is described and explained using the Bias Mismatch Defence in similar fashion to above.

In Chapter 7 I turn to the opposing sort of data introduced by Saxe (2005a); it covers occasions when we are systematically too cynical in our Theory of Mind. For example, persons on different sides of vexed political questions often form very harsh evaluations of their opponents. They see their opponents as biased and unwilling to examine the evidence or assess it impartially. This is explained using the Bias Mismatch Defence with the bias in question being Confirmation Bias. People might be more sympathetic to their opponents if they realised that we all fall victim to it. Nine further experiments are similarly explained.

In Chapter 8 a third variant of Saxe's challenge is introduced: that of 'suspicious congruency' between false beliefs that people have about how minds work and errors they make in their Theory of Mind predictions. This could only happen on Saxe's view if the false beliefs are employed in their Theory of Mind, which means it must be a theory and not a simulation. This is denied. Also, the problem of introspectionism is considered. We believe we have privileged access to our own minds. Theory Theory denies this, implausibly, while Simulation Theory need not. Further data are described where the Bias Mismatch Defence can be employed.

In Chapter 9 the fourth and final variant of Saxe's challenge is discussed. She employs data from the False Belief Task which appears to show that children use the false axiom that 'ignorance means you get it wrong'. For example, they ascribe a false belief when they should ascribe no belief. I explain how this could happen systematically without requiring a Theory Theory view. The explanation relies on a removal of inhibition view, in which removal is known to be difficult for children. They must first discount some knowledge, and then apply it again. This explains why younger children fail while older ones pass.

In Chapter 10 some speculative remarks on the topic of schizophrenia are offered. It is known that schizophrenic subjects exhibit deficits in Theory if Mind, somewhat like autistic subjects. This is considered from a simulationist perspective. Could the loss of a sense of a unified self, which is common in schizophrenia, play a causal role in the Theory of Mind deficits? Or could schizophrenic subjects exhibit impaired Theory of Mind because of their own disturbed emotional states? These explanations appear interesting and are unavailable to Theory Theory, which also cannot explain paired deficits in producing and recognising an emotion. I will close by offering brief Conclusions in Chapter 11.

I will throughout adopt abbreviations and terminology common in the literature. Theory of Mind becomes ToM. I will generally use the abbreviations ST and TT in common with Harris (1992, p. 120), who writes that the debate is 'between advocates of the simulation theory (ST) and the theory-theory (TT)'. I will adjust citations where necessary to reflect this usage. I will also follow Harris (1992, p. 121) when he suggests that we 'suppose that a simulation allows the subject (S) to identify the particular emotion, desire or belief that another person (O) currently entertains'. What this means is that a person, the subject or S, is using ToM to predict the behaviour of a person, the object of ToM or O. S and O could also be Self and Other, but note that O could really be another person, or equally S at a different time or in a counterfactual situation. The idea is that we also use ToM to predict what we ourselves might do in the future, for example. Often in the literature, authors will refer to the simulator and the simulatee; the subject and the object; the person who is simulating and the target of the simulation; a person considering what they themselves might believe and desire at different times or under counterfactual circumstances. As said, I will for the benefit of clarity replace all of these terms with the use of S and O.

Note

1 Mitchell, Currie, and Ziegler (2009b) survey the mirror neurone evidence for Simulation Theory.

2 Simulation theory

Overview

Introduction

The question as to whether simulation or theory form the basis of our ToM abilities remains open and important. As Nagel (2011, p. 14) writes, there is a 'lively current debate over whether our natural 'mind reading' abilities are better understood in terms of simulation or theorising'. I will begin consideration of that debate in this chapter by analysing the competing theories. As Apperly (2008, p. 268) notes, '(ST) accounts were developed as a sceptical response to the claim that TT explains all instances of ToM reasoning'. So, since ST has developed in opposition to TT, we can understand ST by considering TT. I will therefore examine both in this chapter.

There are several variants of each of TT and ST. Keeping all of the variants clear and separate is important, since there is a 'collapse risk' between the various theories. By this term is meant the possibility that one of two apparently separate theories entail elements of another, so that anyone espousing one is committed to the other even if they do not wish to be. For my project in this book, collapse risk between TT and ST would be a serious problem, while collapse risk between different sorts of ST would not be serious. The reason for this is that I am seeking to defend ST against TT, and that project would be complicated if ST and TT were found to be linked in this problematic way. There would not be a separate position to defend. On the other hand, if there turned out to be a real collapse risk between two variants of ST, it would still leave some variants of ST as viable and separate from TT, which is all that is required by a defence of ST.

I will proceed as follows in this chapter. I will first complete these introductory remarks by sketching some initial motivation for considering ST. After that, in the following four sections, I will examine the two most important variants of each of our two competing theoretical and simulational accounts of ToM. Then, I will consider the scientific variant of TT, under which our ToM is theoretically based and the theory used is akin to a scientific theory. This account is the mainstream one in psychology and is the one favoured by Saxe (2005a). At points in the past, it has been called just 'theory-theory', but I will not use that term to avoid confusion, since we now have more than one theoretical account of ToM. Then, I will examine the innate variant of TT, which also claims that our ToM is theoretically based, but denies that the theory is like a scientific theory. On this modular account, which is also known as ToMM, humans are born with the theory that underlies their ToM. Turning to the simulationist views, I will in the subsequent two sections outline the two major variants of ST. Perhaps the major difference between them is whether when S simulates, S becomes like O or rather 'becomes' O. On the first 'replication' variant, what happens is that S examines the situation of O, places himself in that situation, introspects his own consequential mental states, ascribes them to O and then predicts what O will do, if O has those mental states. I will then discuss the rival 'transformation' account: S simply places himself in imagination in O's situation and 'acts' accordingly, with the exception that the acts are to be ascribed to O rather than actually implemented. The transformation account denies that humans have introspective access to their own mental states.

This division into two of the simulationist accounts will involve three claims, which are either asserted or denied by the two rival theories. This suggests further possible simulationist accounts, all of which are of interest and some of which have received support in the literature. I will sketch below what these accounts look like, but will not select a champion. As said, all that is needed for the project of this book is that at least one variant of ST is plausible and distinct from TT; it will remain for further work to decide between them. I will provide some real-life examples of how simulation works; this task will also indicate further potential types of ST. At this point, we will have arrived at a good picture of the various competing accounts of ToM, and so we can turn to the collapse risk between ST and TT. I will cover this in the final section of this chapter. Proponents of TT have laid charges at the door of ST which I will aim to refute. These are of the sort that if simulation employs any theoretical concepts, such as beliefs or desires, then it is really TT. I think this is unreasonable, because no account of our mental lives can get far without beliefs and desires. I call making this charge 'setting the bar too low', because it is too easy for TT proponents to insist that part of ToM is theoretical if the use of beliefs and desires in ToM is enough to be theory use. If that is indeed theory use, then it is not such in any interesting fashion.[1] I will likewise accord little weight to claims of the type that all simulation is theoretical, because using it involves applying the theory that 'simulation works' or 'S is like O'.

Why consider ST?

I will introduce some main motivating factors here; this topic will be covered in more detail in Chapter 4.

The central claim of ST, as set out by Friedman and Petrashek (2009, p. 115), is that 'reasoning about mental states often requires attempting to make one's cognitive system mimic or replicate (simulate) another person's thoughts and feelings'. The motivation for pursuing the ST approach, as Stone and Davies put it, is the fact that 'when we try to understand other people, we are trying to understand objects of the same kind as ourselves' (Carruthers and

Smith 1996, p. 127). So why not assume that we use our access to our own mind to understand other minds? We do not need to introduce extra machinery here. By contrast, Saxe (2005a, p. 174) sets out the opposing TT position as the contention that 'when asked to predict or explain an inference, decision or action, children and adults do not simulate the other person's beliefs in their own mind, but instead deploy an intuitive theory of how the mind works'. An important motivation for ST then is one of parsimony or explanatory power with minimal working parts. We can explain ToM by postulating that we exploit the fact that we all have similar minds so we need not introduce the additional theoretical machinery to explain ToM.

A second advantage for ST over TT derives from the fact that we are trying to explain ToM, which is quite advanced in five-year-old children. The claim that children have developed scientifically a more or less complete body of psychological knowledge by the age of five is already difficult to accept. That difficulty is increased if Onishi and Baillargeon (2005) are correct when they report that 15-month-old infants have sufficient ToM to appear to be surprised by behaviour that is not consonant with false beliefs of others. The implausibility of this scientific approach, with children or infants selecting, confirming and disconfirming hypotheses, was one motivation for TT adherents to propose the alternative innate TT account, but there are problems with that as well, as I will outline below.

ST has received significant empirical support. For example, one study looked at children with SLI – Specific Language Impairment. Farrant, Fletcher, and Maybery (2006, p. 1842) investigated Visual Perspective Taking or VPT, which refers to such tasks for S as stating whether O can see something from O's position, irrespective of whether S can. They note that Harris's version of ST 'predicts that the development of VPT will be delayed' in subjects with SLI. Farrant, Fletcher, and Maybery (2006, p. 1844) point out that Harris 'argued that language facilitates the development of the ability to simulate another's perspective because conversation involves a constant exchange of differing points of view'. Thus, SLI subjects should exhibit developmental delay on both VPT and ToM tasks. This is what is indeed found: Farrant, Fletcher, and Maybery (2006, p. 1842) report that their 'results supported Harris's theory and a role for language in ToM and VPT development'.[2]

A further empirical argument for ST explains emotional empathy in infants. Gordon (1995) notes an observation that a six-month-old exhibited facial signs of sadness on seeing his nurse pretend to cry. Gordon explains this by suggesting that even from a young age we can experience the same emotion as someone else due to a motor mimicry process. When we observe the facial movements of someone else, this will produce similar motor activity in us. We may not know that fact directly because the motor activity can be sub-threshold, i.e. insufficient to cause actual facial movement. Gordon (1995, p. 729) notes that 'motor activity, especially the movement of facial muscles, can drive the emotions'. We then have a mechanism whereby we can 'catch' the emotions of others even when we could not say what those emotions were, even when we are unaware that we have done so, and even when we are six months old. All of these empirical claims are hard to explain on a TT basis but consistent with ST. It would not be the only scenario in which sub-threshold motor activation is held to explain our understanding of others. On the Motor Theory of Speech Perception,[3] we perceive the speech of others by micro-activation of our own speech production musculature.

Goldman (2006, Chapter 6) discusses several further forms of empirical support for ST, including studies of some subjects who have deficits in both experiencing and recognising certain emotions, suggesting that they have damage in a single area responsible for both.

TT(Scientific)

I have chosen the term TT(Scientific) to refer to the scientific version of TT because the authors tend to use the term 'theory-theory' alone. Using that would be confusing since there now are multiple types of TT. As mentioned above, there are two major variants of TT. The two variants of TT are the 'scientific' view – TT(Scientific) – and the 'innate view' – TT(Innate). Both variants of TT hold that there is a body of theoretical knowledge underpinning the abilities of S to predict and explain the behaviour of O which could be expressed as a set of rules or axioms – even though S himself need not necessarily be able to do that. Similarly, more people can apply the rules of grammar correctly than can state them. On TT(Scientific), the body of knowledge that underlies ToM is learned while on TT(Innate) it is not learned. TT(Scientific) holds that the body of knowledge is akin to scientific knowledge, with children developing by improving the body of knowledge in a quasi-scientific way. They would form and test hypotheses, discarding those disconfirmed by data. The data in question would come from observing the behaviour of other individuals.

Below I set out the claims that define TT(Scientific), as set out by Davies and Stone (1995, p. 4).[4] They begin their discussion by stipulating the definition of the thought T as follows: T = '[O] believes that P'. With that in hand, TT(Scientific) is defined by the following set of claims:

- TTa: In order to predict and explain the behaviour of O, S must be able to entertain thoughts of the form (T)
- TTb: To entertain those thoughts, S must have the concept of belief
- TTc: To have the concept of belief, S must have a body of psychological knowledge
- TTd: Development of folk psychological ability is expansion of this body of knowledge
- TTe: This development may be understood as analogous to 'development . . . of bodies of professional scientific knowledge' (Davies and Stone 1995, p. 4)
- TTf: 'Information processing mechanisms' (Davies and Stone 1995, p. 4) are needed to use the body of knowledge.

A major proponent of TT(Scientific) is Gopnik. Gopnik and Wellman (1992, p. 145) summarise TT(Scientific) well when they write that it is: 'the view that the child's early understanding of mind is an implicit theory analogous to scientific theories, and changes in that understanding may be understood as theory changes'. We have here then the claim that even young children are using a theory that they have developed themselves. Any explanation of ToM must apply to young children because they have ToM capacities by the age of five. It is important that the theory postulated be an implicit one, since there seems to be little phenomenology in either children or adults that is consistent with explicit theory use. That is, it seems rare for anyone to explicitly consider pedestrian sequences of deductions like 'Peter believes the ball is in the yard, Peter desires the ball, I conclude that Peter will go into the yard in order to find the ball'. We also have the explicit claim that theory is analogous to scientific ones, meaning that there is hypothesis selection and confirmation. Gopnik and Wellman (1992) explain development in children's ToM abilities on the basis of changes to the theory: viz., improvements in that theory.

TT(Scientific) also looks analogous to science in what it understands a theory to be. Gopnik and Wellman (1992, p. 146) explain that TT(Scientific) involves theoretical constructs which 'are abstract entities postulated, or recruited from elsewhere, to provide a separate causal-explanatory level of analysis that accounts for evidential phenomena'. The abstract entities involved are the mental states of others. They must be abstract, like viruses or electrons, because they cannot be observed directly. Postulating them though allows ToM users to explain evidential phenomena of the sort generated by the behaviour of others.

The way these theoretical entities should interact with each other and the items to be explained should be 'law-like'. As Gopnik and Wellman (1992, p. 148) put it, theories 'should invoke characteristic explanations phrased in terms of these abstract entities and laws'. This means that there ought to be a law-like relation between a postulated mental state and the behaviour that it always or sometimes results in, because it is behaviour that ToM aims to explain. Like scientific theories, under TT(Scientific), the child's ToM allows 'extensions to new types of evidence and false predictions' (Gopnik and Wellman 1992, p. 148). The extension to new evidence is analogous to the way that Kepler's laws of planetary gravitation predicted moons before they were observed. The reference to 'false predictions' means that an incorrect theoretical law will result in ToM errors; a topic that will loom large in this book.

TT(Scientific) is naturally developmental, in that theories in science and in children may be expected to change as they are confronted with new data. The development of children's ToM is naturally explained on TT(Scientific) as reflecting improvements in the specification of the abstract entities postulated in the theory or calibration of the psychological laws that ToM assumes are true. As an example of the former improvement, Gopnik and Wellman (1992, p. 150) suggest that two-year-olds 'have an early theory that is incorrect in that it does not posit the existence of mental representational states, prototypically beliefs'. There will be stages of development as the child matures. Later on, the child will be working with a mature adult concept of belief.

Theories must have laws or axioms. The starting point for suggesting some folk psychological laws ought to be those that the ordinary person would recognise, since we are seeking to axiomatise folk psychology. Such a type of 'common sense belief/desire psychology' is sketched by Fodor in a form which allows the generation of laws. S relies, he writes, on 'causal generalisations' of the form 'If [O] wants that P, and [O] believes that not P unless Q, and [O] believes that it is within his power to bring it about that Q, then ceteris paribus [O] tries to bring it about that Q' (Fodor 1987, p. 13). Fodor's primary argument for this claim is that it explains the widespread success of ToM abilities. The picture here of how reasons for action lead to action is the 'standard' account due to Davidson (1963) in which a reason for action is a combination of a desire and a belief. The belief is that the action will satisfy the desire. This is generally how ordinary people think actions are caused; so an axiomatisation of Davidsonianism seems to be among the laws of folk psychology.

The power of belief/desire psychology is demonstrated by Fodor by showing how it can correctly track through various complexities and background assumptions in the case of the Shakespearean character Hermia. Hermia sees that her lover Lysander is missing while Lysander's rival Demetrius is present and grim-visaged. Hermia uses the generalisation above with Demetrius as O. P is Demetrius's desire to woo Hermia. Demetrius's belief 'that a live Lysander is an impediment to the success of his (Demetrius's) wooing' (Fodor 1987, p. 2) gives Hermia Q to the effect that Demetrius has killed Lysander. The generalisation is indeed powerful here because it explains all of Hermia's mental states together with the facts that Lysander is uncharacteristically absent and Demetrius is grim-visaged.

Gopnik (1993b, p. 99) confirms that one of the 'structural characteristics of theories [is] the fact that they involve coherent law-like generalisations'. Gopnik and Wellman (1992, pp. 150–151) propose a couple of such axioms of ToM: 'Given that an agent desires an object, an agent will act to obtain it. Given that an object is within an viewer's line of sight, the viewer will see it'. Another typical statement of the central thrust of TT is given by Apperly (2008, p. 268), who writes that TT accounts: 'propose that theory of mind abilities are constituted by a set of concepts (belief, desire, etc.) and governing principles about how these concepts interact (e.g. people act to satisfy their desires according to their beliefs)'. Other examples are given by Baron-Cohen (1993, p. 30) who writes that four-year-olds 'make clear, theory-like assertions ("If you haven't seen what it is, then you won't know what it is"; or, "If you want an x, and you think what you're getting is an x, then you'll feel happy", etc.)'. It is clear then that the laws or theoretical axioms connecting mental states to behaviour are central to ToM capacities on the TT(Scientific) account.

Saxe's TT account also constructs ToM on the basis of laws or rules. On the topics of folk physics and folk psychology, Saxe (2005a, p. 174) writes: 'In each case, we could construct a theory (or a body of beliefs) about the entities involved, and the rules governing their interactions'. At this point, Saxe (2005a) cites Gopnik and Wellman (1992) so we know that her preferred account of ToM is TT(Scientific).

TT(Innate)

I will use the term TT(Innate) for the non-scientific variant of TT. The term used by many authors promoting such an account of TT is 'ToMM', standing for Theory of Mind Mechanism. The major proponents of TT(Innate), Scholl and Leslie (1999, p. 133), set out TT(Innate) or ToMM as holding that 'the capacity to acquire ToM has a specific innate basis [...and...] the specific innate capacity takes the form of an architectural module'. So the modularity aspect of the proposal is one way of explaining the innate capacity but a TT proponent could presumably be nativist without being modularist. As Scholl and Leslie (1999, p. 134) admit, their 'claim is not that the entirety of ToM is modular, but only that ToM has a specific innate basis'. Nichols and Stich (2003, p. 117) set out the distinction between TT(Scientific) and TT(Innate) when they write 'In contrast with scientific-theory theorists, who think that the information used in mindreading is acquired, modified, and stored in much the same way that scientific and commonsense theories are, modularity theorists maintain that crucial parts of the information that guides mindreading is stored in one or more modules'. The idea is that the modularity view of TT(Innate) allows for the body of knowledge employed in ToM to be 'located' in an innate module. One claim of TT(Innate) is that 'certain core concepts used in mindreading, including 'BELIEF, PRETENCE and DESIRE' (Nichols and Stich 2003, p. 125)[5] are contained within the innate module for ToM.

Many elements of TT(Innate) will be shared with TT(Scientific), beyond the obvious one that both postulate theories and bodies of knowledge that underlie ToM capacities. Both accounts will see ToM users postulate abstract theoretical entities – mental states. Both will have ToM espouse the Fodorian belief/desire psychology. Both will allow that ToM includes laws of the type proposed above. Therefore our discussion of TT(Innate) can be more brief than that of TT(Scientific) since there is much common ground.

The differences between TT(Innate) and TT(Scientific) lie most prominently in differences in the description of how the body of theoretical knowledge is obtained. TT(Innate), in contrast to TT(Scientific), holds that the body of knowledge underlying ToM is more like the knowledge that underpins the ability to speak and read a language. This is distinct from scientific knowledge for several reasons including that the development of language knowledge does not seem to proceed via the formation and confirmation of hypotheses. The idea is more along the lines that would be termed Chomskian in theoretical linguistics. The languages themselves are not innate, but the ability to learn them may be. This approach has the advantages in linguistics that it explains the fact that children are able to learn languages but also that the one they learn is the one they hear. Similarly, in the TT(Innate) view, ToM abilities develop quickly not because the abilities themselves are innate, but because the ability to acquire the abilities is innate. This account has the same advantages as the linguistic one in terms of explaining the speed with which children acquire ToM abilities and also that they do so in such a way that their ToM predictions will be similar to those of the adults around them.

Only one of the TT(Scientific) claims set out above needs to be changed to arrive at TT(Innate): TTe. This is the one that encapsulates the 'scientific analogy' nature which is characteristic of TT(Scientific). If we change TTe to read as below, we have arrived at a set of claims outlining TT(Innate).

TTeI: This development may be understood as analogous to development of bodies of linguistic knowledge.

Scholl and Leslie note that the fact that development occurs in ToM capacities has been taken to favour TT(Scientific) over their preferred TT(Innate) account, because modules are taken to be static. They oppose this argument by noting that modules may 'come online' at various times. Scholl and Leslie (1999, p. 132) employ a distinction due to Segal, noting that 'Segal distinguishes between synchronic modules (which reflect a static capacity), and diachronic modules (which attain their character from the environment via parameters, as in the case of "Universal Grammar")'. The reference to Universal Grammar here means that the TT(Innate) picture is Chomskian in that innate capacities to develop capacities are postulated. The capacities that develop are not themselves innate. In Universal Grammar, the capacities that develop are the ability to use languages. In ToM, the capacities that develop are the abilities to predict and explain the behaviour of others.

The parameters are an adaptation of another Chomskian idea. The idea is that while there is a very large number of logically possible languages, only a small subset of them are actually used by people. It is logically possible but in practice extremely unhelpful to have a language in which the words for common items change on a daily basis, or in which the surface grammar were not constant. Actually used languages are more sensibly constructed, and might be so because of the way their parameters are set. For example, in the German language, verbs come at the end of sentences. This location could be set by a parameter: a child that learned German would be one that had switched its 'verb location at end of sentence' parameter to TRUE. Other values of that parameter would be possible, but no useful human language would have a parameter like 'nouns change their referent daily' set to TRUE. Mapping these ideas across to ToM, we might find that TT(Innate) postulates a similar set of parameters which define which of several innate capacities to form capacities become operative.[6] Observation by children of the behaviour of others around them would set the parameters in appropriate ways. They might set their parameter 'people who say X believe X' to TRUE. Or, to employ Segal's example, they might have a switch 'labelled prelief/belief' (Carruthers and Smith 1996, p. 151) with the improvement in the child's ToM reflected by the switch changing its value. This particular improvement is the change from a deficient PRELIEF concept that does not distinguish PRETENCE and BELIEF to a mature concept of BELIEF shared with adults.

This would go some way towards explaining how children quickly generate ToM capacities, and how they tend to make similar ToM predictions as do adults in their culture.

ST(Replication)

The definitional ST claims are set out below; it can be seen that they largely oppose the matching TT claims:

- STa: In order to predict and explain the behaviour of O, S 'does not need to entertain thoughts of the form (T), but only thoughts of the form "I believe that P"' (Davies and Stone 1995, p. 6).
- STb: 'To entertain thoughts of just that first-person form, [S] does not need to have the full-blown concept of belief. In fact, the "I believe that P" could just as well be deleted' (Davies and Stone 1995, p. 6).
- STc: S does not need the concept BELIEF to have beliefs.
- STd: Development of folk psychological ability is a case of 'the child gradually becoming more adept at imaginatively identifying with other people' (Davies and Stone 1995, p. 6).
- STe: This development is a gain in skill not knowledge.
- STf: Information processing mechanisms are needed 'to engage in these imaginative tasks' (Davies and Stone 1995, p. 6).

The central thrust of the ST approach can thus be seen to be anti-theoretical, as would be expected. S does not need the concept BELIEF, but just to be able to believe things. S need not be able to think representational thoughts like 'O believes P' but merely note his beliefs.

STe provides a distinction between ST and TT. Recall that TTe insisted that there is a body of knowledge and increases in the scope and quality of that knowledge is what explains children's improvement in ToM abilities. ST denies that there is a body of knowledge and explains the improvement by appealing to improved skill at 'imaginatively identifying' with other people. Provided that we can maintain a clean distinction between skill and knowledge, it can be seen that STe denies both TTe and TTeI, so that on this view, ST is distinct from TT.

Each ST claim is not the exact negation of the corresponding TT claim, though the ST claims are in each case generally opposed to the corresponding TT one. The way Davies and Stone couch STa and STb is initially perhaps a little confusing. They seem to start in STa by insisting that S needs the concept of belief, because while we can accept that S can have a belief without having the concept BELIEF, that does not entail that S has the meta-ability to form the belief 'I believe that P' even when S does in fact believe that P. To see this distinction, observe that we may be prepared to allow that non-human animals believe that P – although this is controversial – but the ascription of 'I believe that P' to non-human animals is absurd. However, in STb we learn that the concept of belief is not needed by S and in a slightly throwaway fashion, Davies and Stone concede that the 'I believe that P' can be dispensed with. I submit that the two approaches are significantly different and the version without 'I believe that P' is both more plausible and expresses the main idea promulgated by ST proponents viz. mind reading can be performed by those who can form beliefs and no mental state concepts including BELIEF are required.

The major proponent of ST(Replication) is Heal. Replication is set out as follows. Heal (2003, pp. 13–14) asserts that if S wishes to predict the action of O, then S will 'endeavour to . . . replicate or re-create [O's] thinking. [S will] place [himself] in what [S] takes to be [O's] initial state by imagining the world as it would appear from [O's] point of view and [S will] then deliberate, reason and reflect to see what decision emerges'. This gives us success conditions for replication. If the function of a thought in S's simulated and contained Replication is the same as the function played in O's un-simulated and unconfined cognition, then pro tanto, the simulation has been successful.

We can obtain more insight into ST(Replication) by considering Heal's response to three objections that have been raised to it.

The first objection aims to disarm the argument in favour of ST that claims it is less complex and demanding than TT. The objection does this by considering the need of ST for ToM users to perform 'initial state matching'. This means that for replication to be successful, S must be able to do two things: 'know what psychological state [O] is in' from external observation and 'put [himself] in the same state' (Heal 2003, p. 14). If this is difficult, we will struggle to understand how replication could often be successful. Heal's response is to claim that the objection misdescribes the target of replication. S is not examining O but rather the situation around O as seen from O's perspective. As Heal (2003, p. 15) notes, '[i]t is what the world makes [S] think which is the basis for the beliefs [S] attributes to [O]'. The objector cannot here continue to urge that it is difficult for S to contemplate the world around O, because S contemplates the world all the time. Moreover, any common errors that S makes in contemplating the world around O will presumably also be made by O, and thus not impede simulation.

The second objection, ascribed by Heal (2003, p. 15) to Dennett, is that ST(Replication) lacks parsimony. The objection urges that replication must involve special beliefs about beliefs and those require more complex mental machinery than merely having beliefs. This objection is met by noting that nothing is required here for simulation purposes that is not already required in S's own case, to enable S to chart actions now, allowing for the fact that S's own beliefs and desires may change in the future. Heal (2003, p. 16) also argues that '[m]ake-believe belief is imagining', and that we already have the capacity to imagine. Heal (2003, p. 16) agrees that it would be absurd to claim that replication can only be successful if S 'believes what [O] believes', so there must be some way of preventing O's beliefs becoming S's beliefs in a way that causes S to act on the beliefs as opposed to ascribing them to O. This leads to a further distinction known as the on-line vs off-line ST distinction which I will discuss below. If S ascribes a belief to O, that belief must be off-line for S and not cause behaviour of S.

The 'make-believe beliefs' or off-line beliefs approach could also work in another way. We could adopt the view in which beliefs are seen as items in the 'belief box'. First, there could be multiple subscripts in the belief box, to speak metaphorically, which tag various beliefs as those of S or those of O.[7] As long as the beliefs tagged 'O' are kept off-line, we would have a mechanism that performed as needed. Second, there could be a contained simulation environment in which beliefs are as effective as they are outside that environment in fecundating other consonant beliefs, but the outputs of which are translated into contained or simulated desires rather than actual desires. The outputs do not leave the contained simulation environment in the form of action proposals. In either case, the simulated beliefs of O stay off-line and do not directly issue in desires or actions of S, as required. The simulated beliefs of O do have effects in S: they are ascribed to O and used to predict his behaviour.

The third objection holds that ST(Replication) requires theoretical elements and thus collapses back into TT. The objection holds that under ST(Replication) there is in S a sequence of thoughts and mental state transitions that replicate those of O in order to explain O's behaviour. The objection suggests that S can only do this by using some theory of how mental state transitions in O are likely to follow from S's view of what O believes. This would mean that replication was less analogous to becoming like O and more like S applying a theory of O to supply the links in a chain of simulation of O. Such an account would have allowed a theoretical element to corrupt the pure simulationist ST(Replication) account, if the objection is successful. Heal's response involves questioning the nature of the links in a chain of simulation. One does not use a theory to get from 'I see p' to 'p' – it is merely a rational transition. This objection is a version of the 'setting the bar too low' error which I will outline below.

ST(Transformation)

The major proponent of ST(Transformation) is Gordon. Intuitively, the distinction between ST(Transformation) and ST(Replication) is that on the former transformation variant of ST, S simulates O by becoming O, while on the latter replication view of simulation, S simulates O by becoming like O. The first idea is clearly only metaphorical, since no-one can in reality become someone else. Gordon sets out three claims, all of which are asserted by ST(Replication) and denied by ST(Transformation). The three claims are that simulation involves:

1. an analogical inference from oneself to others
2. premised on introspectively based ascriptions of mental states to oneself,
3. requiring prior possession of the mental states ascribed.

(Stone and Davies 1995, p. 53)

ST(Transformation) then is anti-Inferentialist, anti-Introspectionist and to coin a phrase, anti-Possessionist. ST(Replication) is Inferentialist, Introspectionist and Possessionist. By the term Possessionist, I mean views claiming that S must possess a mental state before being able to ascribe it to O. Gordon (1992, p. 32) confirms that on his account, S 'is not using one individual, himself, as a model of [O], and there is no implicit inference of any sort from S to [O]'. Instead, the idea is much more to make action predictions without an intervening ascription of mental states. This is done by 'becoming' the other person, or putting oneself in their position, and seeing what one will do. That of course is again somewhat metaphoric, since one rarely finds out what one is going to do by external observation: one merely acts. As Gordon (1992, pp. 31–32) puts it, '[w]hat is relevant is to ask, within a pretend context in which I simulate being [O], "What shall I do now?" . . . Thus, within the context of the simulation, the realisation that now is the time to ϕ spurs me to action'. Here I employ ϕ to stand in for the action proposed in the simulation context. Under normal non-simulation circumstances, the realisation that 'now is the time to ϕ' will cause S to ϕ. Within the simulation context however, the realisation that 'now is the time to ϕ' will cause S to predict that O will ϕ. Gordon's view does not involve any ascription of mental states to S or to O. As he writes, 'people often predict what another will do in a given situation by imagining being in such a situation and then deciding what to do' (Stone and Davies 1995, p. 53). The idea that the ability to pretend is related to the ability to predict behaviour is supported by many studies of autism. As one example, Baron-Cohen (2001, p. 7) notes the well-known finding that autistic subjects have impaired ToM and also that '[m]any studies have reported a lower frequency of pretend play in the spontaneous play of children with autism'.

On Gordon's ST(Transformation) view, we 'transform ourselves in imagination' whereby we 'modify our regular stock of mental states with a complement of artificially induced pretend states, keeping the resulting adjusted stock of mental states off-line' (Stone and Davies 1995, p. 57). On the ST(Transformation) account, there is no need for an inference from S to O by O because S has become O – or successfully placed himself in O's position – and thus now can decide directly what O is likely to do because it can be read off from what S would do. S now knows what O would do because S is in the same situation, except 'off-line'.

As noted, Gordon's ST(Transformation) view is anti-Introspectionist, while on the alternative ST(Replication) account, the way S predicts the mental states of O is by introspecting S's own mental states within the pretend off-line environment within which the simulation of O takes place. S then would have direct introspective access to the mental states of O, or rather the mental states that S ascribes to O as a result of the simulation. So one potential advantage of ST(Transformation) is that it sidesteps questions about mental states and whether they can be introspected. We act; we do not form a mental state which has action as a consequence. ST can still be true even if Introspectionism is false.[8]

Further possible types of ST

As we have seen, ST(Replication) and ST(Transformation) differ from one another in that they assert or deny all of three claims. Yet other positions are

Table 2.1 Possible variants of ST

Position	*Inferentialist*	*Introspectionist*	*Possessionist*
ST(Replication)	✓	✓	✓
ST(Transformation)	×	×	×
ST(3)	✓	×	×
ST(4)	×	✓	×
ST(5)	×	×	✓
ST(6)	✓	✓	×
ST(7)	✓	×	✓
ST(8)	×	✓	✓

possible, and may also be defined in terms of assertion or denial of those three claims. In other words, since the three claims may be asserted or denied independently from one another, there are other possible positions within the logical space available to ST proponents. Some of these positions may even be interesting. I show in Table 2.1 the possibilities in terms of the three claims (Inferentialist, Introspectionist, Possessionist) listed above. Since we have two options (assert or deny) across three options, there are eight possible positions in this logical space as so far analysed.

One such independent position is outlined by Goldman who examines Gordon's motivations for denying each of the three claims. Goldman (2006, p. 186) notes that Gordon thinks that '[t]he analogical inference element . . . threatens to make ST collapse into TT'. This is the collapse risk already noted, which will be examined further below. Goldman also observes that Gordon wishes to avoid Introspectionism because that doctrine is 'philosophically controversial' (Goldman 2006, p. 186). However, it is unclear, as Goldman (2006, p. 186) points out, why Gordon denies Possessionism, observing that Gordon's 'rationale for denying the concept-possession element is elusive'. So we can see that Goldman's account, ST(5), is a position of interest which is viable, distinct from ST(Replication) and ST(Transformation) and ably defended at length by Goldman.[9]

There are also two possible types of Possessionism. One might insist that S needs to possess the mental state concepts in order to ascribe them to O. One might in addition insist that S needs to possess the mental state concepts in order first to recognise them in S before ascribing them to O. We can see that Gordon denies the latter duplex view when he opposes claims that 'to recognize and ascribe one's own mental states and to mentally transfer these states over to [O], [S] would need to be equipped with the concepts of the various mental states' (Stone and Davies 1995, p. 53). It is worth noting that Gordon discusses Introspectionism and Inferentialism in his canonical statement of his position – 'Simulation Without Introspection Or Inference From Me To You' (Stone and Davies 1995, pp. 53–67) – but says very little about Possessionism, consistent with Goldman's claim that Gordon's reasons for denying Possessionism remain opaque. If we agree that these two types of Possessionism are distinct and that both can be held independently of the eight positions specified in Table 2.1, then we have 16 possible variants of ST.

As said at the outset, I will remain neutral in this book between these many possible variants of ST. While they are interesting, which one of them exactly is the best variant and whether it is certain that they do not collapse into each other is not critical to my project. By contrast, collapse of ST into TT would be serious for my project since there would then not be a separate theory from TT to defend. If it transpires that my claims elsewhere commit me to one or other version of ST so be it; all my project requires is that there be at least one viable variant of ST which is distinct from TT.

On-line vs off-line

Stich and Nichols name the ST account the 'off-line ST', but they also note that for Gordon, the 'off-line picture' is 'only an 'ancillary hypothesis' . . . albeit a very plausible one' (Stone and Davies 1995, p. 91). Heal tells us the off-line hypothesis is widely held by supporters of ST, but not by herself. The 'off-line' claim holds that when S simulates O's decision-making, S does something similar but not identical to what S does when S makes a similar decision on his own behalf. S knows for example, that if S desires coffee, and S is outside a coffee shop with available sufficient resources of time and finance, S may well go in. S can extrapolate from this. If S sees O behave in a particular way – viz. entering the coffee shop – S may by analogy with himself as a model use simulation to decide that O has entered the coffee shop because O desired coffee.

Note that we need to be careful with the use of the verb 'to know' here. If knowing that people who want coffee and are outside a coffee shop may go in and buy coffee constitutes a law or axiom or element of a body of knowledge, then ST may have collapsed back into TT. So we need to think of talk of 'knowing' here as meaning 'able to simulate beliefs and desires such that we can find a combination of the key ones which result in the prediction 'enter the coffee shop'. This does not appear to be much more difficult than the following sequence: 'O wants coffee, O is outside the coffee shop, S(off-line) wants coffee, S(off-line) is outside the coffee shop, S(off-line) action: enter coffee shop, predict: O enters coffee shop.

When S runs the simulation, S does not want to be prompted actually to enter the coffee shop himself. This is what is meant by the simulation or the beliefs simulated being off-line. The behaviour of entering the shop should be prompted only by S's own desire for coffee, unless we begin constructing some more complex story in which perhaps S enters because O has and S wants to talk to O. Thus, S's decision-making system is off-line in that S arranges for it to output a specified behaviour, but not actually to execute that behaviour, because S is interested in simulation and not performing that action at this point. The on-line version of ST then sees S as having his practical reasoning system working on actual occurrent beliefs of S. So the postulation is that the system runs as normal but there is no translation into action of the output.

We would also need a mechanism whereby the beliefs S has for standard reasons – e.g. perceptual input – are not contaminated with beliefs S has merely because S needs to have them because O does and S wants to simulate O. This is especially relevant if S needs to predict O's behaviour based on a belief of O's that S knows is a false belief – we must avoid any account where S is required knowingly to have a false belief because that seems impossible. Where on-line simulation does look plausible would be in the grammar-type question discussed by Harris (1992, p. 124). The task is for S to decide which of a set of sentences O will think are grammatical in the common language of S and O. It is very likely that S decides what O will say by forming true beliefs about the grammaticality of the sentences and ascribing them to O as well. Similarly, to adapt Gordon's example, if S and O both form the belief that a tiger is confronting them, S will have no difficulty deciding to run and predicting that O will do so also. Harris (1992, p. 124) concludes his argument by noting plausibly that the TT proposal to explain this, on which the subject has a first order representation of grammar for his own use and a second order meta-representation of other people's grammar, 'strains both credulity and parsimony'. It is simpler to postulate that S forms on-line beliefs about the grammaticality of the sentences – i.e. S actually has those beliefs – and then ascribes those beliefs to O, together with the corresponding behaviour.

The point where it is critical for the system to be off-line is immediately before behaviour. S must be able to infer what desire it was that caused O to enter the coffee shop – or alternatively predict that O will enter the coffee shop if S knows that O has the desire for coffee – without either circumstance causing S to enter the coffee shop or want to do so, unless we again add extraneous factors such as that now S sees O enjoying all the coffee, S wants one as well. But that leaves open all of the stages where S could inhibit behaviour by applying an off-line status. S could inhibit behaviour by any of the following. First, S might have a pretend belief that does not issue in behaviour because it is not S's actual belief. Second, S might in some subsystem allow for a real belief that S desires coffee to operate, but prevent it from having the usual effects of a belief. S would need to restrain it from exiting the subsystem to the extent that it causes other propositions such as 'S desires fluid' or 'S should enter the coffee shop' to become assertible. Third, S might have a real belief, which has real effects in the inference mechanism or a special contained subset of it, but intervene at the last moment before behaviour with an inhibition of action.

Stich and Nichols (1992, p. 247) suggest that off-line ST is unparsimonious. They assert that under off-line ST, we would need to postulate a control mechanism to 'take that system "off-line", feed it "pretend" inputs and interpret its outputs as predictions'. They claim that this task would be 'very non-trivial' (Stich and Nichols 1992, p. 247) but do not provide any evidence for this claim. We also have an everyday example of the decision-making system being taken at least partially off-line: sleep. As O'Shaughnessy (1991, p. 160 observes: '[t]ypically in sleep either simple bodily act-inclinations or sensation-caused act-inclinations [immediately] generate basic bodily willings; and these primitive transactions make no demand upon belief or concept system'. What this means is that when dreaming, we seem to perceive the external world; these apparent percepts sometimes cause us to wish to move in response, but such desires to move do not result in the usual changes in beliefs. If I dream that I walk into the sea, I nevertheless do not believe that I am wet, at least not in the same way as I do if I actually walk into the sea. Thus we have an example of some control mechanism existing or taking effect in that the decision-making system caused me to 'want to walk into the sea'; this then uses 'I am in the sea' as a 'pretend input' and generates the output 'I am wet' as a prediction for my dreaming self in the dream case. There seems to be no special difficulty about doing the same when awake in respect of another person.

In the same vein, as Heal (1998, p. 89) notes, 'we can reason with representations which we do not believe' because otherwise we could not, for example, 'explain what we are doing in arguing by reductio ad absurdum or reasoning hypothetically'. Reductio ad absurdum means to reason by assuming a proposition that is probably false for the sake of argument, and finding that it has absurd consequences. That is taken as proof that the proposition initially assumed is indeed false. On such occasions, it is indeed the case that we have reasoned using propositions that we do not believe and so there must be some mechanism whereby we can hold such propositions off-line. Thus, nothing extra need be postulated for simulation and ST continues to be a parsimonious and elegant explanation of ToM.

My position on the on-line vs off-line debate will be similar to the one I took on the other different types of ST. What is required for my project in this book to succeed is that one of the options be correct; I do not need at this stage to select a champion. Both options look viable; it is fair to suggest that the off-line version has received more support in the literature.

Avoiding collapse between ST and TT

As mentioned, collapse between simulationist and theoretical accounts would be a problem for my project, because I cannot defend ST against TT if they are not separate. TT proponents have sometimes tried to collapse ST back into TT. In this section, I will argue in three ways that ST and TT are separate. These three ways are as follows. I will first in note some plausible distinctions that have been drawn in the literature between ST and TT. Then, I will argue that TT proponents have often been guilty of 'setting the bar too low' in their claims that ST collapses back into TT. They have done this, I suggest, by regarding the employment in any way of any theoretical items like beliefs as sufficient to render an account of ToM theoretical. Since the main challenge to ST nowadays is the denial that it can handle systematic ToM error rather than that it is not distinct from TT, I will treat the collapse challenge only briefly here. Responding to the systematic error challenge is my main project in this book. We will nevertheless learn more about our two competing theories by seeing how obvious or not it is that they are distinct.[10]

Distinctions between ST and TT

I will here briefly outline some plausible distinctions that have been observed between ST and TT. I will suggest in turn that ST and TT employ different data sources; that the Rylean distinction between knowing-how and knowing that will also divide them; that they predict different answers as to whether folk psychology and scientific psychology are continuous and that they differ in the way they handle some real-life examples. In the latter case, I will also be responding to an objection to ST raised by TT proponents.

Different data and processes

One broad-brush and intuitive but clear way of distinguishing ST and TT is given by Arkway when she discusses Heal's position. Arkway (2000, p. 128) writes that a 'simulator looks not at the subject to be understood but at the world around that subject'. This provides a clear contrast with the process under TT accounts in which S will look at O as well as at O's environment, and where we might expect the bulk of the theory to be about people, albeit perhaps people in situations.

Arkway also sees the importance of the off-line nature of some ST accounts, whereby beliefs held by S for simulation purposes of O must be held in quarantine and not result in decisions or behaviour of S. Arkway (2000, p. 128) notes the view of Stich and Nichols that all accounts which posit the off-line use of the decision-making system count as versions of ST. While ST accounts may be on-line as well, there do not seem to be any off-line TT accounts for the simple reason that none are needed. Theoretical reasoning processes normally culminate in some new theoretical beliefs which may become candidates for motivating behaviour, but will not automatically do so.

Knowing how vs knowing that

Freeman writes: '[TT] is intellectualist in that emphasis is put on the child's own [ToM], a theory through which children are held to filter psychological evidence. [ST] is grounded in a consideration of pre-theoretical practical intelligence plus a competence at imagining' (Stone and Davies 1995, p. 68). There is a clear division here between the activity postulated in ToM use. Children are either filtering evidence through a theory, or using their imagination. These activities are very different.

Also, since the divide here is between 'pre-theoretical' and 'theoretical'; we may see it as closely analogous to the distinction due to Ryle (2009, p. 68ff) between knowing-how and knowing-that. TT would involve theoretical knowledge, which would be knowing-that – the possession of propositional knowledge, expressed in the readiness to affirm propositions. The pre-theoretical knowing-how of ST would not involve any propositional knowledge: children can therefore be deemed to be able to perform simulation successfully without thereby necessarily being able to affirm any propositions.[11]

Continuity of folk and scientific psychology

It has been claimed that folk psychology will be superseded by scientific psychology. This would involve ordinary people learning more psychology over perhaps many decades and eventually abandoning their current inaccurate theories of how people think.

The prevalence of error seen in ToM capacities has implications for the accuracy of folk psychology and scientific psychology and whether there is some form of continuity between the two. Gopnik seeks to distinguish TT views from ST views based on these accuracy and continuity points. She writes that both modular and innate TT views suggest 'folk psychology could be, indeed is likely to be, wrong in important ways' (Carruthers and Smith 1996, p. 180). Also, the 'theory-formation view . . . proposes a deep continuity between folk psychology and scientific psychology' (Carruthers and Smith 1996, p. 181) since the latter is a formalisation of the former. Since, as Gopnik states, her views 'stand in contrast to other accounts, such as simulation theory' (Carruthers and Smith 1996, p. 180) we can see that she claims there are two additional distinctions between TT and ST as set out below:

- TTg: folk psychology is wrong in important ways
- STg: not TTg: it is not the case that folk psychology is wrong in important ways
- TTh: there is a continuity between folk psychology and scientific psychology
- STh: not TTh: it is not the case that there is a continuity between folk psychology and scientific psychology.

Thus, ST and TT make different predictions as to whether folk psychology will eventually be superseded by scientific psychology or not. This already distinguishes them, and will do so more clearly to the extent that data or argument makes it look more or less plausible that scientific psychology is superseding folk psychology.

Theory driven vs process driven

This useful distinction arises from an objection to ST which claims that simulation cannot be done without the surreptitious importation of some theoretical elements. If this is true, then ST requires TT and the distinction collapses. This particular objection is ascribed to Dennett by Davies and Stone, who also ascribe the response to Goldman. Dennett asks how simulation can work 'without being a kind of theorising in the end' since there is no difference in principle between when S 'makes believe [S] has [O's] beliefs' and when '[S] makes believes [S] is a suspension bridge' (Davies and Stone 1995, p. 18). There can be no simulation by humans of what it is like to be a suspension bridge; the only knowledge available of how suspension bridges behave is theoretical. This is true, but S may not need to have O's beliefs in the same way that O does.

Responding to the objection, Goldman appeals to standard belief/desire folk psychology, where if S simulates O as having a desire for coffee and a belief that there is coffee in the cup, S will predict that O will drink from the cup. Employing such a form of belief/desire psychology does not commit a position to either ST or TT. As Strijbos and De Bruin (2013, p. 760) show with copious references, the 'assumption that folk psychology is rooted in belief-desire psychology is taken for granted by almost all participants in the debate' whether those participants favour TT, ST or hybrid views. Goldman outlines a 'process-driven' simulation where S 'simulates a sequence of mental states' of O so that S 'wind[s] up in the same (or isomorphic) final states' as long as S and O had i). the same initial states and ii). 'both sequences are driven by the same cognitive process' (Davies and Stone 1995, p. 18). 'Isomorphism' means that S must pass through similar states as O does in reaching his conclusions if S is to simulate O successfully. S need not make believe S has O's beliefs in order to go through an isomorphic process.

Setting the bar too low

There are many examples in the literature of TT proponents making their task too easy by making almost anything count as use of theory. I will set out some examples below, and then consider some useful remarks by Mitchell, Currie, and Ziegler (2009b).[12]

Daniel (1993, p. 39) writes that 'simply . . . resorting to a simulation presupposes that some theory or other is in place', by which he means that we cannot run a simulation without a theory to explain why the simulation has performed as it has. I deny the force of this objection on the grounds that everything is a theory if it counts as being a theory to say 'my simulation will work' or 'this theory tells me how my simulation works'.

Peterson and Riggs set the bar too low twice when they discuss the False Belief Task. Since this is the first of several mentions in this book of the important False Belief Task, I will outline it here. The canonical example of the False Belief Task is described thus: 'A story character, Maxi, puts chocolate into a cupboard x. In his absence his mother displaces the chocolate from x into cupboard y. Subjects have to indicate the box where Maxi will look for the chocolate when he returns' (Wimmer and Perner 1983, p. 106). The point is that subjects must avoid being 'seduced by reality': younger children tend to be impressed by their own knowledge of where the chocolate is actually located – in cupboard y – and thereby fail to take account of the fact that Maxi was not present when the chocolate was moved and therefore fail to predict that Maxi will have a false belief that the chocolate is still in cupboard x. These errors are known as 'realist errors' in ToM. Roughly, it was found that most normal children under four years old would fail the False Belief Task while most would pass at five.

Returning to Peterson and Riggs, we may note their claim that identifying what Maxi is ignorant of 'requires the theoretical understanding that people can be ignorant of things that we are aware of, and also, that if a person is absent when a change takes place, that person may be unaware of that change' (Mitchell and Riggs 2001, p. 91). However, such understanding need not be theoretical. Consider the following simulation alternative. Imagine that you are in a room without windows. It was sunny when you entered the room, but now it is raining. Do you know that it is raining? You can answer this question in the negative very easily by simulating your position in the room without knowing anything about the change in the weather. In addition, you can know by the same simulation that you will continue to remain ignorant about the rain while in the room even though everyone outside will know about it. This suffices to provide you with both of the points listed above.

Similarly, Perner makes the 'setting the bar too low' error when he argues that the Maxi results favour TT over ST. Perner notes that success on the False Belief Task requires omitting the information that Maxi's mother moves the chocolate while Maxi is out playing when assessing what Maxi knows. This is because 'it is far from clear that the critical [information about the movement of the chocolate] is omitted just because one is imagining to be Maxi'; rather what is needed is 'some theoretical knowledge that events that are not perceived are to be omitted' (Mitchell and Riggs 2001, p. 396). It is clear though. Simulate being Maxi playing in the field. Can you see the kitchen? Can you see the chocolate being moved remotely? No, and so you know that Maxi cannot see the chocolate being moved. Moreover, even if a 'rule' about knowledge of remote events is needed, why can it not fall out of the above simulation? Every time a decision about whether someone knows about a remote event is required, the simulation can be run and the result will always be that people do not know about remote events, at least if perception is their mode of access to the remote event in question.

Gopnik sets the bar too low when she suggests that being capable of axiomatisation suffices to make something a theory. We see this when she suggests that phenomenology may fade as expertise grows. This is the 'illusion of expertise', which Gopnik (1993a, p. 10) outlines as an argument for TT, but it can equally be employed against it. Gopnik's idea is that expert chess players, for example, may lose some of the phenomenology initially associated with playing chess. When they learned to play, they learned explicitly and through painful errors. Now many of the results of that learning have been automated. Exactly the same may happen with simulation to solve ToM questions which occur extremely frequently, like 'what will O feel when O gets the X that he wants?' The bar for the truth of TT is set too low if it suffices for TT to be the true account of ToM that ToM propositions can be expressed as axioms. It might just be that the simulations always produce the same outputs when they have the same inputs.[13]

Davies and Stone (2001, p. 146) claim that there is a 'minimal theoretical background for mental simulation' which is the adoption of an assumption that

O is like S. They give several examples of such an assumption, but they all suggest that S must assume that O is relevantly similar to S, or O's processes are relevantly similar to those of S, if S is to simulate O. This is false. While it must *in fact* be the case that the claims made in these assumptions are true for simulation to be successful, S need make no assumptions at all. S merely needs to simulate. There is no such minimal theoretical background.

Similarly, we may consider the argument of Jackson (1999) to the effect that any method which allows us to make predictions about an object or person K is in virtue of that fact a theory of K. Jackson employs the question from the literature about two travellers who are late arriving at the airport. Which is more annoyed, the one who misses his flight by an hour or the one who misses it by five minutes? Jackson (1999, p. 88) believes we need to apply a theoretical axiom to the effect that a mental exercise 'reveal how you would feel in some given situation'. In fact, you just need to perform the mental exercise and have it *be* right without you knowing that it *is* right.

Consideration of the useful commentary of Mitchell, Currie, and Ziegler (2009b) also throws light on the issue of setting the bar too low. They are hybrid theorists with a simulationist bent; Mitchell, Currie, and Ziegler (2009b, p. 513) propose that 'although simulation is primary, rule-based approaches develop as a shortcut'.[14] Within their hybrid approach, the authors present a candidate rule to be used in situations where they believe theory is more likely to be used than simulation.[15]

The allegedly rule-based scenario involves chocolate in the displaced item test. Subjects are asked the standard False Belief Task question as to where Maxi will look for his chocolate when it has been moved in his absence. Mitchell, Currie, and Ziegler (2009b, p. 513) suggest that this is done by those who provide the correct answer by use of a rule to the effect that O will believe that items are where they were when O last saw them. This may be true, but it is of course equally possible to obtain the correct answer by simulation. S can run through an imaginary scenario in which S's chocolate is moved from location A to location B in his absence and predict that S will not have any reason to update his belief set in relation to the chocolate: S predicts that S or O in this scenario continues to believe the chocolate is where it was before he left the scene. The suggestion of Mitchell, Currie, and Ziegler (2009b, p. 513) is that rule use in this scenario might be the 'best method for mentalizing' because it is 'quick, relatively effortless and tolerably accurate'. Indeed, but this assumes that ToM invariably proceeds on the most efficient basis, which would make it an unusual element of human cognition. More importantly, running a simulation in these circumstances would always produce the same result: viz, O does not know to where the chocolate was moved in his absence because S in the simulation also does not know for the same reason. This would mimic rule-based ToM. It is even possible that S remembers in some sense the output of previous relevant simulations to answer this question. This assumes that memory use does not constitute theory use.

Notes

1 See also Blackburn (1992) for discussion of overly promiscuous application of the term 'theory' in accounts of ToM.
2 Simulationists such as Gallese and Goldman (1998) have also appealed to the discovery of 'mirror neurones' to support their claims. These neurones are activated when an action is performed or observed, which lends itself to simulationist accounts. This type of evidence is outside the scope of this book.
3 See for example Liberman (1985), Ivry and Justus (2001), Fadiga *et al.* (2002) and D'Ausilio *et al.* (2009) for the Motor Theory of Speech Perception including the sub-threshold activation elements thereof.
4 Davies and Stone (1995) discuss the TT(Scientific) definitional claims in terms of the False Belief Task. I will discuss this task later, but for now we need not restrict ourselves to one form of ToM test.
5 I will employ the standard practice of capitalising the names of concepts.
6 Scholl and Leslie (1999) in fact oppose Segal's use of parameters to set children's ToM for their ToMM conception of TT(Innate), which is another reason to prefer the label TT(Innate) to their ToMM in the context of this discussion.
7 Such a subscript approach is proposed by Pratt as I will outline in Chapter 9.
8 In any case, many commentators – for a recent example see Rey (2013) – argue that Introspectionism is true, so whether ST is or is not committed to Introspectionism need not be a major concern for simulationists.
9 The charge of collapse risk is brought against Goldman's position. For a persuasive riposte, see Goldman (2009), which also responds convincingly to the anti-Introspectionist critique of Carruthers (2009).
10 Davies and Stone (2001) provide an extended discussion of collapse risk between ST and TT.
11 Note though extended argument from Stanley (2011, p. vii) to the effect that 'knowing how to do something is the same as knowing a fact' with the fact in question being that w is a way to ϕ. This would collapse Ryle's distinction.
12 Further, Garson (2003, p. 511) describes an example of setting the bar too low, being the claim by TT proponents that any use of general knowledge about people constitutes theory use. He also suggests plausibly that substantiating TT requires showing '(at least) that a body of general [folk psychological] information is causally responsible for the course (and success) of [third person ToM] processing' and that connectionist evidence will not support this.
13 There is a reluctance to assent to the assimilation of potentially imprecise simulation to precise axiomatisations. This both illustrates the error I have been discussing and shows a way to reduce collapse risk. The reluctance is paralleled in some ways by the reluctance Soteriou (2013, p. 174) discusses to accepting the above-mentioned Stanley (2011) assimilation of knowing how to do something to possession of propositional knowledge.
14 The primary argument of Mitchell, Currie, and Ziegler (2009b) that favours ST over TT is also valuable. They note that children gradually develop ToM competence. ST predicts this as perspective-taking capacities develop while TT predicts sharp transitions in competence as better rules are acquired.
15 For a useful commentary on Mitchell, Currie, and Ziegler (2009b) and also the criticism that it is empirically unclear whether children develop ToM gradually or with sharp transitions, see Apperly (2009). See also Harris (2009) for further valuable commentary. For an enlightening response from the original authors to these two commentaries, which includes pressing the important claim that TT proponents ought to specify their axioms, see Mitchell, Currie, and Ziegler (2009a).

3 The problem for ST

Introduction

In this chapter I will set out the challenge to ST as urged by Saxe (2005a). The challenge is that ST cannot account for the systematic errors observed when people perform ToM tasks. These errors exist; they are widely reproduced in the psychological literature. This in itself is not a problem for ST, because it can, as Saxe allows and ST proponents have proposed, avail itself of the Wrong Inputs Defence. I will discuss that defence more fully in Chapter 5, but in sum the Wrong Inputs Defence observes that it is not an objection to ST that a simulation is wrong when the inputs to the simulation were wrong. A wrong input could consist in a false belief held by S about the beliefs or desires held by O. Alternatively, it could consist in a false belief held by S about the factual environment around O which is of relevance to whatever behaviour of O's S is seeking to predict or explain. However, Saxe's particular challenge relates not to the errors but to their systematic nature. This means that all or a large proportion of S's will make the same mistaken predictions about O's behaviour in a particular context.

ST does not, according to its opponents, predict that ToM errors will be systematic. In fact, ST should predict a random spread of errors, according to TT proponents. I will outline the TT argument for this here by sketching Ruffman's Two Colours task, to be discussed in more detail later in the chapter. The task involves a child who sees a green bead being moved from a dish containing red and green beads into an opaque bag. An observer A is behind a screen so that A sees that a bead has been removed from the dish but not its colour. Also behind the screen – and thus visible to the child but not to A – is another dish containing yellow beads. The critical question is asked of the child 'what colour does A think the bead in the bag is?'. If the child is simulating, it should place itself in imagination behind the screen and conclude that it cannot see the colour of the bead. So it will give answers randomly spread across red and green (or conceivably also yellow, since there are yellow beads in the other dish that only the child can see) because the child has no reason 'from behind the screen' to pick one colour over another. This is not what is observed, as we will see: the child in fact will mostly say that A thinks the bead is red.

TT, by contrast, has a ready explanation for the systematic nature of the errors. It can postulate a single item of theory, an axiom that is wrong. If everyone has the same incorrect axiom, then everyone will make the same mistaken ToM prediction in all circumstances that activate that axiom. Thus, Saxe can argue that the systematic ToM errors that are observed are good evidence for TT and against ST.

Saxe (2005a) introduces a large variety of experimental evidence to support her claim. The evidence is broken down into several classes. I will consider four classes of data in this book. Later in this book, I will provide a chapter responding to each class of data on behalf of ST, but for now my task is solely to set out the problem. The four classes of data show the following types of systematic ToM error:

- In some experiments, ToM is systematically too 'rosy': S's are unwarrantedly optimistic about the rationality and logic employed in O's decision-making.
- In some experiments, ToM is systematically too 'cynical': S's are unwarrantedly pessimistic about the rationality and logic employed in O's decision-making.
- In some experiments, S's systematically fail to apply Cognitive Dissonance theory, i.e. they do not realise that behaviour inconsistent with beliefs can change beliefs.
- In some experiments, child S's appear systematically to use the false axiom 'ignorance means you get it wrong'.

The first two variants of the challenge are somewhat similar in that they just show opposite directions of the same sort of error. Adults make different sorts of error in different scenarios. The third set of data, from the Two Colours task, relates to children, but is not to be dismissed on that account, because as I will outline, the results which Saxe requires are also obtained with older children who have been thought to be working with more-or-less adult ToM.

The third set of data is rather more theoretical. It is of a Cognitive Penetrability bent in that it claims that false beliefs that S's hold about how minds work can infect S's ToM. This would explain the systematic errors in question. That explanation, on Saxe's account, is only available to TT since TT holds that S's use theory, including any false beliefs about minds, in their ToM. The particular challenge in this fourth case is basically that folk psychology is not as good as scientific psychology. Cognitive Dissonance theory is true, but folk psychology does not incorporate its axioms, and thus fails in certain circumstances to make correct predictions of belief changes.

The fourth set of data is developmental and so somewhat separate to the previous three classes. I will be developing a specific defence for that data in Chapter 9.

There are two charges associated with the argument from error which Saxe (2005a) brings that are linked to the systematic problem for ST. They relate to flexibility and sharpness of transition. One strength of TT is that it postulates different items of theory which can explain why our ToM is too rosy on some occasions and on other occasions too cynical. TT can claim that different situations will involve the application of different false theoretical axioms, and that every time this happens, an error of the same type – rosy or cynical – will be made. There is by corollary a problem for ST on Saxe's account in that it does not have such flexibility. TT also has a natural explanation for the sharp transitions in ToM ability that are observed in children. It can claim that new and improved axioms become available to the child causing a step change in its ability to ascribe false beliefs to others, for example. Although I will not focus on these two further charges associated with Saxe's challenge, much of what follows on systematicity will be relevant to them.

In the next four sections of this chapter, I will introduce each class of data. For now, I will only give one of the experiments cited by Saxe (2005a) in each class as an example. In later chapters, I will retain the separation into four classes but consider many more experiments cited by Saxe within each class.

The 'too rosy' challenge

The class of 'too rosy' data supporting Saxe's systematic error challenge is introduced by her as below.

> Adults, too, have systematically inaccurate and over-simplified beliefs about beliefs that are often self-flattering. 'We are convinced of the rationality of [human] reasoning, highly adept at constructing plausible explanations for our decision behaviour . . . and so on' (Evans 1990, p. 109). That is, we share the conviction that, in general, beliefs follow from relatively dispassionate assessment of facts-of-the-matter and logical reasoning. As a consequence, people's expectations of how they and others should reason and behave correspond more closely to normative theories of logic, probability and utility, than to their actual subsequent behaviour. (Gilovich 1993)
>
> Historically, proposals for when observers use simulation tend to be somewhat *ad hoc*. In fact, if we could accurately simulate other minds, half a century of social psychology would lose much of its power to shock and thrill. The charisma of many famous experiments in social psychology and decision-making derives from the fact that they challenge our too-rosy theories of mind (Ross, Amabile, and Steinmetz 1977). The experiments of Milgram (1963), and Asch (1952), and Tversky and Kahneman (1974), are famous because there is a specific, and vivid, mismatch between what we confidently expect, and what the subjects actually do.
>
> (Saxe 2005a, p. 176)

As one example of Saxe's too rosy data, I will consider the Milgram experiment. I will cover many more in the chapter devoted to explaining this class of data, Chapter 6. This famous experiment involves some deception of the experimental subjects, which means that it has not been widely replicated, because it would not pass modern university ethics panels. It was conducted at Yale in 1961. The context continues to be that of the aftermath of the Second World War, and the preliminaries to the experimental write-up mention that the Nazi regime is an explicit concern. How will ordinary people respond when asked to perform extraordinary acts that are beyond what they would claim are their moral limits? Should we understand the Nazi phenomenon as an aberration, or will ordinary people be generally susceptible to persuasion beyond our expectations when placed in extraordinary circumstances?

There are three protagonists in the Milgram (1963) experiment: the experimenter, the actual subject and the 'dummy subject'. The actual subject is an innocent member of the public. The actual subject believes that the dummy subject is also an innocent member of the public, but this is not the case. In fact, the dummy subject is a collaborator of the experimenter. An apparently random but in fact rigged selection is run to allocate roles between the actual subject and the dummy subject. The two roles are 'learner' and 'teacher' in a word pair learning test. The selection is rigged such that the actual subject is always the teacher, and the dummy subject is always the learner.

The experimenter explains to the actual subject that the experiment is an investigation of how learning may be improved by mild punishment of error. In the standard version of the experiment, the dummy subject is placed in a different room to the actual subject and communicates the word pairs via a panel. Their performance is to be assessed by the actual subject, who is also tasked with applying punishment to them if they make a mistake. The situation is rigged so that the dummy subjects do in fact make many mistakes. The actual subject is now told to apply an electric shock to the dummy subject. They have a range of electric shocks available to apply, beginning from mild and increasing in voltage. In reality of course, no electric shocks are applied at all to the dummy subject. However, they do react as if they were being applied. The intensity of their reaction increases dramatically as the purported shock level increases. Bear in mind that since the dummy subjects are in a different room, their behaviour under the apparent shocks is not seen by the actual subjects. There is no verbal response from the dummy subjects, though the dummy subjects make audible sounds of protest as the experiment proceeds. At extreme levels in fact, they cease to respond to the requests for a new word pair, and '[w]hen the 300-volt shock is administered, the learner pounds on the wall of the room in which he is bound to the electric chair' (Milgram 1963, p. 374).

The actual subjects believe they are administering shocks ranging from 'Moderate' through 'Intense' to 'Danger: Severe Shock' and beyond to the mysterious 'XXX' category. If the actual subject protests that this treatment is unreasonable or unethical or for any reason resists applying the shock, the experimenter encourages them. A fixed scale of four experimenter responses is set as actual subject resistance increases along with dummy subject distress. These 'prods' were in order as follows: 'Please continue, or Please go on; The experiment requires that you continue; It is absolutely essential that you continue; You have no other choice, you must go on' (Milgram 1963, p. 374). We immediately believe here that no-one will comply.

The surprising results though were that: '[o]f the 40 [O's], 26 obeyed the orders of the experimenter to the end, proceeding to punish the victim until they reached the most potent shock available on the shock generator' (Milgram 1963, p. 376). At this juncture, Saxe already has her point: we are amazed that any of the actual subjects will go this far, and we are confident that we ourselves would not.

Crucially for Saxe's view though, there are a fourth group of players, who will provide us with evidence of systematic failure of ToM of the too rosy sort and indeed with hard numerical evidence thereof. Milgram has a group of psychology undergraduates who are later provided with a description of the set-up. They are 'seniors' who 'major' or specialise in psychology, so we may assume that they have no difficulty understanding the set-up or the questions being asked. Milgram (1963, p. 375) writes: '[f]ourteen Yale seniors, all psychology majors, were provided with a detailed description of the experimental situation. They were asked to reflect carefully on it, and to predict the behaviour of 100 hypothetical subjects. . . . All respondents predicted that only an insignificant minority would go through to the end of the shock series. (The estimates ranged from 0 to 3%; i.e. the most 'pessimistic' member of the class predicted that of 100 persons, 3 would continue through to the most potent shock available on the shock generator – 450 volts.)' This provides Saxe with a valuable data point. In the actual experiment, 26/40 = 65 per cent of O's set the dial to 450 volts while the psychology undergraduate S's estimated that that number would be 3 per cent at most.

Since there are now four groups of protagonists in the experiment, there is room for confusion when we view it in our ToM framework. Recall that S is the subject in our terms who is using ToM to predict the behaviour of the object of ToM O. In this framework, the S's are the psychology majors who predicted the behaviour of the actual subjects or teachers, the O's. So the discrepancy between 3 per cent and 65 per cent represents the systematically too rosy ToM error which Saxe requires.

The 'too cynical' challenge

Saxe (2005a) also cites a class of experimental data that tend in the opposite direction to those discussed in the previous section. While her challenge continues to be that there are systematic errors in ToM, the direction of those errors is opposite under different circumstances, and systematically so. As previously, defenders of ST must explain this directionality of error as well as the mere possibility of error. Once again, Saxe will appeal to a wrong theoretical axiom being applied in the various cases, which gives TT an easy response to the data.

Saxe (2005a) introduces this class of data supporting her challenge as below.

> '[L]ay epistemology is not universally charitable. Most adults believe that beliefs are sometimes false, that reasoning can sometimes be distorted – both inevitably, by the limitations of the mind, and wilfully, as in wishful thinking and self-deception – and that all of these are more likely to be true of other people's thinking than of their own' [Pronin, Puccio and Ross (Gilovich, Griffin, and Kahneman 2002, pp. 636–665)]. As a consequence, [S's] sometimes overestimate the prevalence of self-serving reasoning in [O's].
>
> (Kruger and Gilovich 1999; Nisbett and Bellows 1977; Miller and Ratner 1998)

> In one study, Kruger and Gilovich (1999) asked each member of a married couple, separately, to rate how often he or she was responsible for common desirable and undesirable events in the marriage. Then, each was asked to predict how their spouse would assign responsibility on the same scale. Although everyone actually tended to take credit equally for good and bad events, each predicted that their spouse would be self-serving, that is, take more responsibility for good events, and less responsibility for bad ones. . . . Thus whereas reasoning about reasoning is usually characterised by overly optimistic expectations about people's rationality, in specific circumstances (e.g. the culturally acknowledged self-serving bias) observers are overly pessimistic, an effect dubbed 'naïve cynicism'.
>
> [Kruger and Gilovich (1999)]. (Saxe 2005a, p. 177)

Note that there is a possible confusion in the last sentence. There are two 'self-serving biases' at play in this experiment. There is the self-serving bias(O) of O which would involve O making unrealistically positive claims about himself. The second self-serving bias(S) would be in S, where S predicts even more self-serving bias(O) in O than O exhibits. The self-serving bias(S) in S thus paradoxically allows S to predict that S is less self-serving than O and thus more virtuous. It is important to keep these different biases separate.

As before, I will provide here just one example of the sort of experimental data Saxe (2005a) appeals to in this class of too cynical data, while covering many more of her examples in my detailed response on behalf of ST in Chapter 7. Since Saxe herself introduces the marriage partners example and describes it well, I will expand on that.

Kruger and Gilovich (1999, p. 745) had married couples fill out a questionnaire about joint activities of either negative or positive relationship value. Here, 'joint activity' means something that either partner might do, not something that they necessarily both do together. For example, a negative activity would be 'taking out frustrations on partner' while a positive one would be 'resolving conflicts that occur between the two of you'. Each partner was asked to allocate responsibility for such activities by percentage between themselves and their partner. The idea was that the partners should think on a frequency basis. Imagine that there were, for example, 20 occurrences of an activity falling under the given description 'taking out frustrations . . . ' in the last month. This if true means that the total number of such occurrences for which the husband was responsible plus the total number of such occurrences for which the wife was responsible sum to 20. The same pattern should be visible across the board, with no more than 100 per cent of responsibility being allocated across partners and across activities.

The investigation of whether these allocations are biased proceeds by comparing what partners say about themselves and comparing it with what their partners said about themselves on each task. This can then be compared with 100 per cent. If the husband is responsible for 60 per cent of a particular activity, then his wife can claim up to 40 per cent of initiations of this activity for herself, and no bias has been measured. If however the total is more than 100 per cent, then both partners have claimed more responsibility than is actually available and a positive bias has been measured in relation to that activity. Both parties want to claim credit for that activity. On the other hand, if the husband admits to only 30 per cent of responsibility for a given action, and the wife also admits to only 30 per cent, then a negative bias has been observed. Neither party wants to admit responsibility for that activity. As the authors write, 'suppose a wife believes she initiates 60% of the discussions about the relationship and her husband believes he is responsible for 50%. Together, they have assigned 110% of the activity to themselves, yielding a bias score of +10%' (Kruger and Gilovich 1999, p. 745). Initiating discussions about the relationship was a positive activity in the experimenters' paradigm.

By allocating responsibility to himself, the husband naturally also allocates the inverse responsibility to his wife. If he thinks he does 70 per cent of the 'spending time on appearance to please the other' (Kruger and Gilovich 1999, p. 745), then he must also think his wife does 30 per cent. The activities considered in the experiment were such that no-one else could do them other than the two spouses. Since the experimenters have the questionnaires from both spouses, they are now in a position to compare the data, and to cross-reference it with whether the activity is positive for the relationship or negative. But they took a crucial further step in this experiment, which is why Saxe (2005a) cites this particular experiment. Kruger and Gilovich (1999, p. 745) also asked each partner what they thought the other would say. Note that this allows for a sum greater than 100 per cent. If the husband thinks that he does 70 per cent of 'spending time on appearance to please the other', he can consistently also think his wife will claim 70 per cent, while he believes she actually does 30 per cent. The husband can have a biased expectation of bias. Matching that in the other direction, the husband can think that he causes 30 per cent of the arguments, and that his wife therefore actually causes 70 per cent of the arguments, but that she will only admit to causing 30 per cent. If this is the case, then there is a systematic error in ToM in a too cynical direction and Saxe has her data.

This is exactly what is observed; Kruger and Gilovich (1999, p. 745) report that 'couples expected their spouses to claim more than their share of the credit for the desirable activities (M = +9.1%) – but less than their share of the blame for the undesirable activities (M = –16.1%)', where 'M' stands for mean bias. The systematic error in ToM here is then 'biased expectations of bias'. The S's expect their partner O's to be biased. The O's are indeed biased. But they are less biased than the S's predict; the quantum of how self-serving they are is less than predicted. Saxe has indeed provided data which help her in two ways. There is indeed a systematic error in ToM in that S's generally all make the same error. But second, these ToM errors are all in the too cynical direction when the previous ToM errors were all in the too rosy direction. Saxe may now reasonably demand that ST proponents explain this.

The suspicious congruency challenge

A third element of Saxe's challenge bears many resemblances to the previous two considered above, but it has additional theoretical elements. It continues to be data-driven. It again poses a problem for ST proponents since it shows further systematic errors in ToM. As before, I will only introduce the data here by examining one part of it, deferring fuller consideration until I provide an ST response in Chapter 8.

Saxe introduces this variant of her challenge thus: the 'argument from error hinges on this kind of systematicity. When the errors that [S's] make in predicting [O's] action, judgement or inference – or in explaining [S's] own past actions or thoughts (Gopnik 1993a; Bem 1967) are suspiciously congruent with [S's] beliefs about how minds work (Nisbett and Bellows 1977), it seems likely that the S's are deploying those beliefs (or theory) in the process of making the predictions and forming the explanations' (Saxe 2005a, pp. 177–178).

So we see that once again, systematicity of error is the key complaint. One new extension here is that the ToM errors can now occur also in relation to the self, i.e. when S seeks to predict or explain the behaviour of S himself at a previous time or under counterfactual circumstances. Saxe's charge is that if S has false beliefs about the mind, then those false beliefs will on the TT account become false axioms in his ToM. That will not be the case under the ST account for Saxe. So the false axioms can only explain systematic ToM error if TT is true. Therefore TT is true and ST is false, concludes Saxe.

The data Saxe employs in this context come from Bem. Bem (1967) sets out his alternative Self-Perception interpretation of Cognitive Dissonance. I will first outline the mainstream Cognitive Dissonance interpretation before discussing Bem's alternative Self-Perception interpretation.

Bem (1967, p. 183) himself explains Cognitive Dissonance as follows: if 'a person holds two cognitions that are inconsistent with one another, he will experience the pressure of an aversive motivational state called cognitive dissonance, a pressure which he will seek to remove'. Cognitions are thoughts or beliefs. The basic idea here is straightforward: if someone believes P, and then comes across new information that suggests the truth of not P, then a dissonance between the two cognitions has arisen. The person will either decide that the new information is convincing, and hold not P, or decide it is not that convincing, and remain with P, or decide that the situation is unclear, and suspend judgement as to whether P or not P. What they will not do is simultaneously hold P and not P. The desire to avoid this is the 'aversive motivational state' to which Bem refers. Cognitive Dissonance may be seen as arising at root from the need to maintain a coherent belief set.[1]

The nature of Bem's alternative Self-Perception or self-persuasion interpretation of the data is outlined by Saxe when she writes in a later book chapter that 'Bem was the best known advocate, in social psychology, of the view that adults infer the internal reasons for their actions from the externally observable evidence of the actions themselves' (Markman, Klein, and Suhr 2012, Chapter 17). So Self-Perception here means to observe oneself as it were externally. For example, I can tell I am happy by noting that I am smiling. Similarly, I can tell that I have the desire for coffee and the belief that I can buy some in the coffee shop by observing that I am going in to the coffee shop. Naturally, this position is Anti-Introspectionist in that it denies that I can detect internally what my beliefs and desires are; if I could do that, then I would have no need to go down the indirect route of first seeing what I am doing.

We know that Saxe introduces the Bem data in order to support her claim that there are also systematic ToM errors made in relation to the self. She also cites the Nisbett and Bellows paper that argues strongly against Introspectionism. So we may already suspect that Saxe's focus here is on Introspectionism. Fortunately we may confirm this from an expanded version of the challenge Saxe sets out in a later book chapter. She writes that 'by creating experimental situations in which the true explanation of a behaviour is ambiguous (Bem 1967), social psychologists have found systematic evidence that adults reconstruct the best explanation for their own past behavior from current evidence, rather than introspecting and recalling the conscious experience of the event (Nisbett and Bellows 1977)' (Markman, Klein, and Suhr 2012, Chapter 17). This confirms that the challenge is based on a denial of Introspectionism. Saxe holds quite simply that folk psychology asserts that Introspectionism is true while correct scientific psychology on her view asserts that Introspectionism is false. ToM errors will be made in relation to the self as a result.

The type of situation in which these errors should occur will be in relation to past behaviour of the self in circumstances where that behaviour admits of more than one explanation. ToM will employ axioms that assume that Introspectionism is true. Explaining why S is behaving in the way that S is now behaving requires little more than introspecting the currently relevant beliefs and desires of S and applying standard belief/desire psychology. S is entering the coffee shop now because S has the desire for coffee together with the belief that the coffee shop is where S can obtain coffee. A minor extension of this picture to the past also relies on the claim that folk psychology's Introspectionism asserts that there is direct privileged access to one's own memories as well. So, S will explain why S entered the coffee shop previously by introspecting memory to determine that on that previous occasion, S had the same belief/desire pair.

Saxe's claim is that this is a systematic ToM error, because Introspectionism is false. S is mistaken to think that S can introspect to discover that S has/had the belief desire pair in question. That can only be done by considering the external behaviour exhibited by S. On the Saxe/Bem view, S cannot introspect his own beliefs and desires either as they currently are or as they were in the past. By contrast, what S actually does is 'reconstruct the best explanation' for their behaviour. So the direction of causation is reversed for Saxe. S falsely believes that S's own beliefs and desire are recalled and explain the behaviour, while in fact the behaviour explains the beliefs and desires that S imputes to himself. If S entered the coffee shop, it must have been the case that S had the desire for coffee and believed coffee could be obtained in the coffee shop. We can see the strength of Saxe's charge here by considering questions like whether S really does have the ability to recall exactly what of relevance S was believing and desiring when S went into the coffee shop two weeks ago. It seems that 'I desired coffee' is more of a response to 'why else would I be in the coffee shop?' than a recall of a belief; it could well be that on the occasion in question S entered the coffee shop without any particular relevant beliefs foregrounded because S was engrossed in philosophical problems. How often are we certain that we believed something at a point in the past by remembering that belief as opposed to deriving it from external circumstances? So Saxe does have a prima facie case here.

Now we know what Saxe (2005a) is looking for, we may consider the Bem data to see what support she obtains from it. Recall that Bem is working with the Cognitive Dissonance paradigm, but seeking to provide an alternative explanation of it. The particular nature of the Cognitive Dissonance data provided by Bem relates to the strange way that people modify their beliefs if they have behaved in a way that contradicts those beliefs. Even more strangely, they modify their beliefs even if they did not 'own' the behaviour: for example if they are just asked to read out a speech in favour of capital punishment when they are against it, they subsequently become more favourable towards capital punishment. Saxe describes this phenomenon as follows. In the Bem and other experiments, 'participants comply with a request to do an action that doesn't fit well with their prior beliefs and attitudes . . . and only if there was apparently little external pressure compelling the action . . . participants change their reported attitude, claiming that they found the task less boring, or that they agree more with the political position' (Markman, Klein, and Suhr 2012, Chapter 17). So it seems, counter-intuitively, as though people are more likely to change their beliefs based on the dissonance between their behaviour and their action when they did not have a strong motive to behave as they did.

The Bem data show exactly what Saxe (2005a) claims. He successfully replicates some early data due to Festinger and Carlsmith, the pioneers of Cognitive Dissonance theory. In the experiment reported by Bem (1967, p. 188), 75 subjects 'listened to a tape recording which described a college sophomore named Bob Downing, who had participated in an experiment involving two motor tasks'. The two motor tasks were actually extremely dull, involving repeatedly moving pegs from one hole to another. The 75 subjects were divided into three groups of 25: the control group, and two experimental groups called the $1 and the $20 group, for reasons that will become apparent.

After hearing the tape, 'the control subjects were asked to evaluate Bob's attitudes toward the tasks. The experimental subjects were further told that Bob had accepted an offer of $1 ($20) to go into the waiting room, tell the next subject that the tasks were fun, and to be prepared to do this again in the future' (Bem 1967, p. 188). Bob appears to have lied here in a way that is damaging: he has claimed that the experimental tasks are interesting when they are not and he has said this to someone who is about to perform the tasks. Presumably they might be able to avoid the tasks if Bob had been truthful about how dull they were.

Festinger and Carlsmith actually had the participants perform as described i.e. subjects did the tasks and then lied to someone else about them. The participants were paid nothing to lie – in the control group – or $1 or $20 in the two experimental groups. Festinger and Carlsmith found that subjects 'paid $1 evaluated the tasks as significantly more enjoyable than did subjects who had been paid $20' (Bem 1967, p. 187). The control group, which was paid nothing, had no reason to rate the tasks as anything other than as dull as they were. The $1 group, which has been paid an insignificant amount to lie, experiences dissonance between their behaviour in saying that the tasks were enjoyable and their previous perception that they were not enjoyable. They reduce the consequent Cognitive Dissonance by changing their belief about the tasks in the direction of higher enjoyability. The $20 subjects do not exhibit this effect, because they have been 'bribed enough' to lie. So they return to the control group's honest assessment of the tasks as being dull.

Bem runs a similar experiment without anyone actually performing the tasks: the participants listen to the tape about Bob instead of performing the tasks themselves. Similar results are obtained. Participants think that Bob must have been lying when they think he has been paid $20: 'he would say that'. In the control condition, participants revert to the actual assessed enjoyability of the tasks i.e. they were dull. In the $1 case, they think the tasks must have been more enjoyable than they seemed, because Bob was not bribed enough to lie. As Bem reports, these 'successful replications of the functional relation reported by Festinger and Carlsmith provide support for the self-perception analysis. The original subjects may be viewed as simply making self-judgments based on the same kinds of public evidence' that they learned in the community (Bem 1967, p. 189). So the Saxe/Bem point here is that there is no difference between judgements made about oneself in the Festinger and Carlsmith experiment and about others in the Bem replication. Both rely on observation of behaviour, or 'Self-Perception' in Bem's terminology.

Finally we may see the systematic ToM error to which Saxe (Markman, Klein, and Suhr 2012, Chapter 17) adverts here. She concludes as follows: upon 'observing themselves making a choice, or voluntarily acting without a reward, participants made the same inference that an outside observer would make: that they must really have preferred the chosen option, or found the task interesting'. So there is an error in ToM made by S about how O feels about how enjoyable the tasks were, where O can also be S at a previous time. The S's are employing a ToM which does not include Cognitive Dissonance theory and is Introspectionist. So S's do not predict that O will change his view on how enjoyable the tasks were if he was bribed inadequately in order to reduce Cognitive Dissonance. They also hold that Bob must know how much he enjoyed the tasks directly from introspection. On Saxe's view, both of these aspects represent errors in ToM which will systematically appear in all relevant scenarios.

The developmental challenge

A fourth class of experimental data cited by Saxe comes from a set of experiments by Ruffman. They show a systematic ToM error in children in that they assimilate ignorance and false belief. They are unable to distinguish a state of being ignorant of P – i.e. not having a belief that P and not having a belief that not P – from a state of believing falsely that not P. In other words, if you do not know something, you must be wrong about it. Saxe introduces this class of data to support her systematic error challenge as below.

> Four-year-olds, for example, do not yet have differentiated concepts of 'not knowing' and 'getting it wrong', as illustrated elegantly by Ruffman (1996). In one experiment, a child and an adult observer ('A') are seated in front of two dishes of beads. The round dish contains red and green beads, but the square dish contains only yellow beads. Both A and the child watch while a bead from the round dish is moved under cover into an opaque bag. The child, but not A, knows that the chosen bead was green. Then the child is asked 'what colour does A think the bead in the bag is?' The correct answer is that A doesn't know, or (even better) that A thinks it is red or green (but not yellow). Overwhelmingly, though, the children report that A thinks the bead is red. Note that this answer is not simply random: none of the children said A thinks that the bead is yellow. Rather, the actual result is best explained by an inaccurate generalisation in the child's developing ToM: 'ignorance means you get it wrong'. Because A is ignorant of which bead was chosen from the round dish, A must think that it was the wrong colour, a red one.
>
> (Saxe 2005a, p. 175)

The Ruffman paper cited by Saxe includes three experiments each containing several tasks. As above, I will restrict myself here to covering the one task that Saxe describes above for introductory purposes. There will be further discussion in the chapter dedicated to providing a response on behalf of ST, Chapter 9. The particular task Saxe describes is termed by Ruffman the 'Two Colours' task of Experiment 1.[2] Note that Saxe's basic claim here is that the children will be more likely to ascribe a false belief than a true belief, and that this will represent a systematic error in ToM because they should ascribe no beliefs at all.

The Two Colours task was conducted on 71 children, who were split into three groups by age. The younger group included 26 children aged from 4 years 10 months to 5 years 2 months; the middle group 21 children aged from 5 years 3 months to 6 years 11 months and the older group 24 children aged from 7 years 0 months to 7 years 9 months. These children were all asked the test question as to what colour O thinks the bead in the bag is.

Some exclusions and adjustments took place before arriving at the results. A small group of five children actually passed the Two Colours test in the way that an adult would viz. they 'recognised that [A] could hold either a true or a false belief (two from the middle group and three from the oldest group)' (Ruffman 1996, p. 398). The sophistication of this response is underlined by the fact that none of the younger group achieved it. This leaves us with 66 children. At this point, a further 9 children were excluded from the data for not linking seeing and knowing, i.e. they failed to realise that if O sees that P is the case, O knows that P is the case. We now have 57 children split across the three age groups. The numbers ascribing a false belief were as follows: younger group: 15/20; middle group: 16/16; older group: 18/21. This means that across the remaining 57 children, 49 or 86 per cent said that O thinks the bead in the bag is red. While some caveats might be entered about the exclusions and adjustments, Saxe seems entitled to her claim that the Ruffman data show that the children use the incorrect theoretical axiom 'ignorance means you get it wrong'[3] so they make systematic errors in ToM on these tasks.

These data seem distinct from the first two classes of data, because it is not clear that the children are making a too rosy or a too cynical error here. They are just wrong in a systematic way. They are not being too rosy about O because they are not expecting an outcome in which O acquires a true belief. They are also not being too cynical in that it does not seem as though O has much chance under the circumstances of forming a true belief. Note also that there appears to be little development in the older age groups, which makes life difficult for ST proponents who might wish to avoid this class of data supporting Saxe's case by excluding developmental arguments. The idea would be that whatever errors children under five make can be explained just as well by impaired simulation capacities as compared with those of adults. That is ruled out by the data, because children older than around five at the latest – i.e. probably the middle group and the older group – have ToM capacities in many ways that are as good as those of adults.

Of further assistance to Saxe is the Ruffman (1996, p. 399) discussion of what he takes his results to show. He writes that '[i]n line with the predictions of TT, in the Two Colours task a large majority of children were significantly more likely to ascribe a false belief to [O] than to ascribe a true belief [and this] result is inconsistent with ST'. The underlying assumption here is that simulation starts from the beliefs that the child has; and the child has a true belief about the colour of the bead. The child knows that the bead is green because s/he saw it. If then the child is simulating from the starting point of his/her own true beliefs, s/he should be more likely to say that A thinks the bead is green than red.

Ruffman also backs up Saxe's claim that simulation should predict random errors as opposed to the observed systematic ascription of false beliefs under the experimental conditions. He writes that it was 'equally possible that the [bead] could be red or green and hence that [O] could form either belief. If placed in [A's] situation children themselves should have chosen randomly between red and green. Children's failure to do this when assessing [O's] belief suggests that they were not simulating' (Ruffman 1996, p. 399).

Saxe has provided a fourth class of data supporting her claim that there is systematic error in ToM under defined circumstances. She further claims that this can easily be explained by TT since in her view it is an example of the application of a false theoretical axiom 'ignorance means you get it wrong' (Saxe 2005a, p. 175). Again on her account these data cannot be accounted for by ST because ST should predict random errors.

We have now seen four classes of data where Saxe (2005a) has shown systematic error in ToM. These errors pose an as yet unanswered problem for ST. That scenario has been a major factor leading to the consensus hybrid view involving both theory and simulation; in other words, an ST/TT mix. I will in the next chapter therefore consider problems with hybrid views.

Notes

1 See Quine (1951) for discussion of coherent belief sets and their maintenance together with Cherniak (1983) for an update of that account with reference to modern psychology.

2 Saxe makes a number of unimportant errors in describing the data; for example she speaks of the O being an adult observer 'A' when in fact it is a doll named Katy. I will adjust citations from Ruffman to reflect Saxe's terminology because nothing depends on the errors.

3 Though see Friedman and Petrashek (2009) for a denial that children follow this rule.

4 Is going hybrid the solution?

Introduction

Saxe responds to the difficulties raised in the previous chapter for ST by urging the merits of a hybrid account of ToM in which both theory and simulation play a part. In my view though, successful accounts should also describe how the two parts of ToM are to work together. In order to clarify the conceptual geography, I will begin by defining two claims. Assertion or denial of these two claims defines the nature of a position. The two claims are:

- Hybridism: ToM users employ both theoretical and simulational capacities.
- Interactionism: These capacities interact.

Saxe's position is Hybridist and Interactionist, although I will argue below that her position on the Interactionist vs Anti-Interactionist axis is unclear. In any case, Interactionist and Hybridist approaches have serious difficulties which I will outline in this chapter. The difficulties fall into two categories. First, there are problems specific to TT which apply to any Hybridist account involving it. TT has been a mainstream, perhaps dominant account of ToM in psychology, and is now a major constituent of the Hybridist consensus. Indeed, my view is that that consensus is 'simulation-light'; many psychologists prefer the TT account but have been forced to admit some ST into their account of ToM by arguments from the simulationist side. For these reasons, we should not expect to find knock-down arguments that destroy TT's plausibility completely. My method in the first half of this chapter is to canvass some of the arguments that bring TT into question. My view is that these arguments have not found full responses, but in any case, I wish here only to motivate a reconsideration of the merits of a pure ST account as opposed to a pure TT account or the Hybridist position.

I will first examine objections to TT(Scientific), also sketching responses on behalf of the TT(Scientific) side. The six objections to TT(Scientific) are as follows. The first objection, which I think is the most important one, is lack of parsimony. The account requires additional machinery which represents a substantial theoretical cost. The second objection is that TT(Scientific) does not explain default belief attribution. Such an attribution is a useful starting point for

ToM activities because many of us share a great number of beliefs. The third objection to TT(Scientific) suggests that under it, ToM users must solve the frame problem and that finding such a solution is impossible. The fourth objection asks how it can be that all children converge on the same ToM even though their evidential bases are different. The fifth objection notes that normal children achieve some good, quasi-adult ToM capacities by around their fifth birthday at the latest, and suggests that this is an implausibly sophisticated achievement to ascribe to them. The sixth objection examines how science is done and alleges that there is nothing closely or usefully parallel or analogous between scientific inference and the inferences that a child makes in developing its ToM.[1]

Second, I will examine objections specific to TT(Innate). One claims that ToM development cannot be accounted for by TT(Innate) while it is a natural consequence of TT(Scientific). The second objection claims that TT(Innate) cannot account for the facts in relation to default belief attribution: as mentioned above, it is useful for S to start from the assumption that O has the same beliefs as S. The third objection claims that TT(Innate) cannot account for facts in relation to autism; viz. that autistic subjects show deficits in pretend play as well as ToM and that these two deficits ought parsimoniously to be explained together. Several of the objections to TT(Scientific) raise problems for TT(Innate) also.

In the final sections of this chapter, I will consider difficulties relating solely to Hybridist accounts which would occur with all such accounts that combine theory and simulation. In my view, these difficulties are more serious for the consensus Hybridist position than the objections to TT alone. The problems with Hybridism have been much less considered in the literature than the problems specific to TT, which have received numerous responses of varying degrees of success. Since light may be thrown on Saxe's position on these Hybridist issues by some initial exchanges in the literature in response to her key 2005 paper, I will first briefly outline those responses and her replies. Then I will turn to several questions for Hybridist accounts.

One problem arises from the observation that Hybridist accounts are by definition of composite nature. All composite accounts must provide a motivated prescription of interaction between the elements. The first possible answer, and perhaps the simplest, is to combine Hybridism with Anti-Interactionism. This position asserts that there are two elements, theory and simulation, but denies that there is any interaction between the elements. They do not communicate with each other, or use each other's outputs as inputs. There is in addition no third master system combining the two theoretical and simulational systems. Such an Anti-Interactionist account would need to describe how it could come about that there is no interaction. One option might be to specify separate domains of application. Some questions in ToM might always be resolved theoretically, and other questions might always be resolved simulationally. Or, particular questions might generally be solved theoretically and sometimes simulationally. Providing no episode of consideration of a question involved both simulation and theory at the same time, it would still count as an Anti-Interactionist account. There might even be ways of having a particular question considered both theoretically and simulationally on a given occasion, but still qualifying as a non-interactionist account, by some rather *ad hoc* method. One could simply assume that a particular question is considered theoretically and simulationally on a given occasion, but that there is a random basis for selecting which one actually forms the output of ToM on this occasion. Provided the simulation system and the theory system do not interact for any reason including deciding which of them will provide the decision on this occasion, then the account remains Anti-Interactionist.[2]

Dealing with this problem even in the apparently simpler Anti-Interactionist way is not easy. It is not clear which route Saxe takes on Interactionism. She claims that her position is Interactionist when she writes that 'to conclude that a naïve theory of mind, and some capacity to simulate, interact' (Saxe 2005a, p. 175) is a 'better option' (Saxe 2005a, p. 175) than the idea that 'in some contexts, the [S] is a pure simulator, whereas in other contexts [S] uses pure theory' (Saxe 2005a, p. 175). However, we have already seen that she favours the TT(Scientific) account of Gopnik and Wellman, and they are assigned to the Anti-Interactionist camp by Bach (2011), as will be outlined further below.

Objections to TT(Scientific)

TT(Scientific) structure is unparsimonious

The most important objection to TT(Scientific), when viewed from the ST side, is its lack of parsimony. The objection claims that the significant theoretical apparatus that TT(Scientific) postulates is unnecessarily theoretically expensive and cumbersome. Admittedly, the ToM capacities that are explained are themselves complex and sophisticated and therefore one might think that a significant theoretical cost could reasonably be borne in explaining those capacities. However, such theoretical costs are only acceptable when no cheaper theory is available. ST is exactly such a less theoretically costly theory, since it explains ToM capacities by using only machinery that is already present. No additional significant body of knowledge need be postulated, since that 'body of knowledge' can be generated on the fly by the mind of S. The extensive body of knowledge about O that TT(Scientific) postulates also seems unparsimonious because it does not have an obvious use beyond the prediction and explanation of the behaviour of others. Again, why postulate that when the much simpler postulation is available to the effect that S has a mind and can use it to work out what O's mind will do?

In this vein, Nichols and Stich (2003, p. 104) observe that proponents of TT(Scientific) 'have been notably silent on the matter of inference prediction'. Humans are very good at inference prediction: if S knows that O believes P, S will immediately be able to suggest a large range of other propositions that O is very likely to assert or deny. Stich and Nichols ascribe this lack of proposals as reflecting the uncomfortable fact for proponents of TT(Scientific) that the only way for them to explain our success here is 'more theory' (Nichols and Stich 2003, p. 104). And then, the problem is why would evolution 'go to the effort of arranging for us to have a theory about how the inference mechanism works when

[it] could get the job done by using the inference mechanism itself?' (Nichols and Stich 2003, p. 104).

Nichols and Stich plausibly see this objection as paralleled by the grammaticality argument for simulation due to Harris (1992, p. 124). Grammatical judgements are a special case of inference ascription. S and O are assumed to both be native speakers of the same language. We know that S will be very good at assessing what O will say about the grammaticality or otherwise of a set of test sentences. It is much more plausible and parsimonious to say that S does this by simulating O – by deciding what S himself thinks are the grammatical sentences – than that S has a theory of O's grammaticality judgements.[3]

TT(Scientific) does not explain default belief attribution

We are all very good at ascribing a large belief set to others, in the realm of grammar and elsewhere. S can say a great deal about what O's probable perceptual beliefs are based on S's view of O's perspective. S can also predict O's beliefs about a vast range of factual propositions about the world, such as 'Obama is President'. S can also predict a vast range of O's counterfactual beliefs, such as 'If the President resigns, the Vice-President will become President'. Here, TT(Scientific) stands in sharp contrast to the parsimonious ST view. That ST view starts from the idea that S will predict that O will have the same view as S on a particular proposition P. Nichols and Stich (2003, p. 104) set out this problem as follows: 'normal adults readily attribute large numbers of beliefs to other people, even when they have no apparent evidence, and most of these attributions are correct'. By the lack of evidence, they mean that S will often be right about who O thinks is President, even though S has no evidence at all about what O believes about anything, and indeed O may be an unspecified person about whom nothing of relevance is known. We can all predict whether the 5,000th person listed in the Detroit phone book will assert or deny the proposition that 'Obama is President'.

Nichols and Stich (2003, p. 107) point out here that the only recourse for TT(Scientific) is more theory. They canvass one possible response, noting that proponents of TT(Scientific) 'might protest that default attribution is theory mediated, and that the relevant part of the theory is simply the proposition: (1) Most people believe most of what I believe'. But Nichols and Stich (2003, p. 107) respond that this does not allow sufficient sophistication. It would 'generate chaos if the model also contained most of [S's] own beliefs, since some of those beliefs will be incompatible with the discrepant beliefs of [O]'. The problem here arises when S is trying to predict what O believes about P when that is different to what S believes. Imagine that O believes that Obama has resigned. We can see that S will be able to predict successfully a range of other propositions that O will believe: for example, 'the Vice-President will become President'; 'Obama will leave the White House' etc. Note that none of these are true and none of them are believed by S. So for S to simply start from his own beliefs and ascribe them wholesale to O will not do. Some much more sophisticated mechanism to predict what O believes and does not believe is needed. Finding a theory to do that is taxing. Simulating that is easy. S simply needs to imagine that Obama has resigned and ask himself 'in this scenario, what else do I believe?'. It is notable that Nichols and Stich appeal to simulational elements at this point in their own hybrid account.

ToM users must solve the frame problem

The frame problem is a very difficult one, with variants cropping up in several domains of thought. Since it is widely discussed, I will just briefly outline the nature of the problem and then its relevance to ToM, before turning to responses made on behalf of TT(Scientific).

When we make a decision or form a belief, we must consider relevant facts before doing so if we are to do so appropriately. The relevant facts form the 'frame' of a question. For example, if I want to decide whether to take an umbrella, I will learn a relevant fact from the weather forecast: whether it is expected that it will rain. The set of such relevant facts make up the 'frame' of the question. There are other relevant facts which fall into the frame; potentially this number is quite large. Remaining with the example, my decision about the umbrella is defeasible by facts in certain other scenarios. For instance, I may abandon my previous decision to take an umbrella even if I learn from the weather forecast that it is expected to rain if it is also true that I do not expect to be outside for very long during the day.

This leads to the frame problem. I must consider all of the relevant facts, but the number of potentially relevant facts is too large for them all to be considered. But how can I decide whether a potentially relevant fact is an actually relevant fact without considering it? Thus it seems I need to examine every fact I know to see if it is in the frame for a particular question. That task is impossible. On top of this, I need an updated model of the world to reflect the consequences of my actions, which means I need to know what facts to change in the model. Solving the frame problem seems to be extremely difficult. The difficulty of the question takes two forms. In artificial intelligence, it seems impossible to give a computer any algorithmic way of resolving the frame problem. In human psychology, it is also very unclear how we solve the frame problem.[4]

The frame problem translates straightforwardly into problems for ToM. If S is to predict and explain the behaviour of O, how does S decide which of O's probable beliefs and desires are relevant, and which axioms of ToM to apply on any given occasion of prediction and explanation?[5] Since on TT(Scientific), ToM is just the application of axioms to beliefs and desires, there seems little scope to avoid the frame problem. By contrast, ST can employ whatever mechanism we use generally to solve the frame problem when we make decisions. It may be that what that mechanism is exactly will remain forever beyond human knowledge, but there must be an answer, and it may be that it does not use algorithmic mechanics like those employed in ToM on the TT(Scientific) account. This again is a parsimony benefit to ST by comparison with TT. ST requires only that

S can believe P as opposed to theorise about believing P, and we already know S can believe P.[6]

A response to this objection has been supplied by Glymour (2000), who restates the problem in terms of causation. In this form, the problem is knowing what facts to change in the model of the world as a result of a potential action: what effects will be caused by my action? This I need to know in order to decide whether it is a good idea to take the action or not. Glymour (2000, p. 65) writes, contra Hume (2000), that causation can be observed or at least learned: the child learning TT(Scientific) 'notes associations either produced by its actions or otherwise, and the time order of associated events. From that information it infers that some associated features are not causally connected . . . or are more or less directly causally connected'. For example, if the child observes that crying leads to the arrival of parents, it will conclude that the former causes the latter.

As Glymour (2000, p. 65) concedes, however, 'the procedure is reliable only so long as a form of 'closed world' assumption holds, namely that the associations the baby . . . observes are not produced by unobserved or unnoticed common causes'. The difficulty is that if the child always kicks and cries, it would not be able to decide whether it was the kicking or the crying that led to the arrival of the parents. That particular difficulty would be soluble empirically for the child scientist of the TT(Scientific) account: it could kick without crying and see if the parents arrived. However, while using this 'closed world' assumption may work in this special case, the TT(Scientific) account needs it to work for all causal chains in the world connected and unconnected with actions. The child cannot determine whether thunder causes lightning or an unobserved third event – an electrical discharge – causes both by this method because it is not possible to run an experiment with and without the unobserved third event.[7]

ToM is inexplicably convergent

This objection notes that all children in all cultures develop approximately the same ToM at approximately the same time. They make more-or-less the same behavioural predictions and all begin to pass the False Belief Task at around the same age. As Carruthers puts it, 'it remains remarkable that all normal children should end up with the same body of knowledge at about the same time' (Carruthers and Smith 1996, pp. 31–32). On TT(Scientific), the children are supposed to be developing their ToM by forming hypotheses and confirming or disconfirming them based on the behaviour they see around them. The problem for TT(Scientific) is that this behavioural evidence base will be very different in different cultures and so it is hard to explain why there is a cross-cultural convergence in ToM.

The syllogistic form of this argument is as below.

- P1: Children develop their ToM by observing relevant behaviour around them.

- P2: The relevant behaviour around them is culturally specific.
- C: Children develop culturally specific ToM.

The problem for TT(Scientific) is then that the conclusion C to which it seems committed is empirically false. Three potential responses seem available. TT(Scientific) may deny premise P1; it may deny premise P2; or it may accept both and affirm the conclusion against the previously cited empirical data.

On reflection, it seems difficult for TT(Scientific) to deny premise 1 without becoming TT(Innate). Abandoning observation of behaviour as the dataset children use to develop their ToM makes it unclear what that dataset could be without being innate. Children need something with which to challenge their hypotheses and sort the confirmed from the disconfirmed.

TT(Scientific) could deny premise 2. It does seem possible to suggest that the term 'relevant' could do significant work in the argument. This line would attempt to make out that while there are many cultural differences in behaviour between different societies, what matters to the development of ToM is 'deeper'. So while the stockbroker in Manhattan may go to a hot dog stand while the Japanese doctor visits the sushi restaurant, both are acting on similar belief/desire pairs. It is the way belief/desire pairs interact to produce behaviour that is important to the development of ToM; the exact content of the belief/desire pairs is unimportant. While this line seems possible, it has not to my knowledge been attempted in the literature and so it remains to be seen to what extent it would be successful.

The conclusion has been affirmed, by producing additional empirical data at odds with that supporting the claim that ToM is universal. There is some data suggesting that children in different cultures do indeed have different ToM. Strijbos and De Bruin (2013, p. 746) argue that 'there are large differences between the mature folk psychologies of various cultures' and also 'large variations in the [age of] onset of false belief understanding' (Strijbos and De Bruin 2013, p. 747).

Gopnik and Wellman also offer a response to this objection which may be seen as taking the form of affirming the conclusion. They suggest that since adults converge on the same ToM, we should expect children to do so also. Segal observes the inadequacy of this response by noting that we might still 'ask how the adults happened to converge' (Carruthers and Smith 1996, p. 153). Since they deny the conclusion, they may also be denying premise 2, but this is unclear.

Some type of evolutionary explanation might be possible, along the lines of 'everyone has this ToM because this is the ToM that works'. Such a line would have to deal with some very hard questions including that natural selection selects for success and not truth. We would not have the most true ToM, but the ToM that was most beneficial for us. It might be that ToM errors of some sorts are adaptationally fit, for example systematic overestimation of our own capacities as compared with those of others. Again, since none of this has been attempted, we do not know how successful it would be.

ToM is too sophisticated for children

This objection holds that TT(Scientific) ascribes unrealistically complicated abilities to everyone, but especially young children, who seem to acquire ToM abilities when only four of five years old, and possibly much earlier. There is not enough time for children to complete an extensive programme of hypothesis formation, confirmation and disconfirmation and theory building. Moreover, the majority of children must complete the programme, even if they are cognitively disadvantaged. An exception to that rule would be provided by autistic children, who seem to have ToM deficits, but that exception does not seem to be extendable more widely to benefit the TT(Scientific) case. I will canvass two responses to the objection that have been made on behalf of TT(Scientific) and argue that since neither of the responses succeed, this objection sets out a serious problem for TT(Scientific).

One response to this objection has been provided on behalf of TT(Scientific) by Gopnik and Wellman (1992, p. 167), who argue that the objection requires that we have 'some a priori way of measuring the temporal course of conceptual change, of saying what is slow or fast or easy or difficult'. They give as an example the difficulty of assessing how demanding it is to understand the heliocentric theory. Measured 'socially', developing the heliocentric theory may have taken centuries, as the necessary developments in observational technology and mathematical underpinnings were put in place. However, Gopnik and Wellman (1992, p. 167) argue that Kepler did not take a long time to formulate it and also a modern student learns it in 'days, weeks or months'. This response is inadequate for a number of reasons. First, it seems unmotivated to exclude the underpinnings to Kepler's work that were prerequisites to his breakthrough. Even if we exclude work done by others – which is dramatically different to how science actually makes progress – it is hard to believe that Kepler started and finished his work on the heliocentric theory in a short period, even if it culminated in a breakthrough moment. This weakens the analogy and the evidence that both scientific theory change and children's ToM development are similarly quick and easy. Second and relatedly, children are developing and formulating ToM on their own – there are no preschool classes in 'predicting the behaviour of others'. There are two scenarios between which Gopnik and Wellman wish to draw an analogy. In one scenario, we have Kepler using the entire development of science, observational technology and mathematics developed by society that was available to him to develop the heliocentric theory. In the second scenario, children are developing ToM using only what is innate or observable by the pre-five-year-old, who moreover is not born with observational capacities fully developed. Third, Kepler was a very special and talented individual while ToM is acquired by almost all children, including the less special and less talented.

Nichols and Stich also consider this objection, complaining that TT(Scientific) does not explain detailed behaviour prediction in children. The starting point is the observation that children even as young as three are very good at coming up with predictions of behaviour which are highly specific and apt under the exact circumstances of the scenario in question. As Nichols and Stich point out, Gopnik and Wellman attempt to explain this by postulating something akin to a practical syllogism as one of the axioms of the children's ToM. The practical syllogism takes the form 'If an agent desires x, and sees that x exists, he will do things to get x' (Nichols and Stich 2003, p. 108). This appears acceptable as a framework initially, but Nichols and Stich (2003, p. 108) then pose a series of questions which expose severe underdetermination using this axiom of the answers provided by children and their specificity.

Nichols and Stich (2003, p. 108) ask: 'But what "things" will the agent do to get x? If a 3-year-old knows that Mary wants an apple, how does the 3-year-old predict the way in which Mary will satisfy her desire? Will Mary slither on her stomach to the nearest apple?'. This negative point brings out that the three-year-old will exclude a large number of potentially possible but in fact impracticable behaviours aimed at getting x, as well as of course a large number of impossible behaviours. The three-year-old will not predict that Mary will move in an inefficient manner to the nearest apple nor will the three-year-old predict that Mary will teleport to the nearest apple. Already this shows the existence of a set of demands on a TT(Scientific) account which make ToM appear very demanding. Moreover, Nichols and Stich (2003, p. 108) make the positive point that the TT(Scientific) account 'grossly understates the predictive capacities of the young child who can also predict that Mary will walk to the fridge, open the fridge door, pull open the appropriate drawer, pick an apple up with her hands (not with her feet or her elbows), and so on'. All of this together with a myriad similar items must be specified in ToM on the TT(Scientific) account. Much more plausibly and parsimoniously, ST accounts can have the child simply drop in whatever s/he would do if s/he wanted an apple; the child's options will not include teleporting to the apple or the use of feet to pick up apples, and so neither will the child's predictions.

The difficulty of this objection is sharpened if Onishi and Baillargeon (2005) are correct in their claims that 15-month-old infants can succeed on non-linguistic variants of the False Belief Task – because 15-month-old infants are not fully developed linguistically or otherwise as well as proto-scientifically. Strijbos and De Bruin (2013, p. 755) cite several replications of the Onishi and Baillargeon results including 'even 13-month-olds'. These results mean first that the complexity objection is made more difficult for TT because it is now postulated that the ability to handle such complexity arrives at a much earlier age than the four to five years that had generally been accepted previously as the age onset of competence in the False Belief Task. But also, the results mean that TT must account for non-linguistic infants being able to succeed on the False Belief Task.

To prefigure the forthcoming discussion of problems for TT(Innate) briefly, we might note that this complexity objection prompted the shift from TT(Scientific) to TT(Innate). Now it seems however that TT(Innate) is postulating that children who do not yet have the body of knowledge that allows them linguistic capacities – or at least cannot yet use that body of knowledge – can nevertheless use the linguistic-like body of knowledge that allows them ToM capacities, on the TT(Innate) account. This is not impossible, but what independent motivation can be produced for the claim that children can use their ToM body of linguistic knowledge but not their actual linguistic body of knowledge at 13 months?

ToM construction is disanalogous to science

Gopnik and Wellman espouse the weaker claim, as we can see from their discussion of children developing their ToM by changing from an early theory to a more advanced one. They employ the term 'similar' when they write: 'during the period from three to four many children are in a state of transition between the two theories, similar, say to the fifty years between the publication of *De Revolutionibus* and Kepler's discovery of elliptical orbits' (Gopnik and Wellman 1992, p. 156, original emphasis). *De Revolutionibus* is the book in which Copernicus describes the heliocentric theory, so the two stages here may be termed 'descriptive' and then 'explanatory', though of course 'explaining' the fact that the planets orbit the sun by the fact that they have elliptical orbits around the sun opens up further questions that require explanation, such as why the planets have elliptical orbits. The analogy then that Gopnik and Wellman are pushing ought to have this same descriptive/explanatory staging. The descriptive stage could be of observed facts of behaviour while the explanation thereof is the postulated mental states. The further questions would also have analogues, in questions as to why people have those particular mental states.

The stronger claim is more formally put as holding that 'scientific inference and early cognitive development are subserved by the very same mental mechanisms' (Fuller 2013, p. 109). Fuller divides accounts of scientific inference into four types: 'population-level, normative, competence, and performance' and argues that Gopnik as a primary advocate of TT(Scientific) fails to distinguish between them. If that is an exhaustive list of types of scientific inference, then TT(Scientific) proponents must be arguing that there is an analogy between at least one of those types of scientific inference and the child's ToM development process. It is not possible to say to which of the four types of scientific inference TT(Scientific) finds children's development analogous, because a typical claim is that the development of ToM may be understood as analogous to 'development . . . of bodies of professional scientific knowledge' (Davies and Stone 1995, p. 4). In any case, Fuller goes on to give convincing arguments why the strong claim fails in each of the four cases.

The 'population-level' account of scientific inference observes that the various stages of progress described by TT(Scientific) – hypothesis formation, testing, revision etc. – may be conducted by different individuals and in fact often are, as in the Darwinian example Fuller gives. There would then be 'different cognitive dynamics in a typical scientist and a typical child' (Fuller 2013, pp. 113–114) thus destroying the analogy. In the 'normative' account, Fuller allows that Gopnik might on behalf of TT(Scientific) attempt to escape this objection by admitting that science may not proceed with each individual going through hypothesis stages as above, but that it ought to. Fuller (2013, p. 116) raises a powerful objection here: the account is now trying to draw analogies between 'highly idealised scientists on the one hand and more or less actual children on the other'. A second escape which is also somewhat normative is represented by the 'competence' account, covering the last two of Fuller's four types of inference. This uses a 'competence/performance distinction' (Fuller 2013, p. 117) allowing that scientists may not always perform at their best, and it is this which compromises the analogy between scientists as children. Here, Fuller (2013, p. 118) objects that most 'performance conditions that could compromise a given cognitive competence are shared by children and scientists' since both children and scientists can be forgetful or distracted etc.

Turning to the weaker claim, Fuller (2013, p. 109) argues that 'even a weaker analogy between childhood cognitive development and scientific inference has severe limitations [since] scientific inference is subserved by significant levels of cross-domain processing while early cognitive development is not'. Breakthroughs in science are often 'unifying explanations' (Fuller 2013, p. 120) where theories are extended to new domains or hitherto unrecognised similarities between apparently disparate areas are exploited. Children by contrast do not seem to apply lessons from different domains in this way. Fuller thus concludes that there is very little that is analogous between scientific inference and children's cognitive development at all, including their development of ToM abilities.

Objections to TT(Innate)

TT(Innate) cannot parsimoniously account for development

Some commentators have argued that TT(Innate) is less able to account for development than TT(Scientific). TT(Scientific) is inherently developmental: it can easily account for changes in the ToM capacities of children by postulating theory change. That line seems less available to nativist accounts, because if they postulate innate capacities, then at first glance it seems that those capacities are fixed. TT(Innate) proponents have resisted the charge that modularist versions of TT(Innate) cannot account for development in the two ways discussed above. There is the parameterist response of Segal, discussed previously, which suggests that the modules making up ToM may be innate but develop according to the switching of parameters. As the child learns, it does not create new modules, but tunes innate modules by the setting of parameters. For example, it moves from the less advanced ToM which uses PRELIEF – i.e. an unsophisticated combination of PRETENCE and BELIEF – by changing the PRELIEF parameter. Alternatively, the anti-parameterist response of Scholl and Leslie suggests that the modularist can account for development by postulating that modules may come on-line at different points. It does seem as though at the least, the TT(Innate) camp will need additional machinery introduced to their view to account for development.

As Scholl and Leslie (1999, p. 144) point out, Stich and Nichols 'defend a modularity view against a "theory" theory by repeatedly pointing out that a module with enough parameters effectively reduces to a theory'. This is a slightly strange defence, in that it seems in fact to point to collapse risk between TT(Innate) – the 'modularity view' – and TT(Scientific) – the 'theory' theory view. If TT(Innate) is not separate from TT(Scientific), then it cannot be defended by attacking TT(Scientific). However, for our purposes, collapse risk between different sorts of TT is not a concern. In any case, it does appear that both accounting for development of ToM by postulating either a large number of parameters, or a large number of stages of module initiation, represents a significant lack of parsimony and is rather *ad hoc*.

Simulationist accounts can avoid these problems by suggesting as a first approximation that the child can simulate in others what it can do itself. That account is also naturally developmental, but also allows for a less than total correlation between development of the child's own mental capacities and its abilities to simulate those same mental capacities in others because the latter task is more difficult.

TT(Innate) does not explain default belief attribution

Nichols and Stich bring the same objection to TT(Innate) as they did to TT(Scientific). They note that it is a good starting point in ToM for S to attribute all of S's beliefs to O, unless there is a reason not to. This is because that will in broad brush terms supply the right sort of context – a picture of the world – for O's reasoning. Nichols and Stich (2003, p. 120) cite Leslie as arguing that a 'belief that misinforms an agent is a useless, even a dangerous, thing: beliefs ought to be true. Therefore, the optimal default strategy for the [S] is to assume that [O's] beliefs are true'. This approach is successful for many routine exercises of ToM capacities, when S and O share the same true beliefs about the relevant facts of the situation.

Of course, this default strategy needs to be overridden for some scenarios: such as in the False Belief Task because this is precisely about S predicting O's behaviour when S knows that O does not believe or know something that S believes and knows is true. Nichols and Stich note that Leslie can employ this shift away from the default strategy to explain the improvement in ToM that takes place when children begin to pass the False Belief Task. S's who are adults or older children have the ability to avoid default attributing their entire belief set to O and that is why they can pass the False Belief Task. Younger children cannot avoid total default attribution and that is why they fail the False Belief Task. Nichols and Stich (2003, p. 120) cite Leslie describing this as follows: 'the modular Theory-of-Mind-Mechanism, ToMM: "ToMM always makes the current situation available as a possible and even preferred content because (a) the current situation is a truer picture of the world, and (b) beliefs tend to be true"'. Then Nichols and Stich (2003, p. 120) observe that there is a fundamental conflict between this idea and the advertised Fodorean nature of the modules proposed in ToMM or TT(Innate): the conflict flows from the fact that 'an essential characteristic of modules is that they are informationally encapsulated'. So how can 'the current situation' be made available to an encapsulated module? Indeed, 'a cognitive system that has unrestricted access to all of the mind reader's beliefs would be a paradigm case of a non-modular system' (Nichols and Stich 2003, p. 121).

A non-modular version of TT(Innate) might be able to avoid this objection, but no such account has been proposed. Nichols and Stich also say that versions of this objection mean that TT(Innate) cannot explain either detailed behaviour predictions or inference predictions, because both processes need access to other beliefs of S which a module by definition cannot access. In behaviour prediction, the three-year-old needs to access inter alia his beliefs that teleportation is impossible and slithering impractical in order to predict that Mary will walk to the fridge to get an apple. In inference prediction, S needs to access inter alia his belief that the Vice-President is next in line to the Presidency if the President resigns in order to predict successfully what O will say about what will happen next if the President resigns.

A simulationist account of ToM avoids these difficulties because the whole approach is to model O as being like S, meaning that the starting point for S is default belief attribution to O of S's beliefs.

TT(Innate) does not explain autism

Nichols and Stich claim that the TT(Innate) explanation of the deficits and development of autistic subjects is inadequate, which is a serious embarrassment for TT(Innate) since it focussed on autism to provide much of its supporting evidence. They also note in passing that proponents of TT(Scientific) have not addressed in detail the topic of autism, and that this is a problem since autistic subjects have well-known ToM deficits which all plausible accounts of ToM should explain.

The TT(Innate) account of autism begins from two suggestive facts about autistic subjects. They engage in pretend play much less and much later than non-autistic children. Also, they have well-known ToM deficits, passing the False Belief Task much later than non-autistic children, even when matched for IQ. Unsurprisingly, Leslie, who is the main proponent of TT(Innate), argues that these two facts are related. Nichols and Stich (2003, pp. 128–129) set out this view of TT(Innate) as follows: 'Leslie also maintains that mindreading is central to pretence and he holds that ToMM plays a central role in the capacity for pretence . . . It is ToMM . . . that does not develop normally in people with autism'. So the TT(Innate) view is that the undeveloped ToMM in autistic subjects causes both the impaired mind reading and the lack of pretend play that is observed.

One merit of this account is that it explains why children spend so much time pretending that they are, for example, at a tea party with teddy bears that drink pretend tea and, it is pretended, enjoy conversation. The children are in fact exercising their ToMM, which brings important social advantages in childhood and later. The type of exercise involved would be in predicting what teddy might say about the tea he is enjoying, and how he might later say he has had enough tea and it is time to go back to the woods etc. All of this is good practice in ToM use for the children, who we know are predicting the speech and action of teddy because they are supplying teddy with that pretended speech and action.

One aspect of pretence which all accounts of it must explain relates to encapsulation. By this is meant that there must be some way of quarantining propositions held true only within the pretence from the general beliefs of the pretending subject. It would not occur, for example, that an adult who had been pretending to be at the teddy bears' tea party would refuse a cup of tea later on because they had already pretended to drink a cup of tea. Leslie proposes that one of the mental representations underlying the tea party pretence might have the form: I Pretend 'this empty cup contains tea'. So there is a Pretend operator which operates on an actual object, the empty cup, and applies a special proposition to it: that it contains tea. The special proposition is special in that its entailments are not to be used to form further beliefs, as they would be normally. By contrast, if I had already in reality drunk a cup of tea, I would later be disposed to assert the proposition 'I have had a hot drink' which I would not be if I had merely pretended to drink a cup of tea.

Nichols and Stich devote the entire second chapter of their book to denying that mind reading is central to pretence as Leslie claims. Their central objection is simulationist in spirit. It challenges Leslie's Pretend operator which they think is too sophisticated for children to use. Nichols and Stich (2003, p. 51), write that 'the pretence could proceed perfectly well even if the subject did not have the concept of pretence'. So the idea is similar to the simulationist one that S does not need the concept BELIEF in order to have beliefs and requiring the former rather than the latter to explain children's ToM capacities is to demand too much.

As this entire simulationist aspect of the Nichols and Stich account suggests, the ST account of ToM has a ready explanation of links between pretend play and ToM. It can simply say that autistic subjects who are less able to supply pretend dialogue for teddy are by the same token less able to imaginatively project themselves into teddy's position or anyone else's. Since that is exactly what ToM requires on the simulationist account, it is unsurprising that autistic subjects exhibit ToM deficits.

Objections to hybridist accounts

I will first outline what we can learn about the Hybridist aspect of Saxe's position from some brief initial exchanges about her key paper. In support of her stated preferred option, an interacting Hybridist theory, Saxe cites two papers: Ames on everyday ToM use and Epley *et al.* on perspective taking. So after examining the initial exchanges, I will review what benefits Saxe can draw from each of those two papers.

The initial exchanges

A charge that Saxe assumes that ST must rely on mirror neurone pictures of simulation is brought by Goldman and Sebanz (2005, p. 320), who therefore claim that her challenge has no force against any ST not so grounded. Goldman and Sebanz argue that the point Saxe (2005a) makes that the mirror neurone brain regions are not the same as the brain regions for thinking about belief 'doesn't exclude the possibility that non-mirroring simulation is the substrate for the mindreading of beliefs'. Two non-mirroring options for simulation would be 'mental pretence or perspective taking' (Goldman and Sebanz 2005, p. 320). Goldman and Sebanz also claim that the error asymmetry, which Saxe complains cannot be explained by ST, is in fact better explained by it in some cases. They argue that the 'characteristic outcome of poor perspective taking is egocentricity, an error or bias widely reported in the literature' (Goldman and Sebanz 2005, p. 320), meaning that ST predicts the observed effect whereby we 'project [our] own states onto the target' (Goldman and Sebanz 2005, p. 320).

Saxe (2005d, p. 321) responds to these charges with a countercharge that Goldman and Sebanz have 'confuse[d] the source of information (the observer's own experiences) with the cognitive process for detecting that information (mirroring or resonance)'. Since, as Saxe (2005d, p. 321) holds, her 'argument from error is aimed only at the latter', Goldman and Sebanz's charge can have no force. She therefore allows that S's own experience may form part of the background to S's ToM capacities, but denies that the cognitive processing underlying ToM uses either mirroring or resonance to apply that experience.

Gordon has three arguments. First, Gordon (2005, p. 362) argues that the Ruffman data can also be accommodated by ST. Second, Gordon (2005, p. 362) notes that 'Saxe objects to any attempt to "save" ST merely by hypothesizing that the children failed to provide the right inputs to simulation'. Saxe demands that ST explain why the inputs were wrong in the right way, as it were. Gordon's rejoinder is to complain that this is an unfair burden. TT does not explain why there seems to be an axiom holding 'ignorance means you get it wrong' and so ST need not explain it either. Gordon's third and final point is on Cognitive Penetrability. Nichols, Stich, Leslie and Klein explain that a 'capacity is cognitively penetrable . . . if that capacity is affected by the subject's ignorance or knowledge of the domain' (Carruthers and Smith 1996, p. 46). The challenge is that the presence of Cognitive Penetrability in a process is good evidence for that process being a TT process, whereas ST processes would more likely be akin to a 'black box'. Saxe (2005a) urges that if S's have beliefs about how the mind works, and those beliefs are used in a Cognitively Penetrable ToM process, then there will be errors in ToM predictions which reflect those beliefs. This in essence is Saxe's 'suspicious congruency' challenge. Gordon's response is to invert the order of explanation. It is just as likely that the errors cause the beliefs as that the beliefs cause the errors.

Saxe replies by noting that Gordon has only provided an explanation of one ToM error among the many she notes. To be fair to Gordon, he has only been allowed a letter format for his response. However, Saxe is entitled to demand that more of her examples be responded to on behalf of ST, and it is that project I embark on in this book. Saxe (2005c, p. 362) also responds to Gordon by considering his question as to 'why [we should] conclude that "ignorance = being wrong" is actually one of the children's beliefs about the mind?' by answering '[b]ecause in some cases, they say so'. This response seems inadequate because Gordon could point to manifold errors in childrens' beliefs about how the mind works; indeed, we seem to be discussing just that. Ultimately, Saxe (2005c, p. 362) defers the verdict on her argument to subsequent empirical data when she writes 'the power of the argument from error will depend on its ability not just to explain known errors, but also to systematically predict unknown ones'.

Mitchell (2005, p. 363) claims mistakenly that Saxe does not adopt a Hybridist account. He accuses Saxe of insisting that 'because [S's] do not always simulate, they must never do so'. Mitchell's idea is that Saxe has argued for TT by claiming that TT and ST are the only two options and then producing data which are problematic for TT. Mitchell claims that Saxe's approach excludes the possibility of Hybridist accounts between ST and TT. However, Saxe is on safe ground in denying the claim that she is not a Hybridist in her response because she has explicitly espoused Hybridism in her original paper. As we saw above, Saxe (2005a, p. 175) writes that, in comparison with 'having two separate systems for reasoning about other minds' whereby in some scenarios S is a pure simulator and in others S is a pure theorist, a 'better option is to conclude that a naïve theory of mind, and some capacity to simulate, interact [Ames (Malle and Hodges 2005, Chapter 10)] (Epley *et al.* 2004)'. Mitchell may have missed this admission because it occurs only once in the paper as a caption to a figure in a small font. Mitchell may have been misled by Saxe's remarks in the main text to the effect that 'the process that generates the inputs to the simulation might include, or be influenced by, the observer's beliefs about beliefs' so the 'resulting hybrid model can explain all of the errors, but loses the parsimony of a pure Simulation Theory: the 'direct understanding' without 'explicit reflective mediation' (Saxe 2005a, p. 177). It seems as though Saxe is a reluctant Hybridist with a TT bent, since she clearly notes the lack of parsimony inherent in Hybridist theories.

Empathy data cited by Mitchell (2005, p. 363) shows that 'observers make judgements of another person's emotional state in relation to their own feelings (e.g. sad observers more readily perceive sadness in ambiguous facial displays than happy observers) and that this effect is eliminated when observers are prevented from spontaneously mimicking the target's facial expression'. These data comport more easily with ST than with TT because it appears that S's are using their own capacities to express emotions to read the emotions of others. It also illustrates the close links between accuracy of emotional match between S and O and concomitant accuracy of simulation, a point which will concern us much in the rest of this book.

Saxe (2005b, p. 364) responds initially by simply denying Mitchell's first charge: she 'does not claim that "because observers do not always simulate, they must never do so"'. She grants that simulation is active on some occasions.

Her problem though is that 'existing [hybrid] models are unsatisfying' because they define the domains for which simulation is to be used rather than theory by whether mental states are 'brief (simulation) [or] longer-term' or by whether attributions are 'accurate (simulation) [or] inaccurate' (Saxe 2005b, p. 364).[8] These charges seem reasonable, but also expose the difficulty of providing a motivated account of the workings of such a 'more integrated hybrid' (Saxe 2005b, p. 364), as I will argue below.[9]

Which tool when?

This topic as to which element of ToM is used under which circumstance is covered by Ames. On Ames's hybrid account, both theoretical and simulation-type activity form part of ToM capacity. Ames recognises four routes to mental state inference. The first two routes fall into the category of 'evidence-based strategies', which are the theoretical elements of the approach. The second two routes are called 'extra-target strategies'. The first of these is a simulational element. 'Extra-target' means S is to use his own simulational resources to infer the mental states of O, the target. It is unclear whether the fourth route, stereotyping is theoretical or simulational. The four routes to mental state inference are as set out in Table 4.1.

We know that the first 'evidence-based strategy', Route 1, is intended to be theoretical since 'perceivers readily work from the visible evidence of human behaviour to posit invisible underlying mental states' (Malle and Hodges 2005, p. 159). The mental states of O that are posited by S are theoretical entities; O need not in reality have them. As an example of Route 1, Ames gives 'a grabbing hand entails wanting' (Malle and Hodges 2005, p. 159), which would be the theoretical axiom here. Ames notes evidence that even six-month-old infants seem to work on this basis.

The second 'evidence-based strategy', Route 2, also appears theoretical. One example is 'a person beams when proud of her work' (Malle and Hodges 2005, p. 160). The sequence then is that O emits the emotional display of beaming, S uses 'emotional perception' to observe the beaming and interpret it, and S then attributes the emotion of pride to O based on the beaming. The theoretical axiom would be 'persons who beam are proud'.

Route 3 is an 'extra-target strategy' involving projection. This looks very much like a straightforward simulation approach. In other words, S 'assumes [O] has

Table 4.1 Ames's four routes to mental state inference

Strategy Type	*Source of Data*	*Use of Data*
1. Theoretical (evidence-based)	behaviours in context	attribution of mental states
2. Theoretical (evidence-based)	emotional displays	emotion perception
3. Simulational (extra-target)	S's own mental states	projection
4. Unclear (extra-target)	stereotypes	stereotyping

the same mental states that he or she has or would have' (Malle and Hodges 2005, p. 163). Ames's example here is 'I'd be embarrassed if I were in your shoes' (Malle and Hodges 2005, p. 159).

Route 4 is an 'extra-target strategy' involving stereotyping. This means the rather lazy prediction of the type that when S meets an O who is Canadian, S assumes that this O 'loves playing hockey' (Malle and Hodges 2005, p. 163). It is unclear whether this is theoretical or simulational; possibly it is both. There will need to be theoretical axioms like 'all Canadians love playing hockey', possibly combined with simulation of the sort 'if O loves playing hockey and it is O's day off, O is likely to be playing hockey'. Calling route four an extra-target strategy indicates the way that a lazy S will here make the same ToM predictions about all Canadians without reference to which exact Canadian O is being predicted or explained.

The difficulty for Ames relates to the status of his axioms. Returning to 'I'd be embarrassed if I were in your shoes': is this theoretical or simulational? Such an 'embarrassment' axiom is a good candidate for the sort of simulation-generated 'law' that in ST replaces the body of axioms needed by TT. Imagine that the embarrassing situation in question is raising your hand to ask a question in a seminar and finding you have forgotten the question. We will all predict that anyone doing this will feel embarrassed. On TT, that prediction arises because we have a theoretical axiom which states: 'anyone who raises their hand in a seminar to ask a question and then forgets what it is will enter the mental state labelled embarrassment'. On ST, the account is simpler. It merely inputs the pretend belief 'I have just raised my hand to ask a question and forgotten what it is; how do I feel?' and produces the output 'I feel embarrassed'.

Similarly, the ST account of Route 1 would be that when S sees the grabbing hand of O, this may be combined with the simulational output akin to 'when my hand grabs, I want something' to ascribe the wanting to O. This would be another process analogous to that postulated in the Motor Theory of Speech Perception discussed above. This approach is also available for Route 2. S can access the simulational output akin to 'when I beam, my emotional state is pride' and attribute pride to O. So it looks as though there are questions about which method underlies each route to mental state inference. The problem of disentangling the account to provide a detailed description of which route uses theory and simulation – and to what extent and how they interact – looks intractable.

Ames's subtitle is 'which tools are used when?' (Malle and Hodges 2005, p. 158) so he is fully aware that that question is germane and problematic for Hybridist theorists. We already have an indication that the question may be difficult to answer if the same prediction can be formed on both routes. What principled method can be recommended post hoc for deciding which method S actually employed when we only know that S has predicted or explained the embarrassment of O? The example suggests that this may be possible by including in the laws of TT an axiom to the effect that 'people who blush are embarrassed'. However, there is substantial discussion in the literature of how and whether we can distinguish shame and embarrassment, so it would need to be a more complicated axiom than that and some sub-axioms would need to come into play to provide a further subdivision.[10] We may see the Frame Problem rearing its head once more for TT, since rules will be needed to decide what data are relevant to the decision as to which rules shall be used.

An axiom of sorts is provided by Ames who notes that we may forgive someone who has, for example, spilt wine on a white carpet, if they exhibit appropriate remorse. The axiom is '[a]ffect qualifies behaviour in the near term: perceived remorseful affect can lead to ascriptions of good intent to harm-doers in the short run, but repeated harm drives long run ascriptions of bad intent' (Malle and Hodges 2005, p. 162). This in itself illustrates the difficulties of providing laws, but the very name Ames gives his axiom is telling: he calls it a 'contingency'. Now, a contingent event is one which is not certain but perhaps probable, and in this sense of contingency, Ames means to refer to something aiming to provide for the contingent event, should it occur. This again brings out the complexity of axioms problem for TT discussed above. Further complexity may be seen in Ames's description of the inputs: they include 'behaviour [and] arcs of behaviour over time and across situations' while 'affective displays may augment or discount behaviours' (Malle and Hodges 2005, p. 162) and that last factor also has a changing profile of effects over time. The ST account here is rather more simple.

Projection occurs when S 'assumes that [O] has the same mental states that [S] has or would have' (Malle and Hodges 2005, p. 163) so this is straightforwardly identified with simulation. I will not discuss this aspect of the Ames account further since it is just simulational.

To complete the picture, Ames also gives another example of stereotyping: 'Jocks hate romantic comedies' (Malle and Hodges 2005, p. 159). We now have the question though: 'who is a jock?' i.e. to which O should S apply the rule in order to predict that O does not like romantic comedies? The answer had better not be 'anyone who does not like romantic comedies is a jock' or the law has become circular. But there are similar risks involved in the other candidate characteristics. The chain 'jocks like beer'; 'who is a jock?'; 'everyone who likes beer is a jock' is vacuous and so are all the other candidate characteristics. These problems are familiar in philosophy in the form of 'how do we identify what falls under a concept?', to which question none of the available candidate answers – including 'concepts as prototypes' or stereotypes – seems workable.[11]

A similarity rule is proposed by Ames to decide whether a projection or stereotyping approach will be used in a particular use of ToM. He writes that 'perceptions of general similarity guide a trade-off between projection (ascribing [S's] own beliefs and desires to O's) and stereotyping' (Malle and Hodges 2005, p. 160). So the idea is that if S thinks O is like S, then S will simply simulate O on the model of S. That approach will not be used if S perceives a gross dissimilarity between S and O. If, for example, S perceives O as a jock and S himself as not a jock, S will use stereotyping to predict the behaviour of O. The similarity rule is again described as a second 'contingency' (Malle and Hodges 2005, p. 164) by Ames so we have further multiple branches of conditionality. Ames summarises the research as showing that often, 'projection and stereotyping function as alternative strategies that displace each other' (Malle and Hodges 2005, p. 165) which brings out a question deriving from Saxe's citation of this paper as an illustration of a purportedly superior interactionist Hybridist theory. The superiority might come from the two elements working together – i.e. at the same time on the same question – to provide a superior answer to a ToM question, where a superior answer is presumably a more accurate one. The other possibility though is that the interaction takes the form of a division of labour. Some questions may be best answered by simulation and others may be best answered by theory. The superiority may devolve from an apposite selection of methods rather than the application of both. It may be a stretch to call this an interactive Hybridist theory, but it still seems possible. However – what decides which approach is used if S has both routes open?

Handling this division is complex; all four possible routes to mental state inferences proposed in Ames's diagram must be accommodated. Ames offers a third contingency to do this, as follows. 'Cumulative behavioural evidence supersedes extra-target strategies: projection and stereotyping will drive mindreading when behavioural evidence is ambiguous, but as apparent evidence accumulates, inductive judgements will dominate' (Malle and Hodges 2005, p. 166). From our perspective, this means that before there is a sufficient weight of behavioural evidence, some mix of projection and stereotyping – i.e. some mix of simulation and theory – will prevail, but after that, the behavioural evidence will prevail. So we have a complex time development of interactions to handle as well.

We now need to know what mix of simulation/projection and stereotyping/theory operates in the initial stage. One answer to this is that empirically, it seems as though stereotyping is 'a default or initial stage of judgement' (Malle and Hodges 2005, p. 166). This means that S will make stereotypical predictions about O until S has sufficient observations of O to make a less stereotyped prediction. Other accounts though, take the opposite line. Ames mentions one view on which '[w]hen the responses of [O's] are not known, [S's] project their own as a first bet' (Malle and Hodges 2005, p. 166). That account leads on to the Epley *et al.* (2004) perspective-taking account to be discussed in the next section, where S predicts O's behaviour by using S's own projected behaviour as a starting point to be adjusted for O to produce the prediction. That then looks like a simulation starting point with a theoretical adjustment. Ames cites research intended to show that 'time pressure may reduce these adjustments while accuracy incentives may increase them' (Malle and Hodges 2005, p. 166). This gives us one account of interaction. It looks like we have a simulation/theory mix with time pressure increasing the amount of simulation to be expected, or perhaps the probability that the prediction made by ToM will reflect the quick, simulation answer, while accuracy incentives will decrease the probability or weighting of simulation in the final answer. This appears somewhat complicated; the complexity is further increased by Ames's list of items that may boost or inhibit consideration of behavioural evidence viz. 'interaction goals . . . self-relevancy . . . cognitive load . . . time constraints . . . social power' (Malle and Hodges 2005, p. 168).

As I have said elsewhere, my view seeks to reduce the motivation for moving away from pure ST. I offer a strong defence of ST, although only a weak defence would I think have value in the absence of anything else. The weak defence is that on the proposals I present in this book, ST can in fact account for the ToM errors described by Saxe (2005a) and her citations. The stronger defence is that ST can account for those errors more convincingly than TT can. That relies inter alia on the claim that ToM is overly complex on the TT account. This claim remains unshaken by Ames's discussion of a complex interactionist Hybrid.

Perspective taking

Epley *et al.* (2004, p. 328) argue for an 'anchoring and adjustment' paradigm which 'simplifies the complicated assessment of another's perspective by substituting one's own perception and adjusting as needed'. The first element, the substitution, is simulation because it means S uses S as his starting point for arriving at a prediction for O. The adjustment is then added by theoretical means on this interactionist Hybridist account. This model 'is therefore most likely to be engaged when one's own perspective is readily accessible but another's perspective must be inferred' (Epley *et al.* 2004, p. 328). On this account, the model is not invariably engaged, and thus we are entitled to ask when and why on the occasions when it is. Some light may be thrown on that by the supporting claims that it will be in situations when one's own perspective is readily available. That brings up the standard issue of Introspectionism which in turn leads on to a problem for all Hybridist theories. ST tends to be Introspectionist while TT tends to be Anti-Introspectionist. Which way will a Hybridist jump? An account should not simultaneously rely on assertion and denial of Introspectionism.[12]

Epley *et al.* (2004) investigated understanding of ambiguous messages which could be interpreted as sarcastic or not. For example, one message about a comedian was that 'you have to see him yourself to believe how hilarious he really is' (Epley *et al.* 2004, p. 329). The variable that was adjusted was a description of the comedy show that was either positive or negative. S's were then asked to predict whether O's would understand the message as being sarcastic depending both on whether S had the positive or negative description and whether O did. Epley *et al.* (2004, p. 329) found that 'people adopt others' perspectives by adjusting from their own'. This is consistent with a simulational start point – 'own perspective' – and a theoretical adjustment – O had a different description of the event than S did. However, it is also consistent with an entirely simulational account: 'what would I think if I had a different description of the event?'

Another type of adjustment investigated by Epley *et al.* (2004) is where people shift their estimates of the percentages of their peers who will hear something unclear when they themselves know the 'right' answer. For example, there are claims that certain songs contain secret messages when played backwards. The lyrics of a song sound meaningless backwards until one is told what the hidden message is supposed to be, whereupon that hidden message becomes obvious. This is also what is observed, with 88 per cent of informed participants and 0 per cent of uninformed participants believing they heard the message. Epley *et al.* also expected 'informed participants to estimate that a higher percentage of their peers would hear the phrase than participants who were uninformed' (Epley *et al.* 2004, p. 334) and this is indeed what was found. So the anchor here is whether S gets the message, which itself is basically controlled by whether S has been told the content of the message. S is then asked to estimate how many O's will get the message, and does this by starting from whether S did as an anchor. This is in essence a simulational account.

Remarkably, people agree with propositions more if they are nodding their heads when they say them. Epley *et al.* (2004, p. 334) use this result to hypothesise that S's 'who were nodding their heads should be more egocentric and give more extreme responses than participants who were shaking their heads'. This hypothesis was confirmed. There may be a TT account of this. There is an ST one, which is once more based on claims analogous to those made by the Motor Theory of Speech Perception. Simulationists can argue that head nodding influences simulation, since head nodding is what S does when S favours a view. Therefore if S is basing a prediction about O based on S and S is currently nodding, the simulation process will start by modelling O's level of assent as adjusted upwards by S's nodding. It 'looks to S' more like O is favouring a view, or in this case, 'getting the message'.

Accuracy increases over time; Epley *et al.* find that the amount of adjustment increases from the egocentric anchor if time is not an issue while egocentric errors increase for harried S's. This might be explained as meaning that extra time is available to apply theoretical adjustments thus improving accuracy. However, there is a very clear route whereby additional simulation may improve accuracy. This technique is known in mathematics and physics as Monte Carlo simulation. The idea is to run many simulations with slightly shifted input conditions and consider the results of all of them. This provides a better estimation of the outcome when the exact initial conditions are unknown. The name Monte Carlo derives from the fact that the initial conditions are randomly smeared by small amounts reflecting the quantum of uncertainty of those inputs.[13] We may assume that multiple simulations will also allow the human mind to make better ToM judgements if the time is available to perform them; also many simulations could be run in parallel. There is thus no need to retreat to a Hybridist theory, as Goldman (2006, p. 184) does when faced with this question. It is no objection here to say that we do not have phenomenology consistent with running multiple simulations, since we also do not have phenomenology consistent with running a single simulation or using a theory. Although Monte Carlo simulations for physics purposes use theoretical input, they need not do so in all cases of simulation.

The conclusion of Epley *et al.* (2004, p. 338) is replete with caveats: 'individuals' attempts at perspective taking are often something of an integration of theory and simulation. Adults' use of their own perspective as an anchor is similar to using one's self as a source model for predicting others. Additionally, adults' adjustment from that anchor is likely guided by their theories about how different perspectives and psychological states influence judgement and perception.' Perspective taking is 'often' 'something of an integration' i.e. not always; we are not told what 'something' means and we do not know whether to interpret 'integration' as more like 'summation' or 'selection'. The anchoring is 'similar' to simulation. Adjustment is 'likely' guided by theory. We are entitled to ask what evidence supports all of these hedges, what they are intended to carve out, and why, if not to explain inconvenient data. The ST perspective can naturally accept the anchoring side wholesale, so whether the adjustment process must be theoretical is a crucial point. There seems to be no reason at all why it could not be further application of simulation, but with shifted inputs: what would O believe if O was missing facts known to S is a different simulation that allows S to take O's perspective.

All of the theoretical elements in the Hybridist theory here investigated depend on the adjustments in, for example, the lyric perception task, which can be equally well or better explained by additional simulation.

Conclusion

All Hybridists face severe dialectical challenges. The Hybridist line seems to be forced on them by hard cases brought by the other side. Apart from the obvious lack of parsimony, the claim would presumably be that while their preferred ST or TT account does the bulk of the work, some admixture of the other account must be admitted for some questions. Alternatively, some questions may lie entirely in the domain of the other theory. This then entitles us to ask how much of the work is ascribed to the other theory, and what that claim even means. Commentators are here forced into vagueness. For example, Goldman (1993a, p. 107), who is the opposite of Saxe in that he is a reluctant Hybridist with an ST bent, writes that he will: 'make no blanket rejection of "theoretical" inference in self- or other-ascription. I just doubt that that's where all the action is, or even most of it'.

We can understand what it would mean for less than all of the action to be in simulation or theory. That is nothing more than a restatement of the Hybridist position. However, we may legitimately require the Hybridist to say more about the mix. Goldman thinks that 'most of the action' is simulation. Does that mean that 80 per cent of ToM activity is in simulation, and how would such a calculation be made? It might be done by dividing the number of questions resolved by simulation by the total, or the number of propositions, or the occasions of use. All of that would be complicated by any occasions of interactionist ToM use. Bach (2011, p. 28) describes the positions of the Hybridist theorists as involving the following calculation: '[i]f the majority of tasks are given to simulation, then simulation is termed the 'default' process (Goldman), and if the majority is given to theory, then theory is the default process (Nichols and Stich)'. This seems unhelpful since not only is the question unanswerable, but it is not clear what non-circular value has been added by declaring one other of TT or ST the default process.

There is also the question as to where the charge of *ad hoc* domain specification may best be laid. Saxe (2005a, p. 177) claims that historically, 'proposals for when [S's] use simulation tend to be somewhat *ad hoc*'. The problem with this charge for Saxe derives from the fact that Saxe is a Hybridist, accepting a role for ST. Therefore her criticism about the *ad hoc* nature of the domain of application of simulation applies with equal force to her position. Indeed, it is even more virulent, because Saxe has not only the *ad hoc* domain for simulation, but additional *ad hoc* domains for theory and then for the interaction region where simulation and theory interact.

I conclude that moving to a Hybridist account is not the answer, both because of the costs of Hybridism and because of the costs of including a theoretical element. In the next chapter, I will examine previous responses to the problem, before concluding that they too are inadequate – i.e. Saxe has identified a real problem which must be answered and has not been. I will then develop my novel responses.

Notes

1 For further objections see Stich and Nichols (1998), Stich and Nichols (2002), Scholl and Leslie (2001), Bishop and Downes (2002).
2 I will also be pointing out in Chapter 8 that Hybrid positions must make coherent choices across their simulational and theoretical elements in relation to whether they assert or deny Introspectionism, Behaviourism etc.
3 Since TT denies Introspectionism and ST need not, arguments for Introspectionism also indirectly weaken TT. I will consider those in Chapter 8.
4 Fodor (2008, pp. 116–121) sets out the frame problem; Peterson and Riggs (1999, p. 82) consider its difficulty in the ToM context.
5 See also Fodor (1974, p. 102) for persuasive argument to the effect that the notions of 'law' and 'theory' are 'equally murky'. This raises problems that are sidestepped by ST but not by TT.
6 See also Dreyfus (2006) for argument to the effect that '[o]nly if we stand back from our engaged situation in the world and represent things from a detached theoretical perspective do we confront the frame problem' which suggests that TT must face the problem while ST need not.
7 Further difficulties for Glymour would relate to the extended argument presented by Taleb (2007) to the effect that humans ascribe more causation than is justified.
8 I have inserted 'hybrid' where Saxe has 'dual-system' for consistency with the terminology used elsewhere.
9 One argument for Hybridist accounts proposed by Kuhn suggests that they allow both 'self and others to serve as sources of knowledge about self and others' (Mitchell and Riggs 2001, p. 304). That argument has no force since this benefit can be obtained by ST alone. S can simulate S or O to predict the behaviour of either S or O.
10 For a discussion of the difficulty of distinguishing shame from embarrassment, see Zahavi (Webber 2010, Chapter 14).
11 There is an enormous philosophical literature on concepts and what falls under them, which is a measure of the difficulty of the problem. See Wittgenstein (2001), Fodor (1994), Fodor and Lepore (1996), Crane (2003).

12 Nor should an account simultaneously assert or deny Behaviourism, which raises a question as to the advisability of appealing both to the Behaviourist Bem and the anti-Behaviourist Asch.

13 For an example of repeated Monte Carlo simulation being used to produce more accurate predictions, see Short (1992). Also, Salvatore, Dimaggio, and Lysaker (2007) suggest that the ToM deficits in schizophrenia result from an inability to select from the outputs of multiple simulations; see Chapter 10.

5 Bias mismatch defence

Background

As we have seen, going hybrid has many drawbacks, so that does not seem to be the way forward. That would suggest we remain with pure ST. However, as I will explain below, previous defences of ST against the systematic error challenge have proved inadequate. This will show why we need a new defence. I will then go on to give an initial overview of my Bias Mismatch Defence which can be stated very succinctly in the slogan 'simulation does not model bias'. The details of how this defence works in action will emerge more fully in discussion of its application to Saxe's specific challenges in Chapters 6, 7 and 8. I will then outline the various biases involved in Bias Mismatch. I only list the ones I will be employing; there are many more which could doubtless explain many other cases of simulation error. I will then discuss two ways in which Bias Mismatch can occur. Then, I propose Affect Mismatch between S and O as one way in which S and O can be applying different biases, thus causing ToM errors in S. Similarly, another route to Bias Mismatches is provided by System Mismatch under Dual Process Theory, which I discuss afterwards. Here the idea is that if S and O are using different reasoning processes or systems, there are very likely to be simulation errors in S. There are also ways in which System Mismatch and Affect Mismatch can interact and produce simulation errors, which I will close this chapter by discussing.

Why we need a new defence

Simulation Theory has been charged with failure to predict the robust systematic errors that are observed in ToM. Two types of defence have been suggested: a Translation Defence and a Wrong Inputs Defence. Greenwood (1999, p. 35), writes that in ST 'failure can only arise in one of two ways: either the decision maker's practical reasoning system is different from the person whose behaviour is predicted, or the right pretend beliefs and desires are not fed into the system'. This adds up to a concise statement of the Translation Defence and the Wrong Inputs Defence together with a claim that no other options are available.

I will explain both of these two defences, which are offered by Harris (1992). Since the Translation Defence has received much less attention in the literature than the Wrong Inputs Defence, I will spend more time on the latter.

Saxe (2005a, pp. 177–178) sets out her challenge to the Wrong Inputs Defence as follows:

> The pattern of errors described above is not consistent with this kind of Simulation. And, as we shall now see, the most common defence of Simulation Theory against the argument from error also fails: the claim that errors arise from inaccurate inputs to the simulation.

Here, Saxe uses the term 'pattern of errors' to refer to the general problem she raises for ST, that of explaining the systematic ToM errors. Saxe is correct in saying that the Wrong Inputs Defence has been the one more frequently resorted to by ST proponents to explain ToM errors. I will agree that Saxe is right to claim that the Wrong Inputs Defence does not explain the systematic nature of the errors. This is why we need a new defence which I will offer in the next chapters. I will now briefly outline in turn the Wrong Inputs Defence and the Translation Defence. We need not be detained long here, since I agree with Saxe that these defences as originally set out do not have the resources to handle the large array of data that Saxe cites in support of her case.

Wrong inputs defence

I will discuss some of the occasions on which Simulation Theorists have presented the Wrong Inputs Defence before returning to Saxe's specific claims.

Harris (1992, p. 132), responding to Stich and Nichols, puts the Wrong Inputs Defence as follows: 'it is necessary for [S] to feed in pretend inputs that match in the relevant particulars the situation facing the [O] whose actions are to be predicted or explained. Predictive errors will occur if inappropriate pretend inputs are fed in'. Harris deals with three experiments that Stich and Nichols claim are problematic for ST. The three situations deal with Suicide Note Assessors, Lottery Ticket Holders and Shoppers. The first two groups are handled using the Wrong Inputs Defence and the Shoppers are handled using the Translation Defence.

Suicide note assessors

I will refer to the participants in the experiment as O's, since we are interested in ToM errors made about them not by them. In this experiment, O's are presented with apparent evidence suggesting that they are good or bad at a particular task. The task is that of assessing whether a suicide note is fake or real. This evidence is later – after about an hour – fully discredited, since the O's are told that the evidence was false. Surprisingly, O's continue to believe that they are good or bad at the task even though there is now no evidence for that belief. This is not predicted by S's, so we have a systematic ToM error that ST must explain.

Harris (1992, pp. 132–133) responds to the challenge by noting that '[S's] reading about such experiments and attempting to simulate their outcome is presented with a single, integrated account of both the trait information and its disconfirmation [so S's] will find it difficult to reproduce the naive, unsuspecting commitment to the initial information that is entertained by [O's]'. Harris's defence is then the Wrong Inputs Defence in that S's are held to be given both confirmatory and disconfirmatory evidence simultaneously, while the O's have a delay of an hour between presentation of the confirmatory evidence and the disconfirmatory evidence. As Harris (1992, p. 133) remarks, S 'feeds in the pretend inputs in a different way from a naive [O]'. The wrong input that the S has results from the combination of confirmatory and disconfirmatory evidence, which may lead to no belief at all. By contrast, the O's hold the belief – for at least an hour and apparently longer – that they are good or bad at the task.

Stich and Nichols respond to this use by Harris of the Wrong Inputs Defence. They do not have additional properly conducted experimental data to cite, but they have tried a non-controlled version of an experiment that could distinguish between Harris's view and their own. They focus on Harris's point about the time lag between the receipt of the confirmatory and disconfirmatory evidence, and ascribe to Harris the prediction that 'if we presented the information in two distinct phases, separated by an hour or so, people would make the correct prediction'; nevertheless, they find that '[m]ost of [the S's] still got the wrong answer' (Stone and Davies 1995, p. 101).

I will not be raising methodological quibbles about Stich and Nichols not having run a fully controlled experiment, because I am satisfied that such an experiment would confirm their view that the time lag is not the problem. I will be suggesting that the difference is in engagement between the S's and the O's – however well the experiment is described to the S's, it will not be the same as being there and participating.

In any case, the more serious problem for Harris here is that Saxe has introduced a great deal more data to support the challenge to ST. All of the data she introduces would need some kind of special treatment of this kind. I will concede that Stich and Nichols have defeated the time lag extension of the Wrong Inputs Defence offered by Harris, necessitating a new defence, which I will provide. I will also be proposing that the Bias Mismatch Defence takes a unified perspective across the data and is thus not exposed to the charge of being *ad hoc*, which a set of extensions of Harris's defence might be.

Lottery ticket holders

This example relates to an experiment in which O's are more reluctant to return some lottery tickets than they rationally should be. The O's demanded much more money to return tickets they had chosen than to return tickets they were given, even though the tickets had the same chance of winning. The two conditions were referred to as 'choice' and 'no choice' of tickets. S's did not predict this difference in the amount of money demanded by O's. Harris (1992, p. 133) offers the defence that S 'needs to simulate the vacillation and eventual commitment of the [O's]. Moreover, in making that simulation they must also set aside the tacit reminder . . . that any Lottery ticket whether selected or allocated, has the same likelihood of winning'.

The same results are obtained by Nichols, Stich, Leslie and Klein when they re-run the lottery experiment. Nichols, Stich, Leslie and Klein write that Harris complains that 'it would hardly be surprising if the [S's] used the wrong pretend-inputs in making their prediction' (Carruthers and Smith 1996, p. 50) if the delay between buying the tickets and being asked to sell them back was several days for the O's and several minutes for the corresponding questions to the S's. So Harris is once again essaying a time lag extension of the Wrong Inputs Defence. The problem though is that Nichols, Stich, Leslie and Klein reduce the viability of the time lag defence offered by Harris by eliminating the time lag: they show their new S's a video of the actual lottery experiment. For our purposes, the most important element of the Nichols, Stich, and Leslie (1995) reply is to note that 'simulation theory predicts that someone watching the videotape of that part will correctly predict (simulate) the outcome' whatever that outcome is. So the S's should simulate the O's more accurately since the video represents a closer approximation to the actual experiment than merely reading a description of it.

Nichols, Stich, Leslie and Klein have again not employed the scientific methodology of experimental psychologists; they admit their evidence is 'anecdotal' (Stone and Davies 1995, p. 100). This quibble must be raised this time, since Kühberger *et al.* (1995, p. 423) conducted a properly controlled experiment and 'consistently failed to replicate the original difference between choice and no-choice under the conditions used by Nichols *et al.*' so 'it is difficult to use it as a yardstick against which the accuracy of simulation can be assessed'. A reply to these charges is offered by Nichols, Stich, and Leslie (1995, p. 437) who deny that the failure to replicate of Kühberger *et al.* (1995) is a problem for their objection to ST – they introduce further empirical evidence such that the sum 'still weighs heavily against simulation'. I will discuss this further evidence in Chapter 6. It is a point in their favour that there is a great deal more experimental data that ST must explain.

Taking their defeat of the time lag extension of the Wrong Inputs Defence offered by Harris together with the need to explain in a motivated fashion all of the other data, it seems clear that the Wrong Inputs Defence will not save ST here. So once again we see that a new defence is required, which I shall provide.

Translation defence

Harris (1992, p. 132) suggests a second defence beyond the Wrong Inputs Defence when he writes that: 'any simulation process assumes that [O's] behaviour is a faithful translation into action of a decision that is reached by the practical reasoning system. If that assumption is incorrect, the simulation will err.' Here we can see that the simulation could also be wrong even absent wrong inputs if there is a translation error from decision to action. Here, 'error' just means that the way S translates the decision into an action prediction is different from the way that O translates the same decision into action, and so S makes a ToM error in relation to O. We may term this the 'Translation Defence'. Whether we call this ToM error a simulation error depends on whether or not 'translation' is included in 'simulation' or not. I will not consider that question further since our central concerns do not depend upon it.

The Translation Defence is described by Stone and Davies as allowing that 'there may be purely mechanical influences on decision taking that are not captured by mental simulation' (Carruthers and Smith 1996, p. 135). The type of mechanical influence they have in mind would be the ingestion of mind-altering substances. S cannot by simulation predict the behaviour of O after O has consumed a large quantity of alcohol. We can see how alcohol could disrupt the link between the practical reasoning system and the systems controlling action. Also, someone under the influence of alcohol might employ their practical reasoning system perfectly adequately but fail to execute a delicate physical manoeuvre called for by the practical reasoning system.

Shoppers

This example relates to an experiment in which Shoppers chose randomly when there were no rational bases for making a selection. Shoppers were 'asked to say which article of clothing was the best quality' (Nisbett and Wilson 1977, p. 243) from a selection of four identical stockings. It transpires that they choose the right-most pair more often than they would if they chose randomly. Harris (1992, p. 133) responds: 'the shopping-mall experiment . . . I suspect, involves the second source of difficulty identified above: faulty assumptions about what causes the [O's] behaviour rather than an inappropriate choice of pretend inputs'.

The mechanism that Harris proposes is as follows. He thinks that the '[O's] action of choosing the right-most item is not governed by the decision-making system at all' (Harris 1992, p. 133) which would mean that S's would err in simulation because they simulate the operation of the decision-making system which is not in this case operating. This does seem plausible because if the decision-making system is operating, it is at least not operating rationally when it makes a choice on a non-rational basis, as here. Here, calling the decision non-rational refers to the lack of a rational basis for making the particular decision made, which does not exclude the possibility that it is rational to make some decision, and therefore rational to choose one of the pairs of stockings even if there is no reason to choose a particular pair.

Harris's argument for this bypassing of the decision-making system rests on the post facto confabulation that is observed in O's. They do not report having decided to take the right-most item for no particular reason; instead they fabricate a reason based on a false claim about the distinctive qualities of the right-most item. This almost suggests that the decision-making system is called upon subsequently to manufacture a justification for the choice that was made. In any case, Harris seems to be on solid ground when he argues that were O's to be using the decision-making system in the normal way, they would not need to fabricate a reason; neither would they have forgotten the reason they had if they had one, and so the decision-making system is bypassed. As Harris (1992, p. 134) puts it: 'the action of choosing the right-most item is not governed by the decision-making system at all'.

This in essence, is the Translation Defence: S's do not simulate O's bypassing their decision-making system. We might think that S's specifically engage their decision-making system because they have been asked, they believe, to simulate a decision, so this could explain ToM errors. But it does not seem as though we can make much progress by assuming that people bypass their decision-making machinery on a widespread basis. This Translation Defence has in any case not received much support or even attention in the literature. I will therefore not rely on it, meaning a new defence of ST is needed, which I will now provide.

Bias mismatch defence: outline

I claim in my Bias Mismatch Defence that S's simulation of O may fail because S does not simulate the cognitive biases of O. This may occur because S and O are in different affective states. Alternatively, the simulation may fail because S operates with different cognitive biases to O. Dual Process Theory can explain one reason why that may occur. Dual Process Theory postulates two systems of reasoning, the quick but inaccurate System 1 and the slower but more rational System 2. If S and O apply different systems, simulation is again likely to fail.

Is this defence a variant of the two previously discussed defences or a new one? My initial response to that question is to say that its efficacy as a defence is of more importance than its classification. Looking more closely, we may see that one answer would derive from whether we took the view that the Bias Mismatch between S and O meant that S had some wrong inputs to his simulation because S used beliefs that were not biased. That would make the Bias Mismatch Defence a new variant of the Wrong Inputs Defence. Alternatively, one might think that the biases affect reasoning further downstream, just before the beliefs and desires are translated into action. That would make my new Bias Mismatch Defence a variant of the Translation Defence. A third option would be to say that the new Bias Mismatch Defence does not fall into either category and is thus a new type of defence.

Trying to decide where the failure to model bias of O accurately takes place could be seen as being an ill-formed question, since we cannot specify a location where something does not occur. If we had a specified functional location for where the biases are applied in O, then we might be able to say that the difference between those bias-applying locations in O and the same, but not bias-applying, locations in S are where the difference between S and O is found. However, it is possible that these biases are widespread throughout the isomorphic procedure of simulation; or that the question has no answer: as Apperly (2008, p. 281) writes, 'there is no systematic basis for drawing a line between the inputs to a particular reasoning episode and the start of the reasoning itself'. Since we are more interested at this stage in whether the new defence works than in under what category it falls, I will not return to these questions.

The idea behind the defence may be illustrated by considering an example from the book Asch (1952) cited by Saxe (2005a). Consider the following questions, all related to a scenario in which you are given a list of personal characteristics and asked to assess the personality of the person to whom the list applies:

- Would you assess the characteristics fairly?
- Would you assess them regardless of irrelevant features?
- Would you assess them regardless of the order in which they were presented?

I submit that you will answer all of these questions in the affirmative. Moreover, if you were asked whether you would expect someone else to perform in the same way, you would also affirm that, short of any specific information suggesting malice or lack of competence in the other person.

Now look at the following two lists of characteristics from Asch (1952, p. 212):

A intelligent – industrious – impulsive – critical – stubborn – envious
B envious – stubborn – critical – impulsive – industrious – intelligent

Here I contend that, consistent with what Asch found, you will form a more positive impression of the person with the characteristics described in list A than in list B. In this, you will be representative of people generally. As Asch (1952, p. 212) puts it, list A describes 'an able person who possesses certain shortcomings' while list B describes a 'problem' person whose 'abilities are hampered by his serious difficulties' (Asch 1952, p. 212). This means in your original assessment of yourself, you have committed a ToM error, because you failed to forecast that either you or the experimental sample will make such distinct judgements based on a list of characteristics which are the same in each case but merely in reverse order.

Now we come to the shape of the defence. The reason O's assess the characteristics 'unfairly' is that they fall prey to Confirmation Bias. The term Confirmation Bias refers to the 'fundamental tendency to seek information consistent with current . . . beliefs, theories or hypotheses and to avoid the collection of potentially falsifying evidence' Evans (1990, p. 41). In other words, O's tend to look for data confirming what they already believe. Thus, information arriving earlier is given more weight in assessments; the later information has to countervail the earlier information insofar as the later information goes against the earlier data. The reason S's fail to predict this is that simulation here does not model bias. The Bias Mismatch Defence is just this: it is the claim that simulation by S of O can be systematically inaccurate because there can be systematic bias in O which is not simulated by S. Note also here the clear distinction between being asked dispassionate, clinical, salient questions like the ones in the list about how you would do the job and actually being in the situation of assessing the characteristics. We will see this affective mismatch and its analogues on a great many occasions later.

Bias mismatch defence: biases involved

It is well-known that we exhibit many errors in our reasoning due to a large number of cognitive biases. We often use cognitive shortcuts or heuristics which are effectively biases, and as Tversky and Kahneman (1974, p. 1125) put it, 'these heuristics are quite useful, but sometimes they lead to severe and systematic errors'. I set out below a sketch of the biases I will employ in the mismatch defence. How they work will become clearer when I use them later to explain data on systematic ToM error introduced by Saxe (2005a). Naturally, any objections to the effect that I need to use further biases would count as a friendly amendment: I aim to prove that some combination of Bias Mismatches can explain the systematic ToM errors and that can be done using a variety of biases.

Representativeness heuristic

Tversky and Kahneman (1974, p. 1124) define the Representativeness Heuristic as occurring when 'probabilities are evaluated by the degree to which A is representative of B, that is, by the degree to which A resembles B'. Intuitively, we may regard this as stereotyping, because a typical application of the heuristic will involve people deciding that someone is a librarian because they fit the stereotype of a librarian. The error is also known as 'base rate neglect'. Subjects fail to take account of what should be a much more significant factor in the probability estimate viz. the number of people in the population who are librarians.

The Representativeness Heuristic was investigated by giving subjects descriptions of the personalities of a group of persons. Tversky and Kahneman (1974, p. 1124) write that 'subjects were told that the group from which the descriptions had been drawn consisted of 70 engineers and 30 lawyers' or vice versa. The subjects were then asked to assess the probability that a given person was an engineer or a lawyer. The descriptions were slanted to be engineer-like or lawyer-like. For example, a stereotypical engineer will enjoy fixing his car at weekends while a stereotypical lawyer will be tenaciously argumentative in personal situations.

Tversky and Kahneman (1974, p. 1125) found that subjects ignored the population probability data. If given an engineer-like profile, they said the person was probably an engineer, even when they had also been told that the sample consisted of 70 per cent lawyers.

Availability heuristic

Tversky and Kahneman (1973, p. 208) write that '[a] person is said to employ the availability heuristic whenever he estimates frequency or probability by the ease with which instances or associations could be brought to mind'. For example, 'one may assess the divorce rate in a given community by recalling divorces among one's acquaintances' (Tversky and Kahneman 1973, p. 208). This is reasonable as a first approximation, but will be subject to inaccuracy depending on the events of one's life. If one happens to know many divorced people, one will likely overestimate the prevalence of divorce in wider society.

Tversky and Kahneman (1973) measured the Availability Heuristic by asking subjects to rate the probabilities of certain syllables occurring in words. They found that subject's responses were driven by the ease with which they could think of examples, rather than the actual probabilities, even though subjects obviously had a great deal of experience of words in their native languages.

Tversky and Kahneman (1973, p. 212) found that subjects 'erroneously judged words beginning with re to be more frequent than words ending with re'. This came about because it is easier to think of words beginning with re than ending with re, because it is generally easier to think of words with a specified beginning than with a specified ending. This means the words beginning with re were much more available and this produced the faulty probability estimate.

Two further factors feed into availability: salience and Vividness.

Highly salient events will warp probability judgements via their increased availability. Taleb (2008, p. 58) gives several examples including that of someone who heard of someone's relative who was mugged in Central Park. This is likely to be much more salient for them than the statistics relating to muggings in Central Park and therefore much more available. They will likely greatly overestimate the probability of being mugged in Central Park. Such a story is also highly vivid, which leads us to the second factor.

In outlining Vividness, Evans (1990, p. 27) credits Nisbett and Ross with the observation that in our reasoning, we 'overweight vivid, concrete information and underweight dull, pallid and abstract information'. This is intuitively plausible, just from considering that we prefer the vivid to the dull. More vivid information is therefore more available. Evans (1990) again relies on Nisbett and Ross to supply three characteristics of Vividness, which are '(1) emotional interest; (2) concreteness and imageability and (3) temporal and spatial proximity'.

Salient and vivid items are more available and receive higher probability estimates.

Conjunction fallacy

The probability of two events A and B is given by multiplying the probability of event A by event B. For example, if the chance of a coin toss coming up tails is 50 per cent, then the probability of getting two tails in a row is 25 per cent. Since no event can have a probability of more than 100 per cent, there is a law of statistics called the conjunction rule which holds that the probability of both events A and B occurring must be no greater than the probability of event B occurring alone. As Tversky and Kahneman (1983, p. 298) state, '[t]he violation of the conjunction rule in a direct comparison of B to A&B is called the conjunction fallacy'. In other words, the Conjunction Fallacy occurs whenever we assess the probability of two events as higher than one of them alone.

The canonical illustration of the Conjunction Fallacy is the famous 'Linda' experiment. Subjects are told that Linda majored in philosophy, is very bright and as a student 'was deeply concerned with issues of discrimination and social justice' (Tversky and Kahneman 1983, p. 297). Subjects are then asked whether it is more likely that (a) Linda works as a bank teller, or (b) Linda works as a bank teller and is active in the feminist movement. Subjects consistently state that (b) is more probable, even though it is impossible that (b) could be more probable than (a) alone, since (b) includes (a).

The Conjunction Fallacy is closely related to the Representativeness and Availability Heuristics, since what is happening is that a reduction in extension is being combined with an increase in representativeness and availability. Thus it becomes easier to think of examples of a category even when the number of members of that category has decreased. This is what leads us to make the errors in probability estimation. There are also links to what Taleb (2008, Chapter 6) calls the Narrative Fallacy, which combines our tendencies to remember facts linked by a story and over-attribute causation. It is much easier to construct a story about Linda being a committed social activist at college and continuing with those interests later. This is why Tversky and Kahneman (1983, p. 299) found that 85 per cent of subjects rated (b) more likely than (a).

Fundamental attribution error

The Fundamental Attribution Error is defined by Ross, Amabile, and Steinmetz (1977, p. 491) as 'the tendency to underestimate the role of situational determinants and overestimate the degree to which social actions and outcomes reflect the dispositions of relevant actors'.[1] The error reflects our false belief in stable personality: we ascribe the behaviour of others more to their 'characteristics' than to the situation they were in. Darley and Batson (1973, p. 108) found that 'personality variables were not useful in predicting whether a person helped or not': that was explained by whether or not the person was in a hurry. Also, Kamtekar (2004, p. 465) reports on many experiments including honesty studies which showed no 'correlation across behaviour types' e.g. that someone who cheats in a test is not more likely to take money from a box. There seems to be nothing like a character trait of dishonesty. Overall, we often commit the Fundamental Attribution Error, including whenever we say something like 'of course he would do that, that's what he is like' – but there is little evidence supporting the existence of stable character traits and plenty against.

Saxe herself at one point employs the Fundamental Attribution Error in a way that could be seen as a version of the Bias Mismatch Defence. She suggests that 'other people's actions are ascribed to stable traits, whereas one's own actions are generally seen as variable and situation-dependent' (Markman, Klein, and Suhr 2012, Chapter 17) and this leads to ToM error.

Conformity bias

Prentice (2007, p. 18) gives the following definition: 'conformity bias strongly pushes people to conform their judgments to the judgments of their reference group'. Although the pioneer, Asch (1952, p. 467), does not use the term Conformity Bias, he writes that he has observed 'a great desire to be in agreement with the group'; the thwarting of this desire leads to fear, longing and uncertainty. The reference group might be those physically present or a group that the subject identifies with.

The most significant chapter of Asch (1952, pp. 450–501) from the perspective of conformity is Chapter 16, on 'Group Forces in the Modification and Distortion of Judgements'. Asch describes experiments where small groups of individuals are asked to judge which of three test lines are identical in length to a given standard line. All participants call out their answers. A deception is involved, because all but one of the participants are in fact in confederation with the experimenter. They have been instructed to call out obviously false answers. The key question is what will the non-confederated participant – the 'critical subject' – say in the face of such a perplexingly obtuse majority.

The results are that the error rate of the critical subject is 33.2 per cent if the majority is wrong but only 7.4 per cent if the majority is correct. This means that the critical subject is induced to abandon his correct choice in favour of an obviously false group choice with a much higher frequency than can be explained by genuine error. This majority influence meant that 'erroneous announcements contaminated one-third of the estimates of the critical subjects' (Asch 1952, p. 457). This observation forms a clear illustration of the Asch Effect or Conformity Bias. This bias is very strong; Prentice (2007, p. 18) notes that '[m]ore than 60 percent of the subjects gave an obviously incorrect answer at least once'.

False consensus effect

Ross, Greene, and House (1977, p. 279) define the False Consensus Effect when they write that 'social observers tend to perceive a 'false consensus' with respect to the relative commonness of their own responses', where responses might be actions, choices or opinions. So, 'raters estimated particular responses to be relatively common' (Ross, Greene, and House 1977, p. 279) – viz, the ones they had themselves made.

Ross, Greene, and House (1977, p. 279) conducted a number of experiments: one of them was called the 'supermarket story'. Subjects are asked to imagine that they are just leaving a supermarket, when they are asked whether they like shopping there. They reply that they do, since that is in fact the case. It is then revealed that the comments have been filmed, and the subject is requested to sign a release allowing the film to be used in a TV advertisement. The key question is then asked: the subject or 'rater' is asked to estimate the percentage of people who will sign the release.

The results were that raters overestimate the percentages of others who make the same choice they would. Ross, Greene, and House (1977, p. 294) conclude that 'raters' perceptions of social consensus and their social inferences about actors reflect the raters' own behavioural choices'.

Self-presentation bias

Igoe and Sullivan (1993, p. 18) give the definition when they write that '[i]ndividuals show Self-Presentation Bias by projecting personal behaviours that present themselves more positively than others'. The Self-Presentation Bias is perhaps more of a natural psychological tendency than a cognitive bias, though that will not concern us since the effects are the same. Put simply, Self-Presentation Bias expresses the way that people generally wish to show themselves in a positive light. They may do this by selective story-telling or otherwise.

Igoe and Sullivan (1993) measure the rates at which individuals work at hard tasks and find that they systematically over-report their own likelihood of returning to a hard task. Thus, the individuals exhibit Self-Presentation Bias in that they make it appear as though they are more likely to work hard than they really are. Interestingly, the subjects also attributed a lower propensity to return to the task to a fictional character, thus enhancing their own position in relation to others.[2]

Kopcha and Sullivan (2006, p. 628) note that 'self-report data often reflect a phenomenon known as self-presentation bias or social desirability bias – that is, a tendency of individuals to present themselves and their practices in a favourable way'. They measure Self-Presentation Bias in a group of teachers, who all said that they engaged in an array of positively perceived teaching practices more than their colleagues. Similarly, Kopcha and Sullivan (2006, p. 629) cite Self-Presentation Bias as the cause in studies reporting that 'medical professionals often overestimated their level of adherence to the guidelines for clinical practice'. More generally, we may agree with Pronin, Gilovich, and Ross (2004, p. 788) who observe that there is 'mounting evidence that people are motivated to view themselves, their assessments, and their outcomes in a positive light'.

Clustering illusion

Gilovich (1993, p. 16) defines the Clustering Illusion as occurring when we believe falsely that 'random events such as coin flips should alternate between heads and tails more than they do'. For example, in a sequence of 20 tosses of a fair coin, there is a 25 per cent chance of a sequence of six heads, which seems to us far too ordered to be random. Alternatively, consider the probability of the two sets of results of coin tosses: HHHTTT looks much more pattern-rich and therefore improbable than HTHHTT but they actually have the same probability. The Clustering Illusion is the tendency to see patterns in data that are not really there. Gilovich (1993, p. 15) provides further examples including a belief that the random pattern of bomb sites in London actually shows a pattern; this effect is due to selecting the quadrant frame almost in order to arrive at the view that some quadrants of London were more heavily bombed. In general, our abilities to handle random noise are poor; we see patterns everywhere and we even see faces in the side of cliffs.

Confirmation bias

The remaining biases including Confirmation Bias have already been described above, so I will be brief for the rest of this section. As mentioned in Chapter 5, Evans (1990, p. 41) defines Confirmation Bias as the 'fundamental tendency to seek information consistent with current . . . beliefs, theories or hypotheses and to avoid the collection of potentially falsifying evidence'.

Belief perseverance bias

As Nestler (2010, p. 35) observes with copious references, 'belief perseverance has been observed in social perception . . . and self-perception . . . and it is robustly shown that individuals cling to beliefs even when the evidential basis for these beliefs is completely refuted'. The Belief Perseverance Bias was illustrated earlier in the discussion of the suicide note assessors.

Endowment effect

Kühberger *et al.* (1995, p. 432) write that the 'endowment effect . . . means that simply being endowed with a good gives it added value'. It can be seen when students are asked to estimate the price of a visible item such as a mug with a university crest on it. They make an estimate and are then actually given the mug and asked what they would sell it for. It turns out that they demand a much higher price for the mug now that they own it than the figure they gave previously for its value.

The Endowment Effect was in fact behind the results discussed above in relation to the lottery ticket holders. They assigned a higher value to tickets they had chosen than to ones they were given, although the economic value of the tickets was identical irrespective of whether they had chosen them or not. It seems as though their sense of ownership was more awakened by choice.

Position effect

Nisbett and Wilson (1977, p. 243) give the definition when they write that they measured 'a pronounced left-to-right position effect, such that the right-most object in the array was heavily over-chosen' in the experiment with the shoppers. The shoppers had to say which of an array of identical pairs of stockings was of superior quality. This Position Effect was discussed earlier in Chapter 5.

Affect mismatch

My response to Saxe's challenge will be that Bias Mismatch between S and O can supply the missing element of ST to allow it to explain the systematic ToM errors. Often, it will be the case that this Bias Mismatch is in turn a result of Affect Mismatch between S and O. It is acknowledged in the psychological literature that affect can lead to the application of cognitive biases. As Pronin, Puccio and Ross observe, not only do humans add information to the world, but 'perceptions are further biased by their hopes, fears, needs and immediate emotional state' (Gilovich, Griffin, and Kahneman 2002, p. 636).

We do not accurately allow for the biases of others because we are not as exposed as they are to the live situation. Even if we are present, it is much less involving to observe someone hanging from a cliff top by their fingertips than it is actually to be in that situation. S simply cannot feel or imagine the affective position of that O to any significant extent. S is more remote still if S merely hears a dry description of the situation given in a rather clinical fashion. There can be different degrees of such affective detachment, which will impede simulation, as Goldie (1999, p. 410) points out in a discussion of imagining being attacked by a jellyfish. He notes the different affective import of imagining the attack 'whilst sitting at my desk in London, whilst swimming in a pool, and whilst swimming off the coast of South Africa'. The fact that we can so easily do this and so easily agree with Goldie is to my mind in itself an argument for ST. As we will see, much of the empirical data on ToM errors falls into this category: perforce, if it is properly collected data, it has been collected in a scientific manner which excludes S feeling fully engaged in the situation of O.

The same distinctions can apply when S considers the position of S himself. As Goldie (2011, p. 129) notes in a discussion of S's views of S in the past, there are multiple ways in which the S now can differ from O as past S; the gap between S now and then 'can be triply ironic: it can be ironic epistemically – I now know what I did not know then; it can be ironic evaluatively – I now evaluate what happened in a way that I did not at the time; and it can be ironic emotionally'. The irony referred to is the 'dramatic irony' that exists in a theatre when the audience knows something that an observed character does not – this can form an interesting parallel to our examination of S and O. At least the last of these three forms of irony and probably the second as well have a strong affective component. We may also agree that even information asymmetry can have affective import, as suggested by the very term 'dramatic irony'.

One reason why the proponents of TT may have overlooked the significance of this affective mismatch may relate to the larger difficulties that TT has dealing with qualia. Qualia are the 'raw feel' of a mental state; what it is like to see red, for example.[3] TT is associated with Functionalism, which is defined by the claim that mental states are individuated by what they do. Indeed, Heal (2003, p. 28) writes of TT that 'the version best known to philosophers is functionalism'. Shoemaker finds it is necessary to respond to objections that Functionalism cannot handle the phenomenology adequately. There is often 'something it is like' to be in a particular mental state, and this seems to individuate such mental states. As Shoemaker (1975, p. 291) says, the objection against Functionalism and allied doctrines has been that functionalism 'cannot account for the "raw feel" component of mental states'. Even if Shoemaker's defence is ultimately deemed successful, the power of this objection shows how awkwardly the rather analytic TT doctrines sit with an attempt to include affect, phenomenology and 'raw feel'. One of my main claims in this book is that the raw feel of O is not adequately captured by S, sometimes leading S to make simulation errors.

Further evidence for this connection may be derived from Boucher, when she cites Kanner as including affect in the original 1943 definition of autism. She writes that Kanner 'originally suggested that autism . . . results from "an innate inability to form the usual biologically provided affective contact with people"' (Carruthers and Smith 1996, p. 228). Given the well-known association of autism with ToM deficits, we can see that if Kanner's original definition is correct, lack of affective contact with others will impair ToM capacities. Arguing positively for the connection between affect matching and successful mind reading, Biggs (2007) suggests that 'phenomenal simulation' – where S feels something of the qualia of O – may be an aid to mind reading and introduces claims that there is similar neurophysiology occurring in those who experience and merely observe disgust, pain, etc.

In the next two chapters, we will discuss a large number of cases of errors made by S's in assessing what O will do in certain, often stressful situations. Even though there will be processing differences between S and O, there will also be different inputs for S and O: namely, the affect actually felt by O in the situation. If S were able to model the stress of O accurately, it might lead to a reduction in ToM errors. Thus, the Bias Mismatch Defence can be seen as a way of improving the Wrong Inputs Defence by making it available in relation to Saxe's challenges, rather than as an alternative. My priority in any case is to establish that a defence is available; the question as to how that defence should be classified is secondary.

One objection will be to ask why this same bias does not apply when the model is run. S suffers from the same types of cognitive bias as O does. We need this to explain why there can be errors – if exactly the same system is run by S as by O, and there were no wrong inputs, then S would generally not be wrong about the mental state of O. The answer to this is that the specific bias occurs only for O's and not for S's. Why this is so may be because it is just not as engaging to be S as it is to be O – in any situation. Again, it simply is nothing like as fear-inducing to imagine hanging from a cliff by one's fingertips as it is actually to be in that situation. The biases are triggered more by the affect of the situation. While S will doubtless be experiencing some affect, and it may even be sufficiently engaging to trigger some of S's own biases, the affects will not be the same ones as those experienced by O.

One type of Affect Mismatch might be fear differentials. Gordon (1986, p. 161) picks up on the difficulty of adding really experienced fear to the simulation in his early paper, indicating it with his italicisation. He writes: '[i]f I pretend realistically that there is an intruder in the house I might find myself surprisingly brave – or cowardly'. It might even be deleterious to simulate the fear well; S's might become unable to act when faced even with the prospect of danger. It is only possible for S to be surprised about S's bravery if S has a different level of affect, and thus different biases applying, in the simulated case and the real case. Gordon also notes here that self-deception may corrupt the simulation effort. This is highly consistent with the approach I propose here – perhaps S's often deceive themselves about the frequency with which S's use biased thinking. Dennett (1979, p. 37) notes that an affective involvement may lead to self-deception – which we may understand as a failure of ToM – when he writes that if S lacks 'any remarkable emotional stake in the proposition [p] . . . [then S] can quite safely assume that his judgement is not a piece of self-deception'.

White (1988, p. 41) notes, '[S's] do not have the same practical concerns as [O's], because the judgements they are making do not relate to their own behaviours . . . there is less likelihood that accuracy will be low on their list of priorities'. We can see that there will be more affective involvement for the O's who have after all been responsible for the behaviour in question than for the S's who are more dispassionately explaining it. Also, as Goldman (1989, p. 167) observes: the ST 'approach can certainly insist that most simulation is semi-automatic, with relatively little salient phenomenology'. Goldman is countering the objection that if ST is correct, then we should spend more time than we do experiencing vividly what it is like to be in others' shoes, but his point also supports the line I propose here. It might be that one of the conditions of making ST semi-automatic – which is needful given the requirement for efficiency – is that some of the elements, like bias-modelling or full affect simulation, not always be run. As Peterson and Riggs (1999, p. 82) point out, on 'evolutionary grounds, it is plausible to consider strategies which involve minimum processing load'. So the S's might need to exhibit Affect Mismatch on occasions, purely on efficiency grounds.

The proposal is not that the correct bias cannot be added to the simulation; merely that it often is not. As Gordon (1992, p. 20) writes, if you turn back on a country trail because you see a grizzly bear, you may be puzzled by your companion's standing her ground and taking out her pencil and notebook, unless you previously '"prep" yourself with the appropriate intrepid naturalist attitudes and desires'. The reasons you do not generally do this may derive simply from the additional cognitive load involved. As Gordon (1992, p. 25) goes on to observe, it may be that 'readiness for simulation is a prepackaged 'module' called upon automatically'; that would be consistent with evidence suggesting that modelling just the perspectives of others is mandatory, fast but involves significant cognitive load.

As Heal (2000, p. 16) notes, errors in simulation may be because S and O differ in 'the degree of stress they are under in thinking of the problem'. This view leads to a testable prediction of the Bias Mismatch Defence, which is that people with more active imaginations – who are perhaps more able to experience O's affect vicariously – would be less susceptible to Saxe's occasional systematic errors in ToM than others. The view I propose also allows for the relatively high success rate of our folk psychology: in the majority of everyday situations, there is not that much affect involved for either S or O; the lack of full bias modelling makes no difference to the outcome of the situation. This also explains part of why we find unpredictable people disconcerting.

The condition known as Williams Syndrome (WS) provides further evidence available for a link between affective nature and ToM ability. Segal notes the following characteristics of WS: 'average IQ of around 50' (Carruthers and Smith 1996, p. 154); 'general impairments [in. . .] acquisition of . . . theoretical knowledge' (Carruthers and Smith 1996, p. 152); 'high degree of social skills' (Carruthers and Smith 1996, p. 152) combined with good ToM capacities. The social skills are most notable in the syndrome: Bellugi *et al.* (2007, p. 99) note that the 'WS personality is characterised by hyper-sociability, including over-friendliness and heightened approachability toward others'. This sociability will be driven by heightened enjoyment of social situations by WS subjects. They are therefore high affect individuals, when interacting socially. It is suggested by Bellugi *et al.* (2007, p. 100) that social ability and affective involvement go together when they note that WS children's stories 'contained significantly more social and affective evaluative devices' than those of controls. We can see then that empathetic abilities can compensate in ToM for impaired intellectual capacities. The WS subjects are able to develop good ToM capacity despite impairments in their theoretical abilities; which makes it look like affect is more important than theory in ToM.

System mismatch

A further illustration of how the Bias Mismatch Defence may apply can be given by considering Dual Process Theory. Dual Process Theory postulates that there are two cognitive systems we use: System 1 and System 2. The first is quick and dirty; the second is more rational but takes longer. It seems clear that if S and O use different Systems then there will likely be simulation errors. Many simulation errors will occur because O will be using System 1 while S will use System 2, and they give different outputs. Since System 1 basically is the application of biases – of which more below – Dual Process Theory provides another way of applying the Bias Mismatch Defence.

This idea that ToM capacities may be implemented in both systems is supported by Butterfill and Apperly (2013, p. 609), who cite developmental and theoretical evidence to support the claim that 'adults may enjoy efficient but inflexible forms of theory of mind cognition in addition to the full-blown form which involves representing beliefs and other propositional attitudes as such'. This claim is made in the context of their overall argument for a 'minimal ToM' which is less demanding than the full-blown form and might explain the putative or partial ToM abilities of some non-human animals, infants under five and adults under cognitive load. The idea is that if there are easily tracked markers of belief that are analogous to the way that rotten fruit has an unappealing odour, it might be possible to track the 'odour' rather than represent the rottenness or the belief and thus gain most of the benefits of ToM. Adults would have access to ToM in both systems and would employ each system under different circumstances. Strijbos and De Bruin (2013, p. 758) point out that Butterfill and Apperly's two system account of ToM has the advantage that 'they are in principle able to account for the cross-cultural differences in folk psychologies' which is otherwise difficult. They can do this because they can argue that only System 2 full-blown ToM includes a rich belief/desire psychology which might be culturally specific while the simpler System 1 version might be a universal, core, minimal ToM.

An example of ToM implementation in System 1 is given by Kahneman (2011, p. 91) who notes that people judge competence by considering facial features such as 'a strong chin with a slight confident appearing smile'. Someone using their System 1 ToM will therefore predict competent behaviour by a person with such features or will be more likely to vote for them (this experiment was investigating voting intentions). Naturally, there is 'no evidence that these facial features actually predict how well politicians will perform in office'; (Kahneman 2011, p. 91) a fact which is accessible to System 2 ToM, which will not predict that politicians with strong chins are more competent. Thus we can see how systematic differences in predictions of behaviour will result from System Mismatches, whether those mismatches are between different S's or between the same S at different times.

In the same vein but considering only simulation, Goldman (2006, Chapter 6) argues for a division of simulation into low-level and high level (Goldman 2006, Chapter 7) forms which illustrates how simulation might take place in System 1 and System 2 formats respectively. The former quick and automatic simulation is the 'emotional contagion' that takes place when S observes O smiling. S undergoes sub-threshold activation of smiling muscles and feels an attenuated version of O's happiness, thus appreciating something about O's mental state. The latter more rational form of simulation may be complex and explicitly conscious – Goldman's term is 'perspective-taking' (Goldman 2006, p. 292) – where S considers what S would do in a fairly rich specification of O's reasoning process, informed by S's beliefs about O's situation.

Biases are more prevalent in the System 1 mode; indeed the prevalence of biases is definitional of System 1: Kahneman (2011, p. 81) writes that 'the confirmatory bias of System 1 favours uncritical acceptance of suggestions' meaning that Confirmation Bias is a central method of System 1. Similarly, Nagel (2011, p. 8) describes Tversky and Kahneman's investigation of System 1 as being a 'heuristics and biases programme'. Further, as Sloman (1996, p. 15) notes, experiment shows 'conjunction, inclusion-similarity, and inclusion fallacies all resulted from [System 1] based processing'. The conjunction fallacy is the bias exposed in the 'Linda' experiments where people erroneously assess the joint probability of two events as higher than that of one of them. The inclusion similarity fallacy is where people agree that all members of a set share a property but deny that some members do. The inclusion fallacy is that of judging a subset to be larger than a set of which it is a subset. In fact, System 1 includes a wealth of such biases and fallacies.

System 1 employs quick and dirty heuristics because it prioritises speed. These biases are less prevalent in the slower, more rational, more expert System 2. As Nagel (2011, p. 7) points out, '[b]ecause of its speed, and because it does not tie up working memory, System 1 serves as the default mode of judgement'. On the other hand, 'System 2 is slower and more effortful than System 1, in part because it taxes our limited supply of working memory' (Nagel 2011, p. 7). For these reasons, people are more likely to use System 1 when under pressure to make a decision. The O's are generally under pressure to make a decision in many of the examples to be discussed below. This means they will often be using System 1, possibly inappropriately; Nagel (2011, p. 8) writes: 'subjects under immediate pressure to act and subjects distracted by another task may fail to shift up to System 2'.

Nagel (2011, p. 3) usefully uses this dual system approach to argue that we can explain cases where 'two apparently conflicting judgements' are made on the same question when they 'are naturally made in different modes of cognition'. The selection between the two systems is driven by the difficulty of the question to be answered. We might make an 'easy call' that 'one will be . . . meeting someone for lunch . . . in an automatic or heuristic mode – known as 'System 1' in the psychological literature . . . while . . . harder assessment[s] about . . . traffic accident survival must be made in a controlled or analytic mode ('System 2')' (Nagel 2011, p. 3). System 1 is adequate for the simple recall that one is meeting someone for lunch; nothing very important depends on it. A more complicated task such as assessing the chances of survival of someone run over by a car will engage the more complicated and rational System 2, even (or especially) when the S has relevant specialised knowledge or experience. This dual systems approach has found wide application in psychological areas such as decision-making, mathematical cognition as well as ToM.

Sloman (1996, p. 3) agrees that 'several experiments can be interpreted as demonstrations that people can simultaneously believe two contradictory answers to the same reasoning problem' with the explanation being that the two answers originate in different reasoning systems. One experiment he uses to illustrate this is the Tversky and Kahneman (1983) 'Linda' experiment, described earlier. It is notable that some of the groups that committed the Conjunction Fallacy were intelligent and relevantly well-trained. Sloman (1996, p. 12) notes that in a group consisting of 'graduate and medical students with statistical training and a group of doctoral students in the decision science program of the Stanford Business School, more than 80%' made the error. Our surprise at this result illustrates how we may make a ToM error with ourselves as S and the doctoral students as O. We simulate to decide whether this elite group will commit the Conjunction Fallacy and conclude they will not. We are using System 2 to make this prediction. The elite group however could have used System 1 associations to arrive at their answer. So there is a System Mismatch between us and the doctoral students that leads to our ToM error.

System 1 employs associative thought, and 'associative thought uses temporal and similarity relations to draw inferences and make predictions' (Sloman 1996, p. 4). The model for this might be weather forecasting, where absent fully worked out causal rules at the grain necessary, it is still possible to make acceptable generalised predictions by noting for example that in the past, high pressure has been associated with good weather. System 1 is epidemiological. As an illustration of how the two systems might work together or separately on the same type of questions, consider simple arithmetic. If I ask you what is 2 × 3, it is likely that you will not – at least explicitly – perform a calculation, because the answer is very familiar and immediately and effortlessly apparent. These would be the hallmarks of System 1. The question does not need to be much more complex before I can force you to perform a calculation and use System 2. Perhaps 27 + 14 will suffice. Note that it is not required that System 2 be rules-based just because this illustration is.

Sloman (1996, p. 4) notes that 'sometimes people reason in a fashion inconsistent with a rule of probability but in agreement with their judgements of similarity' which is a good summary of the Linda results. It also indicates that on these occasions, people have privileged the results of System 1 over those of System 2. If it were the case that O's reasoned in this way, but that S's used System 2 to simulate them, then we would have the basis for an explanation of how systematic errors in ToM could arise. We would expect such discontinuities since, as Sloman (1996, p. 11) notes, '[o]ne system may be able to mimic the computation performed by the other, but only with effort and inefficiency and even then not necessarily reliably'.

To the extent that simulation is predominantly an activity which takes place under System 1 or employed its constituent biases, then we would expect simulation to be biased. Crucially, however, S's need not apply the same biases as O's, and so S's using System 1 to form a quick view of O's would miss various cognitive biases of the O's and thus make ToM prediction errors about the O's. Alternatively, asking S's in a quasi-scientific setting to predict the behaviour of O's will primarily involve the S's in using System 2 thinking. There is evidence to suggest that some simulation will be a System 2 activity. As Nagel (2011, p. 7) points out, it 'is called into play to handle . . . counterfactual reasoning' and the questions involved in simulation are counterfactual. They take the form 'if I were in situation X, what would I do?'. In that case, S's will have different biases – in particular, they may expect more rationality than is actually applied by the O's – and thus paradoxically, S's will be more likely to make systematic ToM errors when they consider the situation carefully. Nagel (2011, p. 10) notes that S and O must be using the same system for the simulation to be successful when she writes 'if [O] must use System 2 in order to represent a hypothetical possibility and then negate it, then [S] must also switch to System 2 as he retraces the subject's cognitive steps'.

We can therefore be sure that there will be simulation errors when System 2 is used to simulate System 1. It will not be the case though that this argument proves too much: the charge being that simulation is predominantly a System 2 activity and the simulated cognition is predominantly System 1. Nagel (2011, p. 10) writes, 'in many cases the same answer will be endorsed by both systems'. She gives the example of someone responding '1066' on being asked the date of the Battle of Hastings: one might answer that question either reflexively or after research. It is also not the case that all simulation is System 2: Nagel (2011, p. 13) writes that 'there is evidence that routine assessments of the knowledge or belief of others is not inherently taxing but rather modular and automatic'. But again, as mentioned above, when simulation is done using System 1, this will introduce

Table 5.1 Simulation error probability by system type of S and O

	S: System 1	*S: System 2*
O: System 1	Medium; S and O maybe different biases; but perhaps this covers much 'good enough' everyday ToM	High; frequent source of error in many situations where O is under more pressure than S, e.g. Shoppers
O: System 2	Very High; quick simulation of slow reasoning; but this is probably infrequently applied because ineffective	Low; e.g. grammar example discussed above, any occasion where S rationally follows O's rational processes

biases but these will likely be different biases for S than those exhibited by O in O's situation. The fact that it is 'routine' assessments of O's that is automatic suggests that non-routine assessments will be non-automatic.

A further prediction of this view is that the most accurate simulations will take place when both S and O are employing System 2. This can easily be seen to be the case by recalling the example of Harris (1992). If two competent English speakers A and B are asked to decide which of a set of sentences are grammatical and which are non-grammatical, a clear result will become apparent. A will predict that B will make the same classification as A of sentences into the grammatical and non-grammatical categories, and this prediction of A's will be correct. Both A and B are using System 2.

Table 5.1 shows how Dual Process Theory allows for different simulation error probabilities depending on which of System 1 and System 2 are employed by S and O.

Interaction between affect mismatch and system mismatch

At this point, it will be useful to set out how Affect Mismatches can interact with System Mismatches to produce simulation errors. We will be interested in different routes to simulation error; and in predicting when simulation error is likely and when not. In Figure 5.1, the routes to systematic simulation error are shown. At this stage, these are mere template routes for occasions when Bias Mismatch could occur. How these templates work will become clearer in the next chapters when I illustrate examples of these routes in use.

Note that the dashed line is dashed merely to assist with the comprehension of the diagram rather than being a significant element of the argument. The dashed line is the 'yes' line from box 4 to box 3. It is dashed to distinguish it from the other two lines it crosses.

On the Bias Mismatch Defence I propose, whenever there is a Bias Mismatch between S and O there will be systematic simulation error. It can be seen that there are three routes to Bias Mismatch and so three routes to systematic simulation error. There are two routes which do not pass through Bias Mismatch and so do not result in systematic simulation error. I will outline these five routes

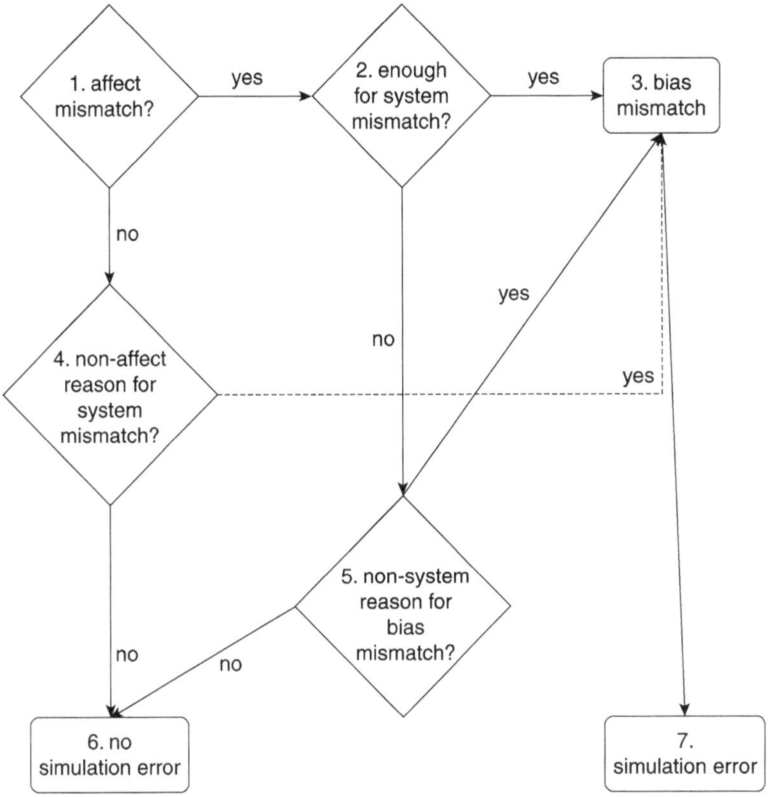

Figure 5.1 Systematic simulation error routes

through Figure 5.1. Each route is named by the sequence of boxes through which it passes. In each case of simulation error, it will be systematic because the Bias Mismatch will take place systematically. These five paths exhaust all possible complete routes through Figure 5.1.

- 1/2/3/7
  - There is an Affect Mismatch between S and O
  - This mismatch is significant enough to cause a System Mismatch between S and O
  - The System Mismatch causes a Bias Mismatch between S and O
  - This route results in systematic simulation error
- 1/2/5/3/7
  - There is an Affect Mismatch between S and O
  - This mismatch is not significant enough to cause a System Mismatch between S and O

  - There is nevertheless a Bias Mismatch between S and O, even though they employ the same system
  - This route results in systematic simulation error

- 1/4/3/7

  - There is no Affect Mismatch between S and O
  - There is nevertheless a System Mismatch between S and O, with non-affective causes
  - This route results in systematic simulation error

- 1/4/6

  - There is no Affect Mismatch between S and O
  - There is no other reason for System Mismatch
  - There is no System Mismatch
  - There is no Bias Mismatch
  - There is no simulation error

- 1/2/5/6

  - There is an Affect Mismatch between S and O
  - The Affect Mismatch does not suffice to cause System Mismatch
  - There is no other reason for System Mismatch
  - There is no System Mismatch
  - There is no Bias Mismatch
  - There is no simulation error.

In the next two chapters, I will outline some of the situations where there is systematic error in ToM and explain how Bias Mismatch between S and O explains the errors in ToM. Saxe suggests a number of relevant circumstances. In some situations, we are 'too rosy' about the reasoning capacities of others and in other types of situation we are too cynical. I will cover both in turn.

Notes

1 See Andrews (2008, p. 13) for argument to the effect that 'folk psychology includes the notion that some behaviour is explained by personality traits', as is consistent with the Fundamental Attribution Error.

2 This assumes a continuity between how people assign properties to themselves and how fictional objects obtain their properties. For more on these vexed questions, see Short (2014).

3 The existence of qualia is intuitively compelling but philosophically controversial. Dennett (1993) argues that qualia do not exist and Chalmers (1997) argues that they do.

6 Bias mismatch defence

'Too rosy' evidence

Introduction

Saxe (2005a) cites Gilovich (1993) as one source of much of the data we will consider in this chapter. It all points to scenarios in which S's are systematically too rosy in their ToM. They predict that O's in the situations described will act more rationally, not to say ethically, than they do. These predictions will not be borne out, as we will see. Gilovich (1993, pp. 9–10) explains that the basic project of his book is to ask why 'questionable and erroneous beliefs are learned, and how they are maintained'. The fact that the beliefs are 'questionable' tells us that there are ToM errors involved. If the beliefs were not questionable, then they would presumably be predicted more often.

We will be interested in any biases that Gilovich cites as explanations of the questionable beliefs, because my proposal is that absence of specifically those biases in S at the time of simulation and as part of the simulation is what accounts for the surprise or the failure of ToM. Naturally I do not claim that S is free of the biases displayed by O; merely that the same biases are not triggered in S or used as part of the simulation because S is not actually in O's situation. That means that the full affective import of O's situation is not felt by S, or S and O may employ different systems of reasoning. So there can be Affect Mismatch or System Mismatch between S and O, leading to Bias Mismatch and systematic simulation error.

Even if O's become motivated to remove their cognitive biases, this is very difficult. Tversky and Kahneman (1973, p. 218) found that undergraduates offered $1 – a significant amount in 1973 – to answer a mathematical problem correctly by avoiding the Availability Heuristic, did not do so. They conclude that: '[e]rroneous intuitions, apparently, are not easily rectified by the introduction of monetary payoffs'. Failure of the S's to simulate cognitive biases in the O's will be a hard-to-remove source of systematic ToM errors in the S's, even when the O's might be expected to be trying hard to remove such biases. The difficulty of removing such biases may sometimes cause ToM errors in the other direction as well: S may apply his own biases. For these reasons, there are many ways of arriving at a mismatch in bias status in S as compared with O, and this will cause simulation errors.

A possible objection here derives from the fact that my account admits that there is widespread error in human cognition. It may be asked how this is possible, if our cognitive systems have evolved to help us survive. I will not address this issue at length, but merely outline the directions of two responses. First, it is clear that we have the biases, and many of them. That is not necessarily irrational, because they save time and we simply do not have enough time or the inclination to consider every question that faces us on a daily basis with the maximum possible cognitive effort. Often, it is better to act on a 'wrong' decision and see what happens than agonise indefinitely. So it is clear that our thinking is not supposed to be even aimed at being error-free. Second, I might appeal to arguments of the sort raised in detail by McKay and Dennett (2009, p. 493), to the effect that some 'misbeliefs' are 'best conceived as design features. Such misbeliefs, unlike occasional lucky falsehoods, would have been systematically adaptive in the evolutionary past'. They give as examples unrealistically positive false beliefs about the self, which improve performance. Note that this could also suggest evolutionary grounds for systematic ToM error, since S employs ToM about S as well as O.

On the other hand, there will be many occasions when ToM succeeds because there is no Bias Mismatch, perhaps because there is no significant affect in either S or O. Or if tasks are selected such that S and O use the same system of reasoning, such as with the Harris (1992) grammar task, then simulation may proceed without error. My account also predicts that there should be occasions of successful simulation by bias matching, which should be empirically testable. It will be important though to ensure that S and O are not just employing the same bias. They would also need to be employing the same bias about the same data. S and O could well both be applying Confirmation Bias, for example, but unless they started with the same beliefs, that would not lead them to seek erroneously to confirm the same prior belief. Very careful experimental design will be needed here.

There can be two forms of evidence for ToM errors, which I will term 'hard' evidence and 'soft' evidence. Hard evidence will be constituted by statistical data on the ToM errors, of the form '75% of S's did not predict O's decision'. This will be the most important data. The softer form of evidence will be where no percentages are given, but we are surprised by the questionable beliefs. The surprise indicates that we have failed to predict the belief. This softer evidence, while still valuable, may suffer from the twin defects that surprise is both subjective and varies from mild to extreme. Moreover, many of the people likely to read this book will have extensive knowledge of the frailty of human reasoning and therefore be unsurprised by any revelations concerning it. It is possible that such S's are not using their ToM at all: they are merely consulting their relevant experience. The hard evidence will be covered in the earlier sections with the soft evidence to follow.

Table 6.1 shows the Bias Mismatch response I will give to each of 11 cases discussed in the works cited by Saxe (2005a), together with the relevant section. I label the cases by the group of people studied. Some of the experiments have

Table 6.1 Response type by group studied: too rosy

Group Studied	*Response*
Shock Appliers	(A): O exhibits Conformity Bias
Fake Prison Guards	(A): O exhibits Conformity Bias
Repenters	(B): S exhibits False Consensus Effect
Quiz Gamers	(B): S exhibits Fundamental Attribution Error
Suicide Note Assessors Redux	(A): O exhibits Belief Perseverance Bias
Lottery Ticket Holders Redux	(A): O exhibits Endowment Effect
Gamblers	(A): O exhibits Confirmation Bias
Women Wanting to Marry	(A): O exhibits Availability Heuristic
Basketball Fans	(A): O exhibits Clustering Illusion
Cancer Cure Assessors	(B): S exhibits Confirmation Bias
Puzzle Solvers	(A): S exhibits Availability Heuristic
Shoppers Redux	(A): O exhibits Position Effect

already been touched on previously. The explanations fall into two broad categories, as set out below:

- (A): O exhibits bias which is not simulated by S [nine entries].
- (B): S exhibits bias when simulating [three entries].

'Too rosy' data

Shock appliers

The Milgram (1963) experiment was introduced in Chapter 3. The results include valuable hard evidence because there are some numerical data concerning S's confounded expectations of the likely behaviour of O's. Recall that 26/40 = 65 per cent of O's set the dial to 450 volts while the psychology undergraduate S's predicted that that number would be 3 per cent at most.

The Bias Mismatch Defence of ST that I propose must now explain this failure to predict. I will do this by noting the significant Affect Mismatch between S and O. The S's, whether ourselves or Yale seniors, consider the question as to how much they would be prepared to shock in a relatively calm, reflective state – precisely one arranged for the seniors so that they could 'reflect carefully' (Milgram 1963, p. 375). The S's are not in this instant under pressure from an authority figure in a lab coat, issuing stringent instructions. We may also imagine that the effects of stress deriving from deference to authority would be much less in modern times than in 1963. All of these factors imply that we are unlikely to apply or to simulate the cognitive bias that tends to make us more obedient than we should be. We as S's fail to simulate the Conformity Bias of the O's, just as the carefully reflecting seniors of Milgram (1963) did.

In accordance with the framework set out previously, I will now explain why this Bias Mismatch arises. On this occasion, there is extreme Affect Mismatch between S and O. The S's are undergraduates sitting calmly, observing in a clinical fashion in the company of their distinguished professor. Nothing much hangs upon what the S's say or do in relation to the experiment; they are expected to make useful psychological comments. Nothing about the calmness and lack of involvement of the S's is true of the O's. As Milgram (1963, p. 375) writes, many of the O's exhibited extreme affect: 'the degree of tension reached extremes that are rarely seen in socio-psychological laboratory studies. . . . Fourteen of the 40 [O's] showed definite signs of nervous laughter and smiling. . . . Full-blown, uncontrollable seizures were observed for 3 [O's]'. There is a very clear affective mismatch between S and O; this explains the absence of the appropriate bias in the simulation which explains this failure of ToM. Milgram (1963, pp. 375–376) even makes remarks suggesting this in interpreting the results he obtained from the Yale seniors: 'it is possible that the remoteness of the respondents from the actual situation, and the difficulty of conveying to them the concrete details of the experiment, could account for the serious underestimation of obedience'.

The hidden S's watching the experiment 'often uttered expressions of disbelief upon seeing a subject administer more powerful shocks to the victim' even though the S's 'had a full acquaintance with the details of the situation' (Milgram 1963, p. 377). Since these observer S's were relatively sophisticated associates of Milgram – 'senior psychology majors' – we may presume that they were much less subject to the bias towards obedience. Or they may have been subject to a different strain of Conformity Bias in that they felt pressure to side with Milgram in his capacity as dispassionate observer. In any case, it is clear that the observers faced much less pressure than the O's, and in fact may have felt countervailing pressure to behave 'clinically'. So we are still entitled to conclude that Affect Mismatch driving Bias Mismatch causes the failure of ST here.

Mind and Language (1992, p. 9) write 'I might conclude, after deliberating, that I would not behave sadistically in the notorious Milgram experiments. But, I might also be convinced, on the basis of scientific evidence that the balance of probability is that I would, in fact, so behave. Here, I will be baffled by the prospect of my action'. The Bias Mismatch Defence I propose in this book eliminates this bafflement. The calm and unhurried simulation of the S's will not reflect at all the various extreme affects O's would face in the Milgram (1963) experiment. The S's would then not suffer from Conformity Bias at all or in the same way as the O's, and so S's simulations would fail.

We know that it is Conformity Bias that causes the unexpected behaviour of the O's, because if the behaviour around them changes, so does theirs. Prentice (2007, p. 27) reports that in some versions of the Milgram (1963) experiment, he had 'two confederates refuse to administer shocks when the dial was turned into the dangerous range [and then] 92.5% of the [O's] defied the experimenter's orders'.[1]

This line must account for the observations made in a re-enactment described by Ross, Amabile, and Steinmetz (1977, p. 492). They write that 'Bierbrauer (1973) . . . showed that even after personally participating in a verbatim reenactment of the classic Milgram (1963) demonstration, raters consistently and dramatically underestimated the extent to which Milgram's subjects would administer dangerous levels of electric shock in accord with the situational forces compelling "obedience"'. My response will be that a 'verbatim reenactment' is still not close enough to the real thing to make it count, affectively, for the S's. Stich and Nichols describe the aim of the Bierbrauer reenactment as 'to study the predictions that would be made by non-participant observers' (Stone and Davies 1995, p. 102). Again, an observer S that is not a participant will not exhibit Conformity Bias to the same extent and about the same cognitions as participant O's.

A slightly greater difficulty is raised for my account when Stich and Nichols note that there were still failures of ToM by S's when 'they themselves played the role of a subject in a vivid reenactment' (Stone and Davies 1995, p. 102). The force of this seems to be that there should not be simulation errors when S and O are identical, because S and O have the same mental machinery. However, two differences are apparent. This objection might suggest that S's should avoid simulation error in relation to themselves as O. This may not be true; it depends on how much 'playing the role' provides the full affective import of actually being in the Milgram (1963) experiment. I suggest that 'playing a role' is very different from 'being' the role. But in any case, the S's were here asked to predict the behaviour of other O's. The idea was that placing them in a closer situation to the one of the O's would give them better insight into the behaviour of the O's. But this will not work at all if there is still scope for Affect Mismatch, which I contend there very clearly is.

In general, many occasions of ToM error arise when S's are given the salient facts and asked to opine on them rationally. This differs dramatically from the affective position of the O's, who simply experience the world without the important, salient or significant facts being given to them as such.

Fake prison guards

Although Saxe (2005a) does not cite the infamous Stanford prison experiment, it is often considered together with Milgram (1963) as providing evidence of unexpected behaviour which may result from excessive deference to deemed authority. The prison experiment had a very simple design. A mock prison was constructed, and the O's were randomly assigned the role of guards and prisoners. The O's answered an 'extensive questionnaire' designed to select those who were 'most stable (physically and mentally), most mature, and least involved in anti-social behaviour' (Haney, Banks, and Zimbardo 1973, p. 73). The O's were all male college students who were mostly middle class. The guards were given the instruction to 'maintain the reasonable degree of order' needed for the 'effective functioning' (Haney, Banks, and Zimbardo 1973, p. 74) of the prison, without being giving further specific instructions as to how this was to be achieved.

The results were that the guards were far more aggressive than expected. As Haney, Banks, and Zimbardo (1973, p. 69) write, '[a]t least a third of the guards were judged to have become far more aggressive and dehumanising toward the prisoners than would ordinarily be predicted in a simulation study'. This is the hard evidence of ToM error; the authors as S's judged the behaviour of the guards as O's and were wrong about a third of them. Note that the experiment was a simulated prison which had no legal authority to hold persons; it was time-limited and yet dramatic and unexpected behaviours were observed. S's will generally fail to simulate O's accurately here in that they will expect that O's in the situation will not display marked aggression in the case of guards and marked passivity in the case of the prisoners.

Despite the apparent normality of the O's and the lack of instructions tending towards this outcome, 'the characteristic nature of their encounters tended to be negative, hostile, affrontive and dehumanising' (Haney, Banks, and Zimbardo 1973, p. 80). A high proportion of the ten prisoners experienced extreme affect: 'five prisoners . . . had to be released early because of extreme emotional depression, crying, rage and acute anxiety' (Haney, Banks, and Zimbardo 1973, p. 81). One prisoner even developed a 'psychosomatic rash' (Haney, Banks, and Zimbardo 1973, p. 81). The guards on the other hand 'enjoyed the extreme control and power they exercised' (Haney, Banks, and Zimbardo 1973, p. 81) and 'on several occasions [they] remained on duty voluntarily and uncomplaining for extra hours – without additional pay' (Haney, Banks, and Zimbardo 1973, p. 81).

The completeness of the failure here of ToM may be gauged from Haney, Banks, and Zimbardo (1973, p. 81) writing that these 'differential reactions to the experience of imprisonment were not suggested by or predictable from the self-report measures of personality and attitude or the interviews taken before the experiment began'. In fact, the study had to be terminated early after six days because of the 'unexpectedly intense reactions' (Haney, Banks, and Zimbardo 1973, p. 88) generated. I will propose that the same explanation may be applied to Haney, Banks, and Zimbardo (1973) as was applied previously to Milgram (1963).

There will be significant affective mismatches between persons outside the experiment who are asked to use their ToM to predict the behaviour of O's in either role in the prison experiment. These mismatches permit the introduction of my proposed Bias Mismatch Defence, to the effect that such affective mismatches cause failure of ToM through inadequate simulation of biases exhibited by O's. There will be different Affect Mismatches between S's and the two subsets of the O's. The failure to simulate the guards accurately will be due to not fully reflecting their enjoyment of power. The failure to simulate the prisoners accurately will be due to not fully reflecting their depression and rage. The main bias active here in both the prisoners and the guards is again Conformity Bias. The prisoners conform with each other and defer to the guards.

The guards also conform with each other. So we have Affect Mismatch driving Bias Mismatch resulting in faulty simulation and systematic ToM error.

'Repenters'

We might expect that people will generally believe that other people agree with them only when there is some reason for that belief, for example testimony to that effect or perhaps polling data. However, Gilovich (1993, pp. 112–113) points out that there is in this respect a 'systematic defect in our ability to estimate the beliefs and attitudes of others' whereby we 'often exaggerate the extent to which other people hold the same beliefs that we do'. This is held to be evidence for a failure in ToM because if people simulated accurately, they would not predict the presence of this agreement where it is absent. However, it can also be seen as positive for the ST account since that predicts such default belief attribution while TT accounts do not, as discussed in Chapter 4.

In fact, Gilovich goes so far as to see the 'imagined agreement' problem as underpinning the wide variety of false beliefs he discusses, since maintaining the false beliefs without the imaginary agreement of others would be much more difficult. On that line, almost all false beliefs would represent a failure of ToM. However, as Gilovich (1993, p. 118) also points out, 'we associate primarily with those who share our own beliefs, values, and habits'; insofar as that is true, we would not have a failure of ToM here at all.

Gilovich (1993, p. 114) cites Ross, Greene, and House (1977) to provide data where we can see this failure. An experiment was conducted in which students were asked if they would be prepared to wear a large sign around campus bearing the legend 'REPENT'. A 'substantial percentage' agreed. The critical question was then asked as to what percentage of their fellow students did they think would also agree to do so. It transpires that student S's thought, roughly, that their peer O's would decide as they had. Ross, Greene, and House (1977, p. 292) report that S's who agreed to wear the sign thought that 63.5 per cent of peer O's would also agree while S's who declined to wear the sign thought that only 23.3 per cent of peer O's would agree to wear it. This of course, is explained by the False Consensus Effect introduced in Chapter 5. The simulation of the S's is derailed by their exhibiting the False Consensus Effect.

My general claim is that the underlying reason for many cases of lack of simulation of cognitive bias is affective mismatch between S and O. Of interest then is the explanation offered by Gilovich (1993, p. 114) for the False Consensus Effect. There is a basic desire to 'maintain a positive assessment of our own judgement' which is particularly likely to play a part when we 'have an emotional investment in the belief'. So, S's emotions can promote the False Consensus Effect. If S's believe particularly passionately that there will be a woman supreme court judge in the next ten years – one of the Ross, Greene, and House (1977) test questions – those S's are more likely to give a mistakenly high estimate of the number of O's who share that view. The effect is reduced or eliminated when the S's do not particularly care about the belief in question. When the test question was about the number of hours of TV watched a week, S's were less likely to think O's were like them. So the False Consensus Effect is exacerbated in relation to beliefs that really matter to the S's. In other words, we have here once again Affect Mismatch driving Bias Mismatch.

Several experiments outlined by Pronin, Puccio and Ross may all be explained on the basis outlined above. Pronin, Puccio and Ross report on a similar experiment, in which the difference was that the sign read 'EAT AT JOE'S' (Gilovich, Griffin, and Kahneman 2002, p. 642). S's who agree to wear the sign believe that O's will agree more than they do, and those who do not agree think that O's will agree less than they do. The False Consensus Effect in S's results in systematic simulation error.

The type of explanations produced for the answers given also favour simulation over theory. S's who thought that only uptight, humourless people would agree to wear the sign thought that many O's would agree, while S's who thought that only attention-seekers or patsy O's who would agree to anything would agree to wear the sign. That looks a lot like S's simulating to find out the answer to 'how would S or O feel in scenario X?' and deciding whether or not S or O will agree to undergo scenario X based on the simulated affect therein.

Similar results were obtained when S's were asked 'whether they preferred music from the 1960s or the 1980s' (Gilovich, Griffin, and Kahneman 2002, p. 642) and what percentage of their peers would agree. S's said that most people would agree with whichever choice they made, even though there was in fact more of an even split between the two choices. This further occurrence of the False Consensus Effect in S's results in systematic simulation error.

Pronin, Puccio and Ross discuss three further experiments conducted in their own lab which they say all show the False Consensus Effect. The first one was on 'Encoding and Decoding Musical Tapping' (Gilovich, Griffin, and Kahneman 2002, p. 643). S tapped out the rhythm of a well-known tune for a listening O who had to identify the tune. S was then asked to estimate the probability that O would recognise the tune. The results were that S's vastly overestimated how easy this would be, because S can 'hear' the tune internally, and does not adjust for the fact that O cannot. S's thought that success rates would vary between 10 per cent and 95 per cent, with an average of 50 per cent, while the actual success rate was a mere 3 per cent. This experiment looks like a slightly unusual illustration of the False Consensus Effect in that it might be best termed as the axiom 'everyone knows what I know' rather than 'everyone believes what I believe'. In some ways, it seems to be an adult version of failing the False Belief Task. We might explain the effects by appealing to the Availability Heuristic in its Vividness incarnation. S's find the tune so vivid in their own mind that they are simply unable to simulate the total lack of Vividness the tune has in the minds of the O's, who just have some dull tapping to interpret. Thus, there is a Bias Mismatch between S and O and so the Bias Mismatch Defence is available.

Quiz gamers

Ross, Amabile, and Steinmetz (1977) investigated the assessment of general knowledge by persons participating in one-on-one quiz game scenarios. The idea being investigated was 'social control', meaning inequalities of power in social settings. For example, if one person works for another person, the latter person will have more social power. Another example discussed by Ross, Amabile, and Steinmetz (1977, p. 493) is that of the dissertation viva at a university. Here, the 'candidate is required to field questions from the idiosyncratic and occasionally esoteric areas of each examiner's interest' while the 'candidate has relatively little time for reflections'. We might expect people involved in such situations of social control to take account of it when making ToM assessments. For example, if the candidate assesses the knowledge of the examiner, he should do so including consideration of the advantages of question selection, time and lack of pressure enjoyed by the examiner. Likewise, if the examiner assesses the knowledge of the candidate, he should take account of the corresponding disadvantages to which the candidate is exposed.

Ross, Amabile, and Steinmetz (1977) proposed to investigate the extent to which assessments of social control played a role in evaluation of others. They arranged for participants to pair off; the questioner would set questions and ask them of the contestant. The questioner set questions based on his own esoteric knowledge. Ross, Amabile, and Steinmetz (1977, p. 486) claim that this models many forms of social interaction, where they say that '[o]ne participant defines the domain and controls the style of the interaction and the other must respond within those limits'. The questioner, then, is in a position of social control in relation to the contestant. The result, naturally enough, was that the contestants were not very successful in answering the questions, lacking the specialised knowledge of the questioner.

After the questions have been answered, the questioners and the contestants both made general knowledge evaluations of each other and themselves. It transpired that of 24 contestants, '20 contestants rated themselves inferior to their questioners' (Ross, Amabile, and Steinmetz 1977, p. 489). So, the vast majority of contestants did not allow for the fact that it is much easier to set questions than to answer them. The contestants as S's made evaluations of the general knowledge of the questioner O's that completely failed to take account of the one-sided nature of the data available to them. Ross, Amabile, and Steinmetz (1977, p. 485) conclude that when 'drawing inferences about [O's], [S's] consistently fail to make adequate allowance for the biasing effects of social roles upon performance'.

This experiment was re-run with observers, who form new S's. The observers produced the same predictions as the participants viz. '[S's] impressions of the [O's] in the quiz game showed the same bias that was evident in the participants' own perceptions. Overall, the questioner is seen as tremendously knowledgeable' (Ross, Amabile, and Steinmetz 1977, p. 491).

What has happened is that the S's of both types have committed the Fundamental Attribution Error. Ross, Amabile, and Steinmetz (1977, p. 491) confirm this when they note that 'the phenomenon we have described represents a special case of a more fundamental attribution error' meaning that S's attribute the underperformance of the O's more to the character of the O's than to the actually more important situational variables viz. the difficulty of the quiz questions. S 'infers broad personal dispositions and anticipates more cross-situational consistency in behaviour than actually occurs' (Ross, Amabile, and Steinmetz 1977, p. 491).

The authors provide a further bias-related explanation for their data when they suggest that 'the various raters' judgements were distorted precisely to the extent that they depended upon biased data samples' (Ross, Amabile, and Steinmetz 1977, p. 493) which would be an example of the Availability Heuristic. This would be because the results of the question and answer session would be highly available since salient yet inaccurate in assessing the general knowledge abilities of participants. S's do not take account of the obvious fact that they have very little data and it is highly selective. So there are two ways of using biases in S to explain the systematic ToM errors made by S here.

Suicide note assessors redux

This experiment was discussed previously in Chapter 5. The experiment, by Ross, Lepper, and Hubbard (1975) is described by Stich and Nichols. In this experiment, O's are given a test which 'indicates that they are unusually good (or unusually bad) at a certain task . . . an hour later it is explained to them that the test results were bogus' (Stone and Davies 1995, p. 100). One of the tasks in the experiment was to assess whether a suicide note was fake or real. The odd result in the experiment is that O's continue to believe that they are unusually good or bad at the task even when the evidence therefore has been dismissed.

Stich and Nichols formed a body of S's from among their students and asked them to predict the results of the test. They found that '[t]he predictions the [S's] offered were more often wrong than right' (Stone and Davies 1995, p. 100). Thus there is some quantification of failure of ToM here; more than half the S's exhibited such a failure. Stich and Nichols adduce this failure as evidence against ST by noting that the students would have exhibited the Belief Perseverance Bias had they taken the test as opposed to been asked to predict its outcome – which we may concede. If so, then they could not have been simulating, according to Stich and Nichols, because they would not have made the error.

This is of course easily explained on the Bias Mismatch Defence I am proposing. The S's simulations failed because they failed to include the Belief Perseverance Bias of the O's in their simulation of the O's. In turn, they failed to include that effect because they were not in the situation faced by the O's, who had an affective involvement resulting from being told something about their competencies which may have been pleasing or displeasing. There was an Affect Mismatch between S and O and a resulting Bias Mismatch leading to systematic ToM error.

The experimental task in the Ross, Lepper, and Hubbard (1975, p. 882) experiment is conducted while wired up to electrodes ostensibly intended to measure physiological responses. We may observe immediately that this is not a low affect scenario for the O's. In addition, the O's were randomly assigned to three groups – success, fail, average – and at least two of these will have had some influence on self-esteem which will in turn have had an affective component. This is confirmed by Ross, Lepper, and Hubbard (1975, p. 883) who note that 'subjects in the success condition reported having felt more satisfaction than subjects in the average condition' who in turn felt more satisfaction than the subjects assigned to the fail condition.

Ross, Lepper, and Hubbard (1975, p. 885) recruited additional experimental subjects who were engaged in 'observing and listening to an entire experiment through a one-way mirror'. They also exhibit the Belief Perseverance Bias about the ability of the O's – they continue to believe that the 'success' O's are better at the task even after they also learn that the O's did not really succeed. This needs to be explained, because on my account so far, these new S's should not have an affective involvement in the prowess of the O's. A further bias-related explanation is available here, though since the Belief Perseverance Bias can also be seen as a result of Confirmation Bias. Ross, Lepper, and Hubbard (1975, p. 880) note that 'once formed, impressions are remarkably perseverant and unresponsive to new input'. That line is also suggested by Pronin, Gilovich, and Ross (2004, p. 796) who write 'biased assimilation of new information, in turn, leads to unwarranted perseverance of beliefs'. The point here then is that the observer S's exhibited Confirmation Bias which introduced simulation error. So we have a further Bias Mismatch explanation of the ToM performance of the new S's.

The remaining subsections cover the soft evidence of ToM error.

Lottery ticket holders redux

This experiment was described previously in Chapter 5. The Endowment Effect is the bias of the O's that the S's do not simulate and this is why the S's simulation fails here.

The S's will be uninterested in the outcome of the lottery, giving them an Affect Mismatch with the O's. Moreover, the S's have the question explained to them in a dispassionate way with the salient points for rational analysis prominent in that explanation. They could then have a System Mismatch with the O's as well. An Affect Mismatch between S and O is also suggested by Kühberger *et al.* (1995, p. 429) when they write that 'resale values would be lower when given in personal interaction with the experimenter rather than anonymously, since [O's] feel under more pressure of potentially having to justify their price'. 'Pressure' means affect for the O's which is not there for the S's. Note also that all of the S's are in the presence of a different experimenter, and will feel different pressures. Together, these factors mean that the Bias Mismatch Defence of ST which I propose predicts the actual outcome – the S's fail to simulate the O's in that the S's suggest lower, more reasonable, resale prices for the lottery tickets. The S's feel pressure to be reasonable while the O's are in the grip of the Endowment Effect.

Nichols, Stich, and Leslie (1995, p. 443) respond to the Kühberger *et al.* (1995) methodological criticisms by introducing new data. This new data is from an experiment showing that S's failed to predict their own later susceptibility to the Endowment Effect. This is of course exactly what my account predicts, since simulation is the basis of ToM when used for all O's, whether the O is another person or the S at another time. There is a Bias Mismatch between S and O at the later time, even though the O is the same person as the S. It is just that the S is not engaged in the actual situation at the time of simulation and so does not feel its affective import. So there can be an Affect Mismatch between S and O even when O is S at the later time. The objection that simulation cannot explain ToM in cases where S and O are identical ignores the fact that additional distinctions are available between S and O apart from their mental machinery, which we may concede is the same.

This idea is consistent with an observation of Kühberger *et al.* (1995, p. 425) who note that 'even five minutes of belonging might be difficult to simulate'. The elements of belonging that might be difficult to simulate might be the affective elements and the biases that are triggered.

In their response to the criticisms of Kühberger *et al.*, Nichols, Stich, and Leslie (1995, p. 440) claim that ST is in trouble even though Kühberger *et al.* cannot identify the factors driving the Endowment Effect because 'whatever subtle features of the situation triggered the difference in selling price, those features were presumably there for the observer subjects to see'. Indeed, but to see is not to feel. The O's are affectively involved much more than the S's.

Similarly, Nichols, Stich, and Leslie (1995, p. 441) note that to 'suggest that successful simulation requires more than the information that was available to our [S's] is to admit that simulation is a marginal ability that would fail in most real life situations'. This is an interesting objection to which my account must respond. No plausible view of ToM can predict high error frequencies across the board when people use their ToM capacities. My account can respond by virtue of the analysis represented by Table 5.1 and Figure 5.1. These allow that there can be scenarios in which the following possibilities apply:

1. there is no Affect Mismatch, no System Mismatch and no Bias Mismatch;
2. there is Affect Mismatch, but no System Mismatch and no Bias Mismatch;
3. there is no System Mismatch and there may be biases but not enough to cause a simulation error;
4. there is a System Mismatch, but the O's were not biased and so there is no Bias Mismatch.

All four of these routes are ones on which my account predicts no simulation error, so my account can respond to the charge brought by Nichols, Stich, and Leslie (1995) to the effect that it makes ToM too error-prone.

Gamblers

Gilovich suggests we make inaccurate predictions of how unhelpful data are evaluated by others, thus indicating a failure of ToM. The others in question are gamblers, in one example. We know that betting shops are profitable which means on average that gamblers are not. We might think then that gamblers are in denial about their losses. They must somehow ignore or forget the data relating to their losses. They must be ignoring data which disconfirms the hypothesis they cling to: that they are successful gamblers.

The surprising element of this case is exactly how people dismiss disconfirmatory data. We may expect that they will simply forget it; they will pay it no attention. As Gilovich (1993, p. 62) says, 'it is commonly believed that people are more inclined to remember information that supports their beliefs than information that contradicts them'. Gilovich has shown however that disconfirmatory data are considered more, not less. He cites an experiment he conducted showing that gamblers remember their losses more than their wins – but they construct narratives in which the losses were actually 'near wins'.[2] As Gilovich (1993, p. 62) writes: 'people often resist the challenge of information that is inconsistent with their beliefs not by ignoring it, but by subjecting it to particularly intense scrutiny'. We work hard to find flaws in the disconfirmatory data so as to accord it a lower weight in our considerations than the unquestioned confirmatory data. Note that this is subtly different type of Confirmation Bias to the one discussed in Chapter 5. There, people seek the wrong sort of data; that which can only tend to confirm their hypothesis. Here, O's are presented with data tending both to confirm and disconfirm their hypothesis, and deal with that scenario in a way that does not optimise the potential value of the data.

The surprise is generated when the question is asked as to whether one should question the quality of new data even-handedly, irrespective of whether it is confirmatory or disconfirmatory. Everyone will answer that question in the affirmative. That could indicate a System Mismatch between S and O, because S is using System 2 to respond to questions about data handling while O is just behaving using System 1. In any case, once again, S's are affectively too remote from the O's situation, since it is known that gambling is highly affectively involving and indeed addictively so. There is then a significant Affect Mismatch between S and O here. As a result, the S's do not simulate the Confirmation Bias of the O's and thus exhibit ToM errors in their simulations.

Women wanting to marry

We expect that people will use the best data available to support decisions, especially when these decisions are important. Decisions in relation to marriage will be among the important ones. What data are available here? Consider the claim: 'an unmarried American woman over 40 is as likely to be killed by a terrorist as to experience matrimony' (Gilovich 1993, p. 100). This claim has a number of properties. It exhibits Vividness, apparent relevance, memorability, and falsehood. Everyone will find out that it is false and no-one will believe it. Not so, alas.

The origin of the claim was a *Newsweek* article published in 1986. It reported accurately on the findings of a Harvard sociology professor in relation to the probability of future marriage: Cherlin (1990, p. 117) writes: 'those who remained single until age 35 would have only a 5% chance; and at age 40 the chance would be a mere 1%'. The claim that this was less than the chance of being killed by a terrorist was added, it is claimed, as a joke. Later studies made very different predictions because they used a better statistical approach, finding 'a 40-year-old had a 17% to 23% chance' (Cherlin 1990, p. 117) of marrying later. Fewer people noticed this more reasonable claim than continued to believe the terrorist claim.

So educated S's here might be surprised by O's who believe the 'terrorist' claim, since it is false and dramatically misleading. It is also possible that educated S's might be unsurprised here as well; this and the previous gamblers case could be two situations of the type I warned of earlier, where sophisticated readers are unsurprised by any facts relating to the frailty of human reason. Nevertheless, S's will struggle to simulate these O's. What is missing in the simulation is the Availability Heuristic. The terrorist claim is exceptionally vivid, which as we saw, makes it highly available. The Affect Mismatch here is also obvious: S's are not affectively involved in the marriage prospects of the O's whereas the O's are so affectively involved. To the extent that the terrorist claim is vivid, because the S in question does feel affectively involved in the issue, we might have a case of successful simulation involving bias matching between S and O.

Basketball fans

There is a belief among basketball fans in the 'hot hand' phenomenon. This holds that players shoot in streaks: if they have just made a shot, they are more likely to make the next shot, and if they have missed, they are more likely to miss. Gilovich (1993, p. 12) studies data relating to an actual team, and finds that the hot hand phenomenon does not exist. On the contrary, 'there was a slight tendency for players to shoot better after missing their last shot'. Since we may expect basketball fans to have a close acquaintance with the relevant data since they spend a lot of time watching the reality generating it unfold, their belief in the hot hand phenomenon is unexpected and thus represents an error in our ToM. Yet more strikingly, the players themselves who are even closer to the raw data also share the false belief in the hot hand phenomenon.

Moreover, for at least those of us calmly considering the phenomenon, the fact that the data are random – or indeed, tending to show that there is an 'anti-hot hand phenomenon' if there is any effect at all – and do not support the phenomenon is made highly salient by its centrality in the discussion. Thus, we are surprised by the first order error; we make a second order error in our ToM because we are told dispassionately about the data. We would simulate better if we were able to place ourselves in the highly non-dispassionate position of a basketball fan, thus reducing the Affect Mismatch between S and O. The Bias Mismatch in play here derives from the fact that the O's fall prey to the Clustering Illusion described in Chapter 5.

Gilovich makes the data more comprehensible for the fans by presenting it in numerical form: there is no statistical tendency for players' hits to follow hits more than misses. We might expect fans presented with this data to accept it, and admit that their previous belief in the hot hand phenomenon was mistaken. This does not happen: Gilovich (1993, p. 13) writes that most people question the data, '[t]he hot hand exists, the argument goes, it just did not show up in our sample of data'. This again we will not expect as S's. The difference of course is that we are not at all committed to the hot hand, we are considering the matter dispassionately, and we will generally believe of ourselves that we will respond to convincing empirical evidence of the falsity of a belief by negating the relevant propositional attitude. That would give us a System Mismatch. The other option is that we as S's do not simulate the Confirmation Bias of the affectively highly involved fans.

O's fall prey to one or other bias, but S's would not, unless they were shown the actual data. Thus, we could convert poor S's to good ones by changing the bias status of the S's. If we ask them whether basketball fans will believe in the hot hand in the face of contrary evidence, they will say no. If we ask them whether they will believe in streaks of shooting based on a sequence of six hits in 20 shots, and show them that sequence as a series of X's and O's, the S's will now be more closely tied in to the actual situation of the fans, and will now model the fans better by matching their Clustering Illusion bias. This would be another example of successful simulation by bias matching.

This conclusion is supported by Gilovich (1993, pp. 16–17) when he points out that professional managers of basketball teams dismissed his findings. Simulation might predict that they would welcome new, relevant and significant scientific data. ST here fails to allow for the major bias that managers will have to show that they know their business. We may have here a further form of Confirmation Bias or Self-Presentation Bias. This accords with the convincing case made in Lewis (2004) that it is possible to use mathematical analysis of player capabilities to outsmart professional baseball sports scouts and managers. The simulations of uninvolved S's will not predict that managers would do anything other than hire the most effective players but in reality they over hire players who are good-looking, have an attractive style or exude confidence because they, and not the modellers, want to avoid being blamed for choosing players who fail. In a variant of the 'no-one gets fired for buying IBM' effect, the managers buy one thing when they choose conventionally rather than optimally: they buy an excuse for failure: 'he looked like a good player and every team wanted him'. This may be the Representativeness Heuristic: 'he looked like good players look therefore he is a good player'. The S's do not include this bias of the O's in their simulation.

We may derive a further confirmation of this conclusion from Figure 2.2 presented by Gilovich (1993, p. 20). This shows the pattern of V-1 bombs falling in London during the war. There was a belief at the time that certain parts of London were safe from the bombs and others were not. As Gilovich (1993, p. 21) argues, this belief is created by dividing the map into quadrants, and observing that there are clusters in some quadrants. He notes that if the map were divided by diagonal lines, 'there are no significant clusters'. The point here is that shown the map, it appears to us that there are clusters: we would correctly simulate the Londoners who falsely believed the safe area/dangerous area hypothesis. But given the data dispassionately together with Gilovich's argument, we agree with him that randomness has fooled the Londoners and we do not simulate them correctly. Our simulation misses out the Clustering Illusion that leads O's to see patterns where none exist, unless we also see the same map. Then we would also exhibit the Clustering Illusion and we would have another instance of successful simulation via bias matching.

Cancer cure assessors

Gilovich (1993, p. 30) cites data relating to whether people believe that cancer patients who engage in 'positive mental imagery' benefit their health status. He reports that people answering this question do not follow the scientifically correct rule based on the fact that instances 'of cancer remission in patients who practice mental imagery do not constitute sufficient evidence that mental imagery helps ameliorate cancer' because there must be a control group i.e. the mental imagery practitioners might have improved anyway. What is needed is not a cure, but a correlation between a change in the independent variable – the practice of imagery – and a change in the dependent variable, the cure rate. Moreover, the cure rate improvement must be reproducible and not occur with changes in other independent variables.

This is an example of examining the wrong data. Gilovich's central charge is that people take evidence for a hypothesis as also confirmatory of that hypothesis, when they should use one dataset to form hypotheses for testing and further datasets to confirm them. He writes: 'willingness to base conclusions on incomplete or unrepresentative information is a common cause of people's questionable and erroneous beliefs' (Gilovich 1993, p. 30). Often, these situations will be instances of Confirmation Bias, where people tend only 'to focus on positive or confirming instances' (Gilovich 1993, p. 33) of a hypothesis they are testing. Whether one is surprised or not by this prevalence of Confirmation Bias – with the surprise being the indication of a failure in ToM – will depend on one's general level of cynicism in relation to the frailty of human reasoning. But one might be surprised at such a widespread lack of quality in data handling. This is not expecting untrained O's to be aware of correct scientific method so much as expecting them not to form scientific conclusions in unscientific ways. Even untrained O's are aware of the idea that A has not caused B if B would have happened anyway. Also note how uncongenial these data are to TT(Scientific), which holds that pre-fives are experts on hypothesis selection and confirmation. What has happened to this expertise during maturation?

There is an affect disparity between the O's who are actually in situations where they must make some decision based on whatever evidence is available and the S's who model that decision-making. The S's face little or no involvement or stress related to the question that the O's are considering. The S's are not exposed to the risk of failing to make a decision, where randomness in the O's may be beneficial in breaking a Buridan's ass-type deadlock. The S's have time to employ System 2 reasoning to come up with a more considered answer while the O's may be under pressure and thus employ System 1. Alternatively, the persons likely to assess non-standard cancer cure approaches which are accessible without training, money or hospital equipment are likely to be persons with cancer or persons who know someone with cancer. This of course is an extremely affectively involving situation; we as S's here have no affective involvement at all. The result is that we as S's do not simulate Confirmation Bias in the O's, thus leading to systematic simulation error.

Puzzle solvers

The paper by Pronin, Puccio and Ross (Gilovich, Griffin, and Kahneman 2002, p. 644) is cited by Saxe (2005a) in her 'too cynical' category, but it reports on one experiment which falls into the 'too rosy' category, so we may consider it here. The experiment in question involves the type of children's game where something seems blindingly obvious to the participants who are 'in on it' and yet extraordinarily opaque to those who are not. So the systematic ToM error is too rosy in that S's overestimate how easy O's will find it to succeed at the game.

The experiment involved asking people to figure out what things existed in 'My World' (Gilovich, Griffin, and Kahneman 2002, p. 644) from a series of clues, and then assessing how many clues would in general be needed by peers to solve the puzzle. For example, one clue was 'My world has trees and grass but not flowers'. The governing principle is that My World contains only things that have double letters in their name. Once one knows this, this factor seems to jump out of the page with extreme Vividness, but before one sees the principle, it is possible to stare blankly at an enormous array of clues, forming and rejecting an immense number of baroque hypotheses. The results were, as expected, that successful solvers vastly overestimated the proportion of the class who would solve the puzzle – they thought that 78 per cent of the class would succeed, while only 21 per cent did. By contrast, those who failed to solve the puzzle gave quite an accurate assessment of how many would succeed – 25 per cent. This is explained by the Bias Mismatch Defence as above, we need only note the extreme Vividness to the solvers of the principle once seen and feed that into the Availability Heuristic.[3]

Shoppers redux

As discussed in Chapter 5, Shoppers were asked to consider which of a set of four identical stockings was the highest quality. They chose the right-most item more often than chance, without reason to do so. When asked why they chose as they did, they confabulated reasons. The reasons they gave involved spurious claims about the superior quality of the selected pair. These claims could only be spurious since the pairs were identical. This I think I can say is surprising without fear of contradiction.

There is an Affect Mismatch between us as S's and the shoppers as O's. It is appropriate to make a quick decision in many low-impact, real-life circumstances. The Shopper O's, we may easily imagine, are already somewhat harried individuals who have moreover been unexpectedly approached to answer unusual questions at a busy time. As Goldman (1992, p. 116) observes in relation to the shopper case, 'one is unlikely to replicate the uncertainties of the live situation' when one simulates. The quickest way for the Shoppers to be able to get on with shopping will be to make a choice. In addition, they might disappoint the authoritative figure of the questioner if they fail to respond, in a similar scenario to that seen in the Milgram (1963) experiments discussed in Chapter 6. S's are exposed to none of these affects and so they do not apply the same biases when they run their simulation.

We may also have a System Mismatch here. The shopping O's are under pressure to make a decision and aware that it is not of the first importance exactly which decision they make. It is often inaccurately reported that Nisbett and Wilson (1977) offered the O's the pair of stockings they selected, in which case they would care somewhat about which pair it was. However, note the exact words of Nisbett and Wilson (1977, p. 243): shoppers 'were asked to say which article of clothing was the best quality'; no mention is made of giving them the stockings. The harried O's use a System 1 heuristic to make a decision. This could be designed to avoid Buridan's ass-type paralysis in decision-making, where one does not know which of two equally good options to choose.[4] The point is that one should just pick one; it does not matter which. The S's are at leisure to simulate the O's and therefore use the more rational System 2.

For one or both of these reasons, there is a Bias Mismatch between S's and O's here. The particular bias involved is dubbed the 'Position Effect' (Nisbett and Wilson 1977, p. 243).

I have generally refrained from challenging experimental procedures on the grounds that accepting it gives the opposing view its best case. I will make an exception for the Shoppers case since it is heavily cited by TT proponents; it is the one experiment of the many reported by Nisbett and Wilson (1977) that is mostly selected for comment. The problem with the Shoppers experiment is its lack of what experimental psychologists term 'ecological validity'. This means that the experimental task should be sufficiently similar to everyday tasks that one may reasonably expect to be measuring elements of everyday behaviour. The Shoppers experiment by contrast focusses on what Johansson *et al.* (2006, p. 689) rightly term 'a rather strange and contrived task' with much less ecological validity than choosing between different stockings.

Part of a better approach is suggested by Heal (2003, p. 83) who notes that 'the rightward bias is irrational and hence not something we need expect simulation to cope with'. There is room to question whether the Position Effect is indeed irrational. Nisbett and Wilson (1977, p. 244) speculate that the Position Effect is in fact a last-seen bias, when they write that it is possible that 'subjects carried into the judgement task the consumer's habit of "shopping around" holding off on choice of early-seen garments on the left in favour of later-seen garments on the right'. It is rational, if asked to select for quality from a range of items, to consider all of the items. It would also be rational, when shopping around, to select the most recent because it is also the currently present item. No one would rationally return to a different shop to obtain an identical item to the one currently under consideration. While this argument would not strictly apply to Nisbett and Wilson's Shoppers, because all of the pairs of stockings are in front of them, there is every possibility that they carry over System 1 shopping heuristics into a selection task with some similarity to shopping – even if it is not very 'ecologically valid'. The fact that it looks like shopping may suffice to switch on shopping behaviours. In any case, whether the Position Effect is rational or not, S's will fail to simulate O's correctly because S's will not simulate O's behaviour in exhibiting the Position Effect.

Notes

1 Goldie (2002, p. 164) attributes the failure to predict behaviour in the Milgram (1963) experiment to the Fundamental Attribution Error. If he is right, the Bias Mismatch Defence still succeeds.

2 See also Taleb (2008) for discussion of the 'narrative fallacy', whereby even constructing stories based on the actual facts can be misleading.

3 Similarly, Pronin, Puccio and Ross give further examples of scenarios where the False Consensus Effect in S causes S to be too optimistic about O's current mental state. The examples are when S gives directions to O and where S asks O to decode musical taps (Gilovich, Griffin, and Kahneman 2002, p. 643).

4 Taleb (2007, Chapter 10) discusses such useful sorts of randomness that help us to avoid Buridan paralysis.

7 Bias mismatch defence

'Too cynical' evidence

Introduction

I will consider three of the papers Saxe (2005a, p. 177) cites with the aim of showing systematically too cynical errors in ToM, as discussed in Chapter 3. These will be as follows: Pronin, Puccio and Ross (Gilovich, Griffin, and Kahneman 2002, pp. 636–665), Kruger and Gilovich (1999) and Miller and Ratner (1998).

I summarise my responses to the elements of this different class of Saxe (2005a) data in Table 7.1. The common link between all of the data considered in this chapter is that S's predict that O's will perform less rationally in their reasoning than they actually do. The Bias Mismatch responses to the remaining systematic ToM errors fall into three broad categories as shown below:

- (A): S and O exhibit various biases [one entry].
- (B): S or S and O exhibit Availability Heuristic [four entries].
- (C): S exhibits Self-Presentation Bias [five entries].

Table 7.1 Response type by group studied: too cynical

Group Studied	*Response*
Conflict Parties	(A): S and O exhibit various biases
Marriage Partners	(B): S and O exhibit Availability Heuristic
Video Gamers	(B): S exhibits Availability Heuristic
Debaters	(B): S and O exhibit Availability Heuristic
Darts Players	(B): S exhibits Availability Heuristic
Blood Donors	(C): S exhibits Self-Presentation Bias
Healthcare Consumers	(C): S exhibits Self-Presentation Bias
Campus Drinkers	(C): S exhibits Self-Presentation Bias
Smokers	(C): S exhibits Self-Presentation Bias
Statement Releasers	(C): S exhibits Self-Presentation Bias

'Too cynical' data

Conflict parties

Saxe (2005a, p. 177) writes that '[m]ost adults believe that reasoning can sometimes be distorted – both inevitably, by the limitations of the mind, and wilfully, as in wishful thinking and self-deception – and that this is more likely to be true of other people's thinking than of their own' and cites Pronin, Puccio and Ross (Gilovich, Griffin, and Kahneman 2002, pp. 636–665) in support. This gives us three key claims. The first is that ToM predicts distortions in reasoning. The second is that these distortions may be voluntary or involuntary. The third is that S's predict more such distortion in O's than in S's. The first claim is not an example of ToM error, since it is true that there are many distortions in reasoning. The third claim seems by contrast to be a clear example of ToM error, since there is no justification across the board for S's reasoning to be less distorted than O's. The second claim is complex and interesting. We can agree that it is true that there are some voluntary and some involuntary distortions, but the truth of that claim would not suffice to make it the case that there is no ToM error here. To avoid error, S's would need not only to recognise that there are voluntary and involuntary distortions of reasoning but also accurately to identify occasions when each are occurring.

The particular focus of Pronin, Puccio and Ross is on how predictions of biased reasoning can bring parties into conflict so I use this as a title for the section. We might also use the term 'biased expectations of bias' to describe the focus of the authors. I will be arguing that the second claim is at the heart of their position. Conflict is caused not because ToM predicts bias in others, but because it wrongly sees bias as voluntary.

Debates about political questions are often highly affectively involving and often lead to conflict at some level. Pronin, Puccio and Ross give as examples debates about 'capital punishment, abortion policy [and] the Middle East' (Gilovich, Griffin, and Kahneman 2002, p. 637). S's considering the positions of O's who oppose their particular views on such topics will form negative views of the reasoning abilities of the O's. S's make 'harsh evaluations of [O's] on the other side, whose perceptions and arguments . . . appear biased and self-serving' (Gilovich, Griffin, and Kahneman 2002, p. 637). This is systematically too cynical ToM. The authors tell us that what fosters this is the way that partisans 'accept at face value arguments and evidence congruent with their interests and beliefs' (Gilovich, Griffin, and Kahneman 2002, p. 637) while subjecting opposing arguments to intense scrutiny. This of course is a definition of Confirmation Bias.

So the ToM errors here result from S failing to simulate Confirmation Bias in the O's in the right way. The S's are excessively cynical about the intentions or genuineness of the O's. The S's expect in one sense that the O's will exhibit biased reasoning, but do not ascribe it to Confirmation Bias – which may be an unavoidable aspect of human reasoning – but to a partisan and deliberate failure properly to examine the facts and arguments. If simulation modelled bias in the right way, then we would expect the S's to predict the reasoning of the O's more accurately and also ascribe it less to deliberate partiality of the O's, which might reduce conflict. The key point for the Bias Mismatch Defence continues to be that the process is still well described as a simulation failure due to inaccurate bias modelling in S.

This conflict situation will be exacerbated if the S's also apply their own Confirmation Bias to the subject matter, because this will open the gap wider between S and O. This argument is intuitively compelling and empirical well-supported by citations supplied by Pronin, Puccio and Ross. In one citation, Edwards and Smith (1996) discuss a 'disconfirmation bias'; i.e. S's tend to apply a negative confirmation bias to the positions espoused by O's. The arguments of the O's are subjected to more intense scrutiny. The effects are worsened by Affect Mismatch: S's and O's may become passionately attached to their positions. As Edwards and Smith (1996, p. 20) note, 'affective and motivational factors influence cognitive processes to produce biased conclusions'. In sum, the overly cynical ToM errors here can be explained by S applying Confirmation Bias to S's own positions, a negative Confirmation Bias to O's positions and then also failing to allow for O's own Confirmation Bias.[1]

Pronin, Puccio and Ross also note how the Availability Heuristic, the Representativeness Heuristic and Cognitive Dissonance reduction – which I will argue in Chapter 8 can be seen as just another bias – can all lead to conflict. I suggest the same mechanism applies here as described above. S's see 'self-serving or ideologically determined biases in [O's] views' (Gilovich, Griffin, and Kahneman 2002, p. 637). Again, if the S's simulated correctly, they would be aware that these biases are unavoidable. So we have the failed simulation of three more types of bias generating systematically too cynical ToM errors here.

Pronin, Puccio and Ross also describe how the False Consensus Effect may make teachers see students as 'inattentive, unmotivated or even stupid' (Gilovich, Griffin, and Kahneman 2002, p. 644) because the teacher fails to set aside her own mastery of the subject. This is an example of Bias Mismatch in that S applies a bias and thus fails to simulate O correctly. Similarly, they discuss an 'inadequate allowance' thesis in the context of a word game (Gilovich, Griffin, and Kahneman 2002, pp. 644–646). S's who know the answer overestimate how easy it is to find the answer due to the False Consensus Effect. They then make 'unwarranted negative inferences' about the O's. So a bias in S's leads them to make systematically too cynical ToM predictions.

Marriage partners

As discussed previously in Chapter 3, the predictions of marriage partners of one another's assessments of contributions to various activities were studied by Kruger and Gilovich (1999), being the second 'too cynical' citation of Saxe (2005a). They considered an array of positive and negative marriage activities, such as dog walking, or beginning arguments. They asked each S to rate S's own contribution to each activity, O's contribution to each activity, and crucially, to state what S thought O would say that O's contribution to each activity was. The hypothesis was that S's would predict that O's would be self-serving in their responses, i.e. O's would claim more responsibility than justified for positive activities and admit less responsibility that justified for negative activities.

The hypothesis was confirmed. Kruger and Gilovich (1999, p. 745) reported that 'couples expected their spouses to claim more than their share of the credit for the desirable activities . . . – but less than their share of the blame for the undesirable activities'. The spouses did indeed claim more than their share of the credit and accept less than their share of the blame. So the S's exhibited no systematic ToM errors in relation to the nature of credit and blame claims by the O's. The ToM errors were related to the amount of such differential claims. The O's engaged in making such differential claims to a lesser extent than predicted by the S's. The S's were thus 'too cynical' here in their ToM, in that they predicted more significantly differential claims to be made by the O's. These errors were symmetrical in that both spouses made them in relation to each other.

The explanation here is that both S and O exhibit the Availability Heuristic. The activities of each S are more available to that S than the activities of O are available to that S. This means that S's are likely to claim more responsibility for both positive and negative activities than is warranted. Then, these S's will make the opposite error in relation to O. As Kruger and Gilovich (1999, p. 744) point out, S's 'may be surprised to find that others often claim too much responsibility for [negative] activities as well'. This can be explained on the Bias Mismatch Defence for which I have been arguing. There is a Bias Mismatch between the S's and the O's. The S's are failing to allow for the application of the Availability Heuristic by the O's.

We have a Bias Mismatch though in a special sense of that term. Both partners exhibit the Availability Heuristic, but they do so about different topics. This is how they can both apply the same bias but still make simulation errors. In each case, one partner as S employs the Availability Heuristic to overstate S's own contribution to the activities and understate the contribution of the other partner as O. Since the mirror image of this process occurs in the other partner when they are in the role of S, both of them come to overstate their own contribution and understate that of the other partner. This has the results seen: both partners predict that the other partner will be more self-serving than they actually are. This is why the partners are surprised when the other partner admits more responsibility than expected. Each S applies his own Availability Heuristic but does not simulate it in the O, leading to simulation error. Kruger and Gilovich (1999, p. 744) confirm this when they note the potential adverse effects of not allowing for the biases of others when they write that: '[i]nstead of attributing another person's inflated assessment to the availability bias, people are likely to see it as a motivated grab for excess credit'.

This Availability Heuristic explanation of these data is also given by the original experimenters. Kruger and Gilovich (1999, p. 743) write of those original experimenters having: 'offered an information-processing interpretation of this bias, one based on the differential availability of one's own and another person's contributions. Simply put, people have an easier time remembering their own input than someone else's'. So, as Tversky and Kahneman (1973, p. 207) point out, 'reliance on the Availability Heuristic leads to systematic biases' and we have explained exactly the systematic ToM errors which Saxe (2005a) cites.

Video gamers

The same explanation is available for a total of four studies reported by the same authors. In the second of four studies reported in the paper Saxe cites, Kruger and Gilovich (1999) examined assessments of bias in players of a two-person video game. This was a co-operative game where both players had to work together against a common enemy. There were two players and an observer. After the game, all three assessed the contributions of both players on eight parameters, evenly divided between negative contributions and positive contributions. Also, the players estimated how much each player would claim he contributed on each parameter, and what the observer would say.

As with the marriage partners, the video gamers expected more self-serving bias than was actually the case. 'Participants expected their teammates to credit themselves with 23.0% more responsibility for the desirable game elements' and 'less than their share of the blame for the undesirable game outcomes' but in 'actuality, players took 8.3% more credit for the undesirable outcomes of the game' (Kruger and Gilovich 1999, p. 751). These results can be explained on the same grounds as the Marriage Partners case: S exhibited the Availability Heuristic.

The players thought that the observer would say the same as they did – i.e. unsurprisingly, the players thought that their opinions were objectively valid. This means they were unaware of the operation of the Availability Heuristic so did not correct for it. Pronin, Puccio and Ross cite evidence to the effect that 'people are often unaware of their own unawareness' in the context of bias (Gilovich, Griffin, and Kahneman 2002, p. 662).

Debaters

This study aimed to investigate a 'more motivationally charged situation' (Kruger and Gilovich 1999, p. 748) with the aim of examining whether motivation affected ToM errors. Kruger and Gilovich (1999) did this by studying undergraduates taking a debating course, who wanted to do well, since they sought careers in law and politics and the like. Participants debated a political topic in teams of two, and were subsequently asked anonymously to apportion responsibility for positive and negative aspects of the debate between themselves, their teammates and their opponents. They were also asked to predict what apportionments the teammates and opponents would make. There are two factors in play here. There is to some extent an objective fact of the matter about who did what in the debate – or at least a less subjective reality such as one might expect from an impartial observer. The second factor is a subjective 'overlay' on the objective facts, reflecting the hypothesis that S's would give themselves more credit for positive aspects of the debate but also expect O's to do the same.

The results were consistent with the hypothesis that S's would predict more self-serving bias in the O's than the O's actually exhibited. Kruger and Gilovich (1999, p. 749) found that 'debaters expected their opponents to claim 69.8% more of the credit for the desirable outcomes than for the undesirable outcomes' but 'this assumption was wildly exaggerated' since '[d]ebaters in fact credited their own team with 21.0% more of the credit for the desirable outcomes than for the undesirable outcomes'. This prediction of biased estimation still appeared when S's considered their teammates, but much less so, with S's predicting teammate O's would claim '26.0% more of the credit for the desirable outcomes than for the undesirable outcomes' (Kruger and Gilovich 1999, p. 749).

These results can again be accounted for by assuming that the S's applied the Availability Heuristic, with some extension from themselves to their teammates. In short, there is a hierarchy of availability which follows the order S; teammate O; opponent O. Thus we can explain why S's predicted that their teammate O's would take some more credit for desirable outcomes than justified, and opponent O's a lot more. It is because S's own activities are somewhat more available than those of teammate O's and much more available than those of opponent O's. This line is suggested when Pronin, Puccio and Ross summarise the literature in writing '[i]intergroup enmity can arise from simple availability and representativeness biases' (Gilovich, Griffin, and Kahneman 2002, p. 637).

S's 'thought their opponents would claim . . . 32.7% less than their fair share of the undesirable debate elements' (Kruger and Gilovich 1999, p. 750). In partial contrast, they thought their teammate O's would also admit less than their full share of responsibility for undesirable debate elements, but would not do so to the same extent as the opponent O's. The reality was that O's of both types admitted to more responsibility than expected. This can be explained by an extension of the 'marriage partners' account to allow for the additional participants in this experiment. S exhibits the Availability Heuristic such that S's own actions loomed larger in the debate on both positive and negative sides than those of the teammate O's. S also exhibits the same heuristic in relation to the even less available actions of opponent O's. These biases explain the systematically too cynical ToM of S in this scenario together with the different levels of cynicism in relation to teammate O's and opponent O's.

Darts players

Kruger and Gilovich (1999, p. 751) found in the final study reported in the paper Saxe cites that 'darts players thought their opponents would be more self-serving than their teammates and more self-serving than they actually were'. These results are similar to the ones about the debaters and can be explained in the same way using a hierarchy of availability.

Table 7.2 Actual versus estimated number of individuals volunteering to give blood for payment or no payment

Volunteer Rate		
Incentive	Actual	Estimated
Payment	73%	63%
No Payment	63%	32%

Blood donors

Five studies in Saxe's final 'too cynical' citation (Miller and Ratner 1998), are claimed to show evidence of systematic cynicism in ToM. I will be explaining them all by appealing to Self-Presentation Bias in the S's.[2] In each case, responses by participants are likely to be dominated by what they think they should say – or what shows them in a positive light – rather than what they actually think. Note that participants need not be aware of the operation of Self-Presentation Bias.

The first Miller and Ratner study examined the number of S's who would donate blood with and without payment and compared this to the estimates of the S's as to how many O's would donate blood with and without payment.

The results of the study are shown in Table 7.2. Miller and Ratner (1998, p. 54) found that '(63%) indicated they would agree to give blood if not paid, and . . . (73%) said they would agree to give blood if paid $15'. So the cash incentive had little effect because there were only an additional 10 per cent of participants whose minds were changed by the payment.

However, S's 'estimated that roughly twice as many [O's] would agree to donate blood for $15 as would agree to donate blood for free'; the S's estimated that 63 per cent of O's would donate for payment whereas only 32 per cent would donate without payment. This study then is an example of too cynical ToM, because the S's expected that more of the O's would agree to donate only if paid than was actually the case. So the challenge here for ST is that the S's predicted that the O's would be more motivated by payment than by altruism than was in fact the case; and the S's made this too cynical prediction even though the S's themselves were not in general more motivated by payment than by altruism.

One way for S's to promote a positive self-image in this experimental scenario is to make it look as though they are uncommonly altruistic. This they can do by saying that they would themselves volunteer to give blood for no payment but also by saying that few others would do so. It is not sufficient merely to volunteer if everyone else does as well. So the data are explained by Self-Presentation Bias in the S's.

Healthcare consumers

The second Miller and Ratner study examined the effect of sex on views of a putative US government programme to make abortion available at public expense.

A large majority of S's agreed that such a programme would benefit women more than men. They also thought that this would mean that women would be more in favour of the programme than men. Miller and Ratner (1998, p. 56) write that the 'majority of [S's] in this study perceived women to have a greater stake in, and to be more supportive of, a proposed health care plan than men'. This was a systematically too cynical ToM error though, since in fact 'there was no difference in the degree of support expressed by men and women' (Miller and Ratner 1998, p. 56).

One way for S's to promote a positive self-image here as in the other experiments in this class is to maintain that S is less subject to biased reasoning than O's. So both male and female S's here thought that S's own opinion was free of bias but that O's opinion would be heavily biased by self-interest. Self-Presentation Bias in S explains this desire to predict that O is more prone to bias than S, and in this case to predict wrongly that female O's would favour the programme more than male O's.

Campus drinkers

The third Miller and Ratner study related to attitudes to alcohol pricing on campus. We learn that there was a ban on the sale of kegs of beer at Princeton which affected younger ('sophomore') undergraduates more than older ('senior') ones, because the latter were members of dining fraternities untouched by the ban. There were then, two questions. The first was whether there was an interaction between whether undergraduates were junior or senior and whether they favoured or opposed the ban. The second was whether there was an expectation undergraduates would reason in a self-serving way viz. junior undergraduates would be predicted to oppose the ban more strongly than senior ones. The results were the same as those in the two studies reported above: the 'majority of participants in this study perceived Princeton sophomores to be more adversely affected by, and to be more opposed to, the keg ban than Princeton seniors' but in fact 'there was no difference in the opposition expressed by sophomores and seniors' (Miller and Ratner 1998, p. 57). Again, this is explained by the S's ascribing more biased reasoning to O's than to themselves. It could also be that the sophomores wanted to think something like 'my peers are more addicted to alcohol than I am, so they will oppose the ban, while I am health-conscious enough to favour it'. Either way, the results are driven by Self-Presentation Bias in the S's.

Smokers

The fourth Miller and Ratner study looked at whether smokers and non-smokers favoured smoking bans, and whether smokers and non-smokers were expected to reason in their own interests. There was a change here to the prior studies. The prior studies had shown predictions that there would be a relationship between self-interest and reasoning in scenarios where no such relationship existed. The hypothesis in the smoking study was that there would be such a relationship, but that its strength would be overestimated. As Miller and Ratner (1998, p. 57) point out, they 'do not claim that vested interest never affects attitudes, only that it does not affect attitudes as much as lay theories assume'. The hypothesis was borne out by the results. Over-prediction by S's of self-serving bias in O's combined with S maintaining the belief that S is himself free from such self-serving bias explains the data and represents Self-Presentation Bias in S. This explains the systematic error in S's ToM in this scenario.

Statement releasers

The fifth Miller and Ratner study looked at behaviour rather than attitudes. Participants were told of a purported health threat that affected either only men or only women, and a proposed cut in government funding of research into it. The questions were whether participants would agree to release a statement about the cut to a local political organisation; whether members of the sex with a vested interest would agree more than members of the opposite sex; and whether S's would predict that O's with a vested interest would agree more. As before, 'participants' predictions significantly overestimated the actual impact of self-interest on behaviour' (Miller and Ratner 1998, p. 59) in that S's predicted that the affected group would release more than the unaffected group, even though in reality both groups exhibited similar high release rates. Over-prediction by S's of self-serving bias in O's combined with S maintaining the belief that S is himself free from such self-serving bias explains the data and represents Self-Presentation Bias in S. This explains the systematic error in S's ToM in this scenario.

Discussion

In some scenarios, reports systematically fail to reflect ToM outputs, thus impairing Saxe's ability to draw conclusions about ToM predictions based on what people say. For example, 'people engage in many acts of genuine compassion, but they do not explain these acts in terms of compassion' (Miller and Ratner 1998, p. 61). Instead, they explain their charitable acts by saying things like 'it got me out of the house' or 'it gave me something to do'. This is readily understandable – people do not wish to be seen as performing charitable acts merely through Self-Presentation Bias. However, it does mean that although people may know the true reason for their action – they felt compassionate – they may say something else. In fact, it seems as though they gave a false, ostensibly self-interested reason, rather than a true compassionate one. One question here is the extent to which someone who says 'it got me out of the house' expects to be believed or themselves believes that that is why they performed the charitable act, which further complexity makes drawing ToM conclusions still more fraught. But in general here, we can see how Self-Presentation Bias may influence ostensible reports about motives, and so presumably also reports about motives of others. Then what S's say about the motives of O's may not reflect what their ToM tells them about the motives of O's. So what S's say would not give us completely pure and transparent data on ToM errors.

Miller and Ratner (1998, p. 60) themselves throw some doubt on whether and how closely they were examining ToM when they write 'it is important to note that we did not ask participants to predict their peers' "true" attitudes or feelings, only to predict how their peers would respond to the same measure to which they themselves had responded'. It seems as though ToM should be what is examined when one asks what S's predict O's 'true attitudes or feelings' because attitudes and feelings are mental attributes. This need not mean that predictions of behaviour fall outside the purview of ToM, but it can mean that 'wide ToM' including factors beyond attitudes to questions may figure. There may also, for example, be Self-Presentation Bias effects. S's may expect O's to answer political questions in a politically correct manner, and O's may in fact do this. For example, the male undergraduates may have secretly opposed the publicly funded abortion more than they admitted, but have decided it would be a poor presentational choice to admit this. All of this can still figure in a ToM debate, but it makes the situation considerably more complex. I will postpone further discussion of such Introspectionist issues to Chapter 8.

In conclusion, all of the 'too cynical' data as well as the 'too rosy' data can be explained by appealing to the Bias Mismatch Defence.

Notes

1 See also Kunda (1990) for discussion of selective memory access to bolster biased positions, and Short (2012) for arguments from Nietzsche to the effect that such memory selection is a feature of active and strong individuals.

2 Pronin, Puccio and Ross also discuss the Self-Presentation Bias in terms of a 'holier than thou' effect (Gilovich, Griffin, and Kahneman 2002, p. 665).

8 Suspicious congruency

Introduction

I will now cover Saxe's third challenge, that of 'suspicious congruency' between ToM errors and folk theories about minds. Recall that the challenge was that it is suspicious if ToM errors made by S about O 'or in explaining [S's] own past actions or thoughts (Gopnik 1993a; Bem 1967) are suspiciously congruent with [S's] beliefs about how minds work (Nisbett and Bellows 1977)' (Saxe 2005a, pp. 177–178). The idea is that the congruency arises because S deploys those beliefs in making the ToM error. So the idea is that if S has a false theoretical axiom in his ToM, then that axiom will cause ToM errors systematically, whenever a situation occurs in which the axiom is deployed. This would give TT an easy explanation of the systematic errors which explanation would not be available to ST, since ST does not postulate axioms.

I will first make some brief remarks prompted by Saxe's position here, before outlining the topics for the rest of this chapter. There is some tension between Saxe's stated adherence to the Hybridist position and her challenge here and elsewhere to ST, because of course ST is an essential element of Hybridist accounts. One escape for Saxe here may be available to her deriving from her distinction of ST into stronger and weaker versions. Saxe (2005a, p. 174) defines what she means by a 'strong version' of ST when she writes that ST 'in its stronger versions, proposes that people need not use a naïve theory of psychology, or indeed any mental state concepts, when predicting and explaining actions'. So only strong ST denies that there is any element of theory use in ToM, or at least that simulation does not involve any mental state concepts. Weak ST on her view permits such a role and thus weak ST would allow a Hybridist account of the type Saxe favours.

My claim by contrast is that not allowing ST any mental state concepts makes the setting the bar too low error which I discussed in Chapter 2. We may ask whether Saxe avoids this error. Saxe's claims are that ToM is theoretical if it (i) uses a naïve theory, or (ii) employs mental state concepts. The first claim is true but appears circular and therefore uninformative. The second claim is more interesting. It says that S's may be deemed to be employing a theory if they 'use' mental state concepts in applying their ToM capacities. Significant work is being done by 'use' here; one can ascribe multiple senses to the term which will be rather important in assessing the claim. There is an available distinction here that is paralleled by one in philosophy of language between the 'use' of a term and its 'mention'.[1] If ST merely 'mentions' mental state concepts through which S progresses, replicating O's progress, then the 'employment' of mental state concepts does not become theoretical. S can replicate the effects of the beliefs of O without ever considering or becoming liable to assent to or representing any propositions of the form 'O believes that p'. So I claim here as elsewhere that ToM may 'mention' mental state concepts as it progresses in S through states isomorphic to those of O without thereby collapsing back into TT. I will now outline the main business of this chapter.

I will argue that the variant of Saxe's systematic error charge that she sets out as above is closely related to other problems that have been raised for ST. The first related challenge is that of Cognitive Penetrability. Leslie and German explain that term as follows: 'a process is cognitively penetrable if knowledge or representation can influence the outcome of the process in a "rational" way, e.g. through entering into a sequence of inference' (Stone and Davies 1995, p. 123). The idea then is that if a process is Cognitively Penetrable, then it is not modular according to one of the Fodorean definitions of modularity, which is informational encapsulation. Encapsulated processes, commonly known as black boxes, may receive starting inputs, but they then process those inputs without further influence from outside the module. So Cognitive Penetrability is the opposite, approximately, of informational encapsulation. Saxe's charge here then is that ToM processes are Cognitively Penetrable, since the systematic ToM errors show that. And TT is better placed on her view to accommodate that, since it need only postulate that the defective theoretical axiom that S harbours cognitively penetrates his ToM and causes the errors.

The second related challenge amounts to a denial of Introspectionism. Rey (2013, p. 260) cites Shoemaker to define Introspectionism as the claim that 'each mind has a special access to its own contents'. Introspection is the name for that special access. If Introspectionism is true, then we know our own mental states from the inside as it were, and we do not need to infer them by observing our behaviour. If we did need to make such inferences, then we would be similarly placed in terms of ascribing mental states to ourselves and to others. As we have seen in Chapter 2, there are versions of ST which assert Introspectionism and versions which deny it. Saxe's TT(Scientific) on the other hand denies Introspectionism. So arguments in favour of Introspectionism would be problematic for TT(Scientific) but not problematic for ST. In the next two sections, I will discuss these two issues of Cognitive Penetrability and Introspectionism, focussing on what we can learn about the issues from papers cited by Saxe (2005a).

This will lead on to further consideration of how we know our own mental states. Saxe (2005a, p. 177) cites Bem (1967) to support her claim that there are ToM errors made by S in relation to S. Bem is arguing for Self-Perception Theory, which asserts the claim mentioned above that the way that S finds out about S's own occurrent mental states is to 'perceive' himself or in others words,

S finds out what his mental states are by seeing how S behaves.[2] In this chapter, I will examine this account, favoured by Saxe (2005a). One part of this examination will be consideration of experiments cited by Bem (1967) concerning viewers of homoerotic images. I will show that there is an early appeal to what we can see as a form of the Bias Mismatch Defence in the Bramel (1962) experiment cited by Bem (1967).

I will conclude that consideration of all three of these issues loads TT with significant theoretical costs that ST as augmented with the Bias Mismatch Defence need not pay.

Cognitive penetrability

If TT is the correct account of ToM, then false beliefs that S has about how minds work can penetrate S's ToM and cause systematic errors. This would be the 'suspicious congruency' of which Saxe complains. On her line, if S is using simulation however, ToM cannot exhibit Cognitive Penetrability and there can be no influence from what S believes about how the mind works to what S predicts about O using his ToM. As Stich and Nichols put it, 'the simulation theory entails that [ToM] predictions are cognitively impenetrable' (Stone and Davies 1995, p. 94). The idea is then that on ST, S's do not need to know how minds work to simulate them, they merely have to have a mind that works in the way that other minds work. Or as Saxe (2005a, p. 177) puts it, 'the argument from error is directed against pure [ST], according to which the [S's] mind is a "resonating" black box, a working model that can be fed inputs and produces outputs, though the [S] has no idea how the model works'. On this account then, showing Cognitive Penetrability of ToM processes would favour TT over ST.

It is allowed though by Leslie and German that the off-line version of ST need not be Cognitively Penetrable. They write that the 'radical simulationist claim is that common sense psychology is cognitively impenetrable to theory of mind knowledge because . . . [S] simply runs the action planning device that generates [S's] own behaviour' (Stone and Davies 1995, pp. 123–124). This account does not need ToM knowledge, and so ST parsimoniously claims that none exists, also obviating the difficult requirement of explaining where the knowledge comes from. If there is no ToM knowledge, it cannot penetrate anything. Since the off-line version of ST is very much a live option, we may conclude that the challenge of Cognititve Penetrability is not a serious one for simulationists.

Surprisingly, even some TT proponents agree. Botterill and Carruthers (1999), even while arguing for TT against ST, are relatively unimpressed by this argument and indeed deem it misnamed. They believe that their arguments are 'a good deal more convincing than a rather technical one pressed by Stich and Nichols'. Botterill and Carruthers (1999, p. 88) think the objection would be better named 'the theoretical fallibility argument' because 'if there is some area in which [O's] regularly tend to behave irrationally in ways which are surprising to [S's] . . . then [S's] are probably relying on theoretical knowledge' (Botterill and Carruthers 1999, p. 88). Botterill and Carruthers then go on to say that while they think this argument is valid in abstract terms, it lacks empirical backing, i.e. they are unconvinced that the lottery experiment discussed by Stich and Nichols (see Chapters 5 and 6) are clear enough examples of 'theoretical fallibility'. Until these examples are provided, Botterill and Carruthers (1999, p. 88) hold that 'the cognitive-penetrability/theoretical fallibility argument remains an argument in search of its premises'. It may be that they would be more satisfied by the further examples supplied by Saxe (2005a), but of course I claim to have dealt with that new data using the Bias Mismatch Defence. Stich and Nichols also concede that the Cognitive Penetrability objection applies only to on-line versions of ST when they allow that 'if the off-line simulation theory is right, what we don't know won't hurt us – predictions about people's behaviour are "cognitively impenetrable"' (Stone and Davies 1995, p. 94).

For more on Cognitive Penetrability, we may consider Greenwood (1999), cited by Saxe (2005a, p. 178) in support of her challenge to the Wrong Inputs Defence. Greenwood says he will challenge the claim that failure to predict the outcome of experiments shows that ToM is Cognitively Penetrable, because this claim rests on 'the doubtful assumption that our ability to verbally predict another's behaviour is a reliable measure of our ability to anticipate it'. The problem is with the verbal nature of the test, according to Greenwood; he allows that non-verbal tests of ToM predictions would constitute a good test of ST.

The experiment discussed by Greenwood is again the lottery one. Recall that the ToM error in question is the failure of S's to predict that O's will demand higher prices for lottery tickets they have chosen than ones they are simply given, even though there is no difference in value or the probability of winning. Greenwood (1999, p. 35) aims to supply two ways in which off-line ST can accommodate this ToM failure while maintaining that 'simulation is 'cognitively impenetrable' in the sense of not being dependent on information'.

One way Greenwood proposes to account for the ToM errors is to complain that the simulation faculty is not engaged because the scenarios of the S's are not realistic enough, which we may understand as meaning 'sufficiently relevantly similar' to the situation of the O's. This approach has some commonalities with my Bias Mismatch Defence. It relies on the distinct environments of S as opposed to O, and may involve Affect Mismatch between S and O. However, Greenwood's claim is that these distinctions decommission simulation in S, while mine is that the simulations run, but the distinct situations allow for Bias Mismatches.

The second way of accounting for these ToM errors proposed by Greenwood is the verbal distinction flagged above. Greenwood (1999, p. 44) writes that the 'verbal prediction of [O] behaviours in novel experimental situations is not the normal condition (never mind the optimal condition) under which everyday simulation is held to operate'. The idea then is that S's failure to report accurately on what O will do does not constitute evidence for S's failure to simulate accurately what O will do – error on report does not mean simulation error, in other words.

Naturally, Greenwood must now explain why there is inaccurate report and accurate simulation. The way he does this is to propose that where we see Cognitive Penetrability is in the report and not in the simulation. So we might simulate correctly but then have the output of the simulation corrupted or overridden by what we believe about what people do. This is interesting as an idea, but does run the risk of allowing the Cognitive Penetrability objection some purchase. Stich and Nichols might justifiably complain that verbal report is a fundamental domain in respect of how we find out about people and the shunting off of Cognitive Penetrability problem into that domain does little to insulate simulation from the problem.

The response offered by Greenwood (1999, p. 44) here is to claim that it is known that 'many of our cognitive capacities are disassociated from our 'verbal reporting' systems', with the example being given of the 'backward masking' phenomenon. This is seen, for example, in the Sperling (1960, p. 1) data, where subjects are shown a 3 × 3 array of numbers for a short time. They can report on average three numbers, but if cued to give numbers from a specific row after the display has disappeared, they can give all three numbers rather than just one, as might be expected. This can be interpreted as meaning that they 'see more than is remembered'. Greenwood (1999, p. 45) characterises the data as meaning 'subjects can select numbers or letters previously presented, but will deny recognition when the number or letters are represented to them (Sperling, 1960)'. So this does seem to be an example of a situation where there is information cognitively available in some respect but not reportable.

Greenwood (1999) then considers the Nisbett and Wilson (1977) critique of Introspectionism. That critique claims that we cannot trust verbal reporting of cognitive processes, because the data tend to show that we are inaccurate when we list factors that influenced our reasoning. As I mentioned in Chapter 5, the Shoppers who exhibited Position Effect are the most frequently discussed element of Nisbett and Wilson (1977). The point urged by Greenwood (1999, p. 46) is that if we cannot accurately verbally report on our cognitive processes, then that inability should equally 'apply to experimental evaluations of our ability to anticipate the behaviour of others based upon simulation of their psychological processes and states'. So simulation can be the cognitive mechanism underlying ToM, but because we do not have access to that and other cognitive mechanisms, we cannot verbally report that accurately either. The conclusion that Greenwood reaches is that there is 'no fingerpost' in the Stich and Nichols strategy, meaning that lack of accurate verbal report does not point a metaphorical finger inexorably in the direction of lack of accurate simulation.

I conclude that Cognitive Penetrability is not a problem for simulationist accounts, because two escape routes have been made available. One is to deny that Cognitive Penetrability is a problem for off-line simulationist accounts and the other is to deny that Cognitive Penetrability is shown by verbal reports indicating ToM error.

Introspectionism

There are two seminal papers in this area with the same lead author. One, Nisbett and Bellows (1977) is cited by Saxe (2005a, p. 178). The other is Nisbett and Wilson (1977). I will first describe the experiment outlined in Nisbett and Bellows

(1977) and argue that it too is susceptible to the Bias Mismatch Defence. I will then argue that the denial of Introspectionism is problematic for TT by considering objections that have been raised to Nisbett and Wilson (1977).

Verbal reports about causal influences

The central claim of Nisbett and Bellows (1977, p. 613) is that '[r]eports about cognitive processes may be based less on introspection than on a priori causal theories' which supports Saxe's denial of Introspectionism on behalf of TT.[3]

The experiment involved investigation of the assessment of a 'job application portfolio'. In particular, it studied whether what people said had influenced their thinking. Participants or 'assessors' were asked to evaluate the quality of the job application. There were also 'observer' participants who were supposedly to comment on the reasoning of the assessors. The study examined both what assessors reported about what had influenced them and what observers thought would be influential.[4]

In the study, five factors were adjusted meaning that half of the experimental subjects were given information relevant to a factor and half were not. The aim was to find out which factors influenced the opinions of the assessors about the applicant and which did not. The five factors that were manipulated are shown in Table 8.1 (Nisbett and Bellows 1977, p. 615).

The assessors were asked to make four judgements about the applicant. The four judgements were as shown in Table 8.2 (Nisbett and Bellows 1977, p. 617). The question then was how much the five factors in Table 8.1 influenced the four judgements in Table 8.2 and how much the assessors and the observers thought the factors had influenced the judgements of the assessors. This question was investigated by asking assessors all possible variations of factor and judgement questions, for example: '[h]ow did the person's physical appearance influence: a. how much you like the person?' (Nisbett and Bellows 1977, p. 618).

The results were that assessors and observers were both inaccurate about which were the important factors. Nisbett and Bellows (1977, p. 613) found that for the assessors, 'reports about the effects of the factors on the judgements were in general highly inaccurate' and for the observers, 'predictions were extremely similar to [assessor] reports', i.e. observers made accurate predictions of the assessors' inaccurate reports. The observers are avoiding ToM error in that they

Table 8.1 Job applicant: factors

Factor No.	*Factor Description*
1	Applicant is physically attractive
2	Applicant has excellent academic record
3	Applicant spilled coffee in interview
4	Applicant is in constant pain from auto accident
5	Applicant will later be met in person by assessor

Table 8.2 Job applicant: judgements

Judgement No.	*Judgement Question*
1	'How much do you think you would like this person?'
2	'How sympathetic would this person be to the feelings of others?'
3	'How intelligent do you think the person is?'
4	'How flexible would the person be in solving problems?'

correctly predict error in the assessors; though perhaps not as such. Where we can see ToM error is in the reported importance of factors: both assessors and observers were apparently wrong about which factors influenced them most. ST must explain these errors.

Here, we may note the highly apt question of White (1988, p. 41): 'should I admit to liking someone a lot more simply because they are described as highly intelligent, or physically attractive? What will the experimenter think of me if I do?'. This brings out the idea that inaccuracy of verbal report may be motivated by Self-Presentation Bias rather than tending to show the absence of introspective access. It is immediately apparent that discussion of the Table 8.1 factors courts controversy, which also suggests that reports about which of them were important are influenced by Self-Presentation Bias. I will be arguing in fact that this bias means that the assessors' reports of what influenced them are inaccurate because they want to show themselves in a positive light. So the Bias Mismatch Defence will be available. This will raise the immediate objection that Self-Presentation Bias would not explain the predictions of the observers, because the observers do not wish to present the assessors in a positive light. This objection fails though, because the questions put to the observers were in fact about themselves. Nisbett and Bellows (1977, p. 622) asked assessors '[h]ow did the person's physical appearance influence: a. how much you like the person?' and they asked observers '[s]uppose you knew the person was quite physically attractive. How would that influence: a. how much you would like the person?'. What should have been done to provide ToM data untainted by Self-Presentation Bias would be to ask the questions of the assessors and then ask the observers what they thought would have been said by the assessors.

Both assessors and observers appeared to give inaccurate reports about what factors influenced the judgements. This happened in two different directions. All participants said that important factors were unimportant and also said that unimportant factors were important. For example, Nisbett and Bellows (1977, p. 620) report that for the 'flexibility judgement, the effect of anticipated contact was very great, . . . yet subjects reported that it was slight and reported that one other factor (academic credentials) was more influential'. The question to ask here is again whether it is in fact sensible to expect people to admit that the prospect of meeting someone greatly improves their view of their qualities. We may expect Self-Presentation Bias to dominate responses.

We may also expect psychology undergraduates to assert that academic credentials are important in deciding whether they like someone, since by doing that they can show themselves in a positive light of relevance to their status. This explains participants' claims that 'the factor having the largest effect on the liking judgement was the academic credentials factor' (Nisbett and Bellows 1977, p. 620). Self-Presentation Bias factors will be most important in verbal reporting here. Consider one of the verbal reports elicited by Nisbett and Bellows when asking whether intelligence influenced liking: 'Intelligence is very important to me in a person. All of the people I like best are very smart' (Nisbett and Bellows 1977, p. 623). Few undergraduates would deny that. S exhibiting Self-Presentation Bias is the best explanation of the data in this experiment.

The Nisbett and Bellows (1977) argument also needs to be viewed in the context of the Nisbett and Wilson (1977) critique of Introspectionism, to which I will now turn.

The critique of introspectionism

There has been a large amount of argument in the literature for and against Introspectionism. TT denies Introspectionism, while ST has versions which assert it and which deny it. Thus, objections to the critique of Introspectionism provided by Nisbett and Wilson (1977) indirectly support ST. I will canvass only a few of these objections here.

Evans (1990, p. 104), cited in Saxe (2005a, p. 176), describes Nisbett and Wilson (1977) as 'highly controversial'; listing challenges to the work based on claims that Nisbett and Wilson need cleaner distinctions between (i) 'mental processes and their products' (Evans 1990, p. 105) and between (ii). 'awareness and verbal reportability' (Evans 1990, p. 105) of mental processes. These objections are also seen in White (1988), which challenges the entirety of the Anti-Introspectionist line of Nisbett and Wilson. White (1988, p. 13) discusses studies aimed at testing the proposal that 'people lack "introspective access" to their own mental processes' and concludes of those studies that 'none has achieved unambiguous support for, or falsification of, even the weak form of the proposal' (White 1988, p. 13).

One of White's powerful objections to the denial of Introspectionism relates to the unobservable modality distinction he attributes to Nisbett and Wilson. White (1988, p. 14) points out that on their account, 'an accurate report by an actor is not sufficient to demonstrate 'access' to the process'; to do that, the report 'must be more accurate than an observer's guess'. The point is that the Anti-Introspectionist seems to beg the question against the Introspectionist here by attempting to insist that if the actor could have done as well by observation only of external behaviour, then that is what the actor must have done. White (1988, p. 30) goes on to list 11 reasons why an experimenter might judge a verbal report inaccurate, only one of which is what Nisbett and Wilson require – viz. inaccuracy caused by lack of introspective access.

Similarly, Johansson *et al.* (2006, p. 674) note that it is 'incumbent on one who takes a position that denies the possibility of introspective access to higher order processes to account for these reports by specifying their source'. Any appeal to a poorly functioning theory here begs the question against ST. The authors also note that not only was there severe difficulty in assessing the quality of access evinced in apparently introspective reports, but that this was exacerbated by the ST/TT debate: it was an 'exceedingly complex task to unravel all the possible influences on report in an actor–observer paradigm . . . and this was before the whole [ST] vs. [TT] debate' (Johansson *et al.* 2006, p. 674). It would thus involve a circularity to attempt to use a purported fact of the matter in the Introspectionism vs Anti-Introspectionism question to decide the ST vs TT question since the latter is critical to the former. At the close of their paper, Johansson *et al.* (2006, p. 690) call for renewed investigation of introspection and the Nisbett and Wilson data since 'far too little has been said about telling more than we can know'. Since they are writing relatively recently – they are commenting in 2006 on a 1977 paper – we can agree with them that more work is needed here.

There is even a problem defining the term 'introspection'. White (1988, p. 17) offers 'one's awareness of being aware' and contrasts it with 'consciousness', 'conscious experience' and 'awareness'; all of which terms do seem discrete. All of these entities may stand in particular relationships to one another, so an account must be complex. White charges Nisbett and Wilson (1977) with assuming an account without argument – viz. that introspection is like perception in that 'the self' uses it to observe its mental processes. If so, then 'inaccurate verbal report shows only that subjects developed a poor hypothesis from their introspections' (White 1988, p. 20).

The Nisbett and Wilson paper is described by Goldman (1993b, p. 27) as being the 'best-known psychological critique of introspective access . . . to higher order cognitive processes'. Goldman (1993b, p. 27) points out that what Nisbett and Wilson 'mean by 'process,' however, is causal process; and what their evidence really addresses is people's putative access to the causes of their behaviour'. This is true, Nisbett and Wilson discuss a panoply of surprising data in which subjects think X because of irrelevant stimulus Y and then confabulate the more plausible sounding Z as a cause of their thinking X. As Goldman (1993b, p. 27) concludes though, the paper 'leaves it open that [subjects] do have introspective access to the mere occurrence of certain types of mental events'. That is as much Introspectionism as ST needs.

Subsequent partial recantation by the second author is described by Goldman (2004, p. 7) in a later paper. He notes how Wilson allows in 2002 that there can be 'introspective access to a specific memory that just came to mind' but argues that this is not a major concession since what the original 1977 paper aimed to 'deny was that people have introspective access to the causes of behaviour, or to cognitive processes' (Goldman 2004, p. 7). This is then further caveated with an allowance that introspection may work for the conscious self and not the unconscious: 'to the extent that people's responses are caused by the conscious self, they have privileged access to the actual causes of these responses' (Goldman 2004, p. 7). So in practice, this would mean that the shopper choosing the 7 denier because she likes 7 deniers would have introspective access to that cause of her behaviour, but the shopper choosing the right-most stockings because of the Position Effect would not. This is consistent with the Bias Mismatch Defence. As Goldman (2004, p. 14) points out, this restriction of introspection to the conscious does not 'threaten the actual truth ratio of spontaneous introspective reports, because they almost always do address conscious events'.

Self-perception theory

I outlined some of the Bem (1967) data in Chapter 3. Saxe (2005a, p. 176) cites Bem (1967) in support of TT's denial of Introspectionism, and to produce another set of systematic ToM errors made by S about himself. These errors must be explained by ST. I will first briefly point out the need for theoretical coherence across the components of Hybrid accounts before turning to the experimental data. In relation to that data, I will argue that we can again apply the Bias Mismatch Defence in relation to these data and in fact that has already been done by Bem and some of the experimenters on which he comments.

Bem (1967, p. 184) commits himself to strong Behaviourism when he writes 'the alternative formulation to be presented here eschews any reference to hypothetical internal processes . . . [s]uch an approach has been called 'radical' Behaviourism'. Botterill and Carruthers (1999, p. 46) bemoan how it was 'embarrassing' when 'scientific psychology . . . ignore[d] the intentional states [folk psychology] postulates . . . during its Behaviourist phase'. Saxe of course is not committed to Behaviourism by her citation of the Behaviourist Bem or to its denial by her citation of the Gestalt psychologist Asch.[5] We may insist though that no position may credibly both assert and deny Behaviourism in the same way as no position may credibly both assert and deny Introspectionism. Hybridists must make the same choice for the theoretical and simulational components of their view, so they are committed to Gordon's Anti-Introspectionist version of ST. They also seem to need a Behaviourist version of ST, which I am not sure has been described in the literature.

I now turn to the Bem data. There is an explanation of the Festinger and Carlsmith data described previously, or its replication by Bem, in terms of Bias Mismatch. The charge brought by Saxe is effectively that because people do not know about Cognitive Dissonance theory and Cognitive Dissonance theory is true, they will make systematic ToM errors about scenarios when there is Cognitive Dissonance. In other words, if O changes some of his beliefs because they are dissonant with some of O's subsequent behaviour, S will not predict this. We can translate this into Saxe's suspicious congruency terminology. Here, she claims that false theories that S holds about how the mind works will penetrate S's ToM and lead S to make congruent systematic ToM errors. The false theory in question is basically the negation of Cognitive Dissonance theory. Spelling it out, S's false belief is approximately 'it is not the case that the predictions of

Cognitive Dissonance theory should be used to make predictions about the behaviour of O'.

We can see the application of Bias Mismatch if we consider the aversive motivational force to harmonise dissonant cognitions to be a bias. That is not much of a stretch. Bear in mind that in the Bem (1967) interpersonal replication data, what is happening is not highly rational, so the term bias seems appropriate. The experimental participants changed their beliefs based on subsequent behaviour when ideally their beliefs should just be influenced by facts and deductions. I will term this Dissonance Reduction Bias. If we see the data as showing that S's simulation of O does not model Dissonance Reduction Bias, then we have explained the systematic ToM errors in this class of data using the Bias Mismatch Defence. O experiences the aversive bias and S does not simulate it, even when O is S himself. Since the motivational force is 'aversive', we can also see a way in which an Affect Mismatch can open up between S and O.

The plausibility of considering the cognitive force involved in Cognitive Dissonance reduction to be a bias is shown by a consideration of some of the relevant literature. Kunda (1990, p. 480) argues that 'motivation may affect reasoning through reliance on a biased set of cognitive processes' where the motivation in question is the avoidance of dissonance. The strategies and beliefs applied are different depending on whether the reasoning involved has accuracy goals or directional goals. If the former is the case, then the strategies and beliefs applied in the reasoning will be those considered most likely to produce an accurate conclusion. By contrast, if a particular conclusion is sought whether it is accurate or not – i.e. a directional goal – then strategies and beliefs most likely to produce that conclusion will be applied. For example, a smoker will apply biased reasoning 'to dispel the notion that smoking might be harmful' (Kunda 1990, p. 480) because otherwise the smoker's behaviour in smoking would be dissonant with his belief that smoking is harmful. Segal (2014) discusses similar biases in relation to the Cognitive Dissonance experiences by alcoholics who continue to drink despite overwhelming evidence that this is extremely harmful and indeed fatal to them. We can see that the type of reasoning involved in Dissonance Reduction Bias is of this directional type since the aim is to form beliefs that are less dissonant with the behaviour than the pre-existing beliefs.

One mechanism which can facilitate directional reasoning is memory selectivity. For example, 'people who want to believe that they will be academically successful may recall more of their past academic successes than of their failures' (Kunda 1990, p. 483).[6] We can easily adapt this to the Bem data. The hypothesis would be that Bob would reduce the dissonance between having initially believed the tasks were dull and his behaviour in claiming that they were not dull by only remembering the enjoyable aspects of the tasks. The S's asked to assess Bob's feelings about the tasks, who we should recall replicated the Festinger and Carlsmith data where the experimental subjects actually performed the tasks, will not simulate this memory selectivity.

Kunda (1990, p. 484) comments on the Festinger and Carlsmith subjects, arguing that if they 'were motivated to espouse attitudes corresponding to their dissonance-arousing behaviour, it seems likely that in their attempt to do so, they accessed their initial attitudes and were constrained by them. However, they may have accessed a biased subset of these initial attitudes'. This could be a memory selectivity effect but need not be. It might also be a premature termination of reasoning effect of the 'satisficing' form viz. a search of prior attitudes to the enjoyability of the tasks ends when the desired positive attitude has been found. Thus the subjects may access the attitude that 'the tasks involved enjoyable dexterity challenges' and terminate their attitude search there; not proceeding to the other attitude that 'the dexterity enjoyability was subsequently outweighed by finger numbness'.

There may also be a role for another Tversky and Kahneman (1974) bias, the Anchoring Heuristic. This, remarkably, involves the influence of random numbers that are known to be random on probability estimates. If a person is asked to estimate the number of African member states of the UN, they will give a much higher estimate if they have previously seen the number 65 appear on a wheel of fortune than if they saw 10. This seems to be an 'anchoring and adjustment' bias in that people reach estimated probabilities by commencing with a starting number and adjusting it until it seems sensible. The striking point is that the starting number can be any number at all. The suggestion here as to how this could apply to the dissonance reduction data is that the dissonant behaviour serves as the anchor for the enjoyability rating of the tasks which is then adjusted until plausible. Kunda makes the point that this interpretation is not in competition with her memory-selectivity explanation; both may be true as the explanation of how biases can effect dissonance reduction.

Naturally, dissonance in the data under discussion also results from the fact that the participants or Bob have lied to someone who they expect will be harmed by the lie: the stooge who will perform the dull tasks. Participants will exhibit a variant of Self-Presentation Bias in relation to themselves: they will presumably mostly want to view themselves positively. A positive self-image can only accrue to someone who does not generally lie at the expense of others for no particular reason. Note that this type of interpretation can explain the shape of the data where the \$1 subjects rated the tasks as much more enjoyable than the \$20 subjects, possibly because the \$1 subjects had lied for a paltry sum. Kunda (1990, p. 485) plausibly proposes her selective memory view again here, noting evidence that: '[p]ositive self-characterisations may be maintained not only by biased recall and construction of one's own traits and behaviours but also through biased construction of the traits'.

This leads on to the most obvious way of viewing dissonance reduction as a bias: the employment of Confirmation Bias as a primary mechanism to reduce dissonance. Kunda (1990, p. 495) identifies her memory selectivity mechanism as a cause of Confirmation Bias when she writes that 'the tendency to confirm hypotheses appears to be due to a process of biased memory search'. Combining this with the idea that almost everyone wishes to maintain a positive self-image gives us the idea suggested by McKee and Diethelm (2010, pp. 1309–1310) who suggest in connection with Cognitive Dissonance that 'confirmation bias is how we deal with evidence that challenges our strongly held beliefs and that would otherwise threaten our self-perceived status as intelligent and moral individuals'.

Going further, Cohan identifies six cognitive biases as being caused by Cognitive Dissonance. All of these have been employed at various points in the arguments I have been making to explain simulation errors. He discusses corporate hierarchies in particular, but that does not detract from the validity of his comments for our purposes, since humans are organised social creatures. Cohan (2002, p. 283) writes: 'Cognitive dissonance manifests in various types of bias . . . ':

1. Confirmation Bias.
2. Belief Perseverance Bias.
3. The Entity effect whereby 'peoples' hypotheses often take on a life of their own' (Cohan 2002, p. 284) and in particular may survive being completely discredited – which seems related to the Belief Perseverance Bias.
4. Motivated reasoning, which describes the (Kunda 1990) results discussed above.
5. Group cohesion effects, whereby once a group 'commits to an idea or a course of action, there is a strong motivation to resist evidence that it was the wrong move' (Cohan 2002, p. 284) – which seems related to Confirmation Bias.
6. The False Consensus Effect.

Cohan discusses the deleterious effects of all of these biases resulting from Cognitive Dissonance in the bankruptcy of Enron. The common factor is that there was a dissonance between the cognition 'I work for a successful company' and various data showing the contrary that were apparent to anyone who looked for them. Confirmation Bias is an excellent way of avoiding such data or minimising its import. Similarly, the Belief Perseverance Bias manifests itself in the persistence of the belief that the company was successful even if such contrary data were to be acknowledged. Motivated reasoning, employing memory selectivity or otherwise, explains how people could be directing their reasoning to the desired goal of concluding that the company is successful when it is not. All of this is facilitated by group cohesion effects and the False Consensus Effect, which here takes the form 'everyone around me in the company thinks it is successful, so anything leading me to suspect otherwise must be wrong'. So it is indeed plausible that Cognitive Dissonance can manifest itself in these several biases, which strengthens the case I have sought to prove, that dissonance reduction can be regarded as an unsimulated bias.

We may ask whether there is a tension between two parts of Saxe's position. She is concerned about Cognitive Penetrability of ToM, which she says exists and shows that TT is true. If it is indeed true that ToM is influenced by beliefs about the mind, why can we not tell people about Cognitive Dissonance theory such that they believe it and thereby improve their ToM? Also, we would expect experts in the field to have improved ToM abilities. They know about for example the Fundamental Attribution Error and could be expected to include it in their ToM predictions, if TT is true. Moreover, that should suggest a reduced tendency to commit such errors, since ToM is often used in relation to the self as well as others. Such experts should often find their ToM telling them 'in scenario X, I am likely to commit the Fundamental Attribution Error'. Since they know that this would be a mistake, they would avoid it. Do we see experts in psychology exhibit fewer cognitive biases? I think not. This line also blocks any 'me too' defence of TT against the position I defend in this book to the effect that TT may also not allow for biases, unless TT proponents drop Cognitive Penetrability as a challenge.

Finally, there is mention by Bem (1972, p. 25) of a third interpretation of the data, beyond mainstream Cognitive Dissonance theory and his own Self-Perception interpretation. Bem discusses this third 'Alexander-Knight' interpretation of the data, in a more detailed and comprehensive survey than the paper Saxe cites. Bem writes that in this third interpretation 'the results of many experiments can be predicted from a knowledge of the most socially desirable response to the situation'. This would be a case of successful prediction or elimination of ToM error by bias matching, with the bias in question being Self-Presentation Bias. S simply predicts that O will say what S would say in the simulated conditions, and what S would say is driven by what would make S look good in the circumstances. For example, as discussed above, S will successfully predict that O will say that O's reasons for selecting a particular job candidate were her intelligence and not her attractiveness.

One element which is prominent in the more comprehensive 1972 Bem review paper is frequent recourse to simulation language, when compared with the shorter 1967 Bem paper cited by Saxe. Bem discusses the importance of matching the experimental conditions as closely as possible when attempting to simulate them in such a way that the Self-Perception interpretation of Cognitive Dissonance data is available. It is important, Bem (1972, p. 29) writes, 'to note just what a successful simulation means. It implies the same thing that a successful computer simulation implies, namely, that the process model embodied in the "program" is functionally equivalent to the process being simulated, and, further, that the selection of the input statements was not in error'. Quite so. This is very close to a Goldman-like statement of the need for isomorphism of process if simulation is to avoid ToM error together with a statement of the Wrong Inputs Defence.

There is also a Bias Mismatch explanation for other data cited by Bem which I will cover in the next section.

Image viewers

I will consider some further data discussed in Bem (1967) relating to responses to homoerotic images. The data does not derive from an experiment Bem himself conducted; he reviews an experiment that was reported on by Bramel (1962).

There were two participants in the experiment, who both underwent the same procedure. Each participant, according to Bem (1967, p. 196) 'was first led to view himself favourably or unfavourably on a number of personality characteristics and then given information that implied that he was sexually aroused by homoerotic pictures. This information was in the form of numerical readings from a meter which was supposedly measuring . . . sexual arousal to the stimulus pictures'. The participants were led by Bramel (1962, p. 122) to form favourable or unfavourable assessments of themselves across the parameters of 'creativity, hostility, egocentricity, and over-all maturity'. They were also introduced briefly to the O's they were partnered with and then filled in a questionnaire on which they could give their assessments of how favourably they viewed the O's and in particular, how favourably they viewed him on the key attributes of creativity, hostility etc.

The numerical readings from a 'galvanometer' were in fact pre-set to read higher when pictures of attractive and partially undressed men were shown than when pictures of unattractive and fully dressed men were shown, thus making all participants believe that they had some level of homosexual tendencies whether they did or not. The idea was that a Cognitive Dissonance will now arise between the favourable self-images held by the participants, and the unfavourable impact on their self-image of the new information appearing to show latent homosexual tendencies.[7] Moreover, this dissonance will arise more strongly for the participants who have previously been led to view themselves favourably. Participants should now seek to reduce the dissonance between the two cognitions. The experimenters have ruled out the idea of discounting the data by extensively discussing the reliability of the galvanometer, a technique that might be less convincing today.

The ToM element of the study derives from investigating 'S's prediction of the meter readings that were obtained from his "partner", another male [O] who was participating in the experiment concurrently' (Bem 1967, p. 196). The experimenter correctly predicted from dissonance theory that a systematic ToM error would now arise, in that the S's who had been previously led to view themselves more favourably would 'attribute a higher amount of homosexual arousal to [O's] than would S's in the unfavourable condition, who would find the information less dissonant with their self-image' (Bem 1967, p. 196). The results bear this out: 'subjects in the high dissonance condition attributed to their partner about the same degree of arousal as they themselves appeared to be having. Those in the low dissonance condition in general attributed to their partner a level of arousal less than their own' (Bramel 1962, p. 129).

The reason this is a systematic error is that O's level of arousal will be unrelated to S's self-image. What has gone wrong is that S has a flawed axiom in his ToM. He views homosexuality unfavourably, is unaware of Cognitive Dissonance theory, and believes that O is like himself. The flawed axiom derived therefrom will be something like 'uncreative O's will be more aroused by homoerotic images' or 'hostile O's will be more aroused by homoerotic images'. Naturally these axioms are both false.

Bem himself explains the Bramel data by appealing to the Halo Effect. This is our tendency for 'cross-talk' between our attitudes to someone. If we assess that they are a good speaker, we are likely to adjust positively our assessment of even unrelated attributes, such as appearance. Nisbett and Wilson (1977, p. 244) write of one of their reviewed experiments that it was an 'experimental demonstration of the halo effect [which] showed that the manipulated warmth or coldness of an individual's personality had a large effect on ratings of the attractiveness of his appearance, speech, and mannerisms'. Along these lines, Bem (1967, p. 196) writes that in the homoerotic data a 'simple "halo effect" is evident: S's attribute high readings to partners toward whom they had generally unfavourable attitudes'. This means that S's attributed higher levels of arousal to partner O's in response to the homoerotic images if they had independently formed a negative impression of the O's for unrelated reasons. This means that we can appeal once again to a variant of the Bias Mismatch Defence. The S's make a systematic error of ToM in that they attribute higher levels of arousal to the O's than are warranted for no valid reason. They do this because they fall victim to the Halo Effect. Similarly, we fail to predict this response of the S's when we use them as our O's. We do not predict their behaviour because we do not simulate in them their application of the Halo Effect.

Notes

1 See Davidson (2001) for the use-mention distinction.
2 There are clear links here also to Behaviourism, which is the claim that stimuli may be related directly to behaviour without postulating the existence of mental states as intermediaries.
3 See also Gopnik (1993a), cited in Saxe (2005a, p. 177), for an extended TT denial of Introspectionism.
4 I will be denying that the observers were in fact reporting on the assessors; the way the questions were put to observers meant they were commenting on themselves and this difference vitiates any ToM conclusions to be gained from this study.
5 Asch was a Gestalt psychologists as opposed to a Behaviourist, as we can see from King and Wertheimer (1992, 124) when they write of 'the profound and independent Gestalt orientation of' Asch. As to whether Gestalt psychology and Behaviourism are compatible, see Ogden (1933).
6 See also McKay and Dennett (2009) for more examples of such beneficial selectivity.
7 I do not pretend that this experiment would pass modern ethical guidelines.

9 Partial simulation defence

Introduction

I will now turn to the fourth variant of Saxe's challenge, which was the claim that children use the false ToM axiom 'ignorance means you get it wrong'. The Ruffman (1996) data were held to show this axiom in use. Before discussing a different view of that data, I will briefly outline Gordon's theoretical response to Saxe's challenge. Gordon (2005, p. 362) argues that '[b]ecause [the children] can hide a fact only by negating it, they collapse ignorance into being wrong'. The idea is that the children first become aware that they have to somehow ignore a fact they know, if they are to simulate someone who does not know that fact. This basic idea is also at the root of the alternative partial modelling process explanation I will be outlining in this chapter. More sophisticated children, and adults, will be able in their simulations to ascribe disjunctive true beliefs later than they will be able to ascribe false beliefs because the former is more difficult. My approach then is a specific variant of the general defence Goldman (1993b, p. 27) suggests when he writes that '[d]efenders of ST might explain these developmental data in a different fashion by positing not fundamental changes of theory but increases in flexibility of simulation'.

I will first describe the approach to ToM called adaptive modelling proposed by Peterson and Riggs (1999). I will then set out the standard modelling process we may ascribe to the child before adjusting it for the Peterson and Riggs (1999) adaptive approach. The aim is to set out a response to Saxe's challenge, which response I will term a Partial Simulation Defence. The key idea of the Partial Simulation Defence is that children must learn to perform two tasks when simulating. The child as S must first learn to simulate O as lacking a piece of data that the S himself has. The child must also learn to deal with the consequences of this lack of data in O correctly, as will be outlined below. Since there are two tasks, children can acquire the ability to do one before they acquire the ability to do the other. They can, therefore, be able to conduct only a partial simulation. As I will show, this Partial Simulation Defence explains the data without appealing to theory and thus provides a defence of ST against TT. This is important because, as Friedman and Petrashek (2009, p. 115) observe, 'simulation theorists have not provided a convincing account for why children should predict that ignorance should lead to false belief' and this has led to Hybridist accounts being proposed.

ToM as adaptive modelling

Peterson and Riggs (1999) suggest a model of ToM which was developed using considerations of efficiency arising from database theory. The idea is that if particular approaches to obtaining data from databases are known to be more efficient than others when computers operate on databases, it may well be that the processing of evolved humans is similar, since efficiency is a key figure of merit for human cognitive processes also.

Peterson and Riggs (1999, p. 81) call their approach 'adaptive modelling'. The task they describe is for system-A to simulate or model system-B, where system-B can be another person or a counterfactual situation. System-A corresponds to S in our notation and system-B corresponds to O. Their general format for adaptive modelling is set out in Table 9.1.

Peterson and Riggs (1999) apply this view to the Maxi-type False Belief Tasks. They introduce two forms of reasoning they see as underlying ToM abilities, SD and MD. SD stands for Standard Derivation and MD for Modified Derivation. The idea is that SD reasoning involves no changes to known facts or perspectives. MD will then account for the changes to generate a view from somewhere else, being either another person, or oneself at another time, or a counterfactual. An example of SD is shown in Table 9.2 (Peterson and Riggs 1999, p. 83).

The authors extend their approach using MD, which will now allow for ToM application when O is missing a fact, or for analysis of counterfactual changes. The counterfactual analysis permits the generation of answers to questions like 'if the car had been towed to the pound, where would it be now?'. It also permits

Table 9.1 General format for adaptive modelling

Stage Number	*Stage Description*
1	Identify differences between system-A and system-B
2	Temporarily implement these differences in system-A
3	Run the adapted system-A
4	Attribute the result to system-B

Table 9.2 SD: standard derivation

Derivation Type	*Derivation Description*
Query	Where is the car?
Base-fact	The car was parked outside work at time t1
Norm	Things generally stay where they are put
Default Answer	Outside work

Table 9.3 MD: modified derivation

Derivation Type	*Derivation Description*
Instruction	Ignore(The car was moved to the car-pound at time t2)
Query	Where is the car?
Base-fact	The car was parked outside work at time t1
Norm	Things generally stay where they are put
Defeating fact	The car was moved to the car-pound at time t2
Default answer	Outside work

Table 9.4 General adaptive modelling strategy

Stage Number	*Stage Description*
1	S identifies the thing which O does not know
2	S implements this as an 'ignore' instruction to S's system
3	S runs S's system while sustaining the instruction
4	S attributes the result to O

the further extension to false belief type questions like 'where would O believe the car to be?' under circumstances where O is not aware that the car has been towed. The relevant example of MD is now as shown in Table 9.3 (Peterson and Riggs 1999, p. 86).

On the Peterson and Riggs (1999) model, improvements in ToM abilities in developing children are due to improved abilities to run MD, i.e. they gain in ability to reason with counterfactuals. A failure of ToM would be due to failure to implement the 'Ignore' instruction correctly.

The general adaptive modelling strategy for mind reading in the Maxi Task is as set out in Table 9.4 (Peterson and Riggs 1999, p. 90).

In summary, the adaptive modelling approach holds that for S to predict successfully the behaviour of O, S must determine what it is that O does not know and then 'run S's own system' implementing an Ignore instruction in relation to what it is that O does not know. It will be apparent that the term 'run S's own system' is in need of significant unpacking, which will also fix which type of explanation is involved. This unpacking will be done later when the approach is used.

Unadapted modelling process

Saxe's challenge has a response on the Peterson and Riggs (1999) model described above. I will first outline how the child reasons about the colour of the sweet before modifying that approach in light of the Peterson and Riggs model to cover the child's simulation of others.

In Figure 9.1 the pattern of reasoning for the child in the Ruffman experiment is shown.

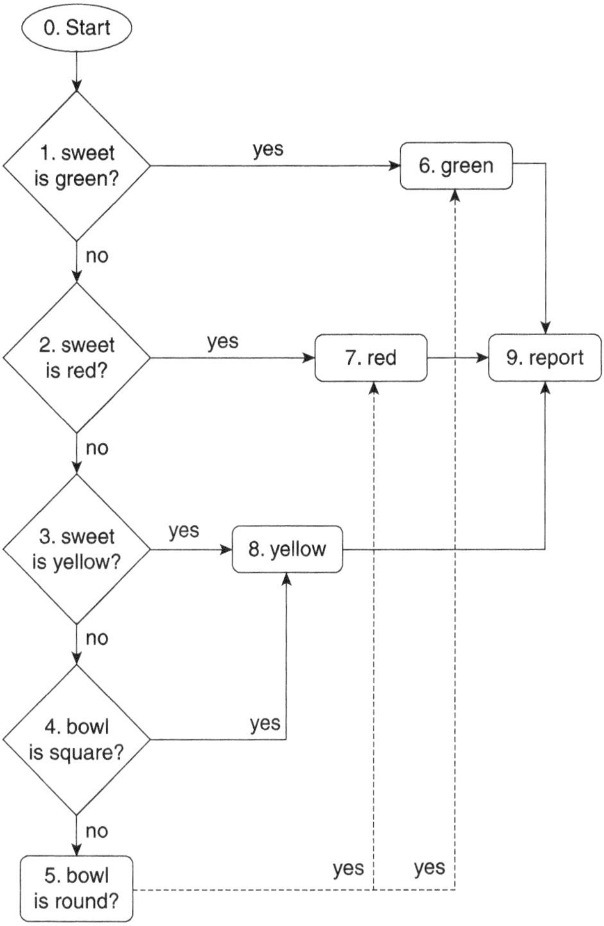

Figure 9.1 Decision tree for child in Ruffman experiment

Initially this decision tree is intended to represent the child's own reasoning in deciding the colour of the sweet. Below, I will reuse the diagram to show how the child simulates the observer. All routes on the diagram run from 0 to 9. The starting point from the child's perspective is simply to look at the sweet to see what colour it is. If the child can see the sweet, there is no need for the child to engage in reasoning from the shape of the bowl from which the sweet came to decide the colour of the sweet. The diagram shows the visual colour determination split out into several stages which are possibly otiose as a reflection of reality, but useful for our current purposes. The first question that the child asks then, when it sees the sweet, is whether it is green. If it is indeed green, the child can set the 'green' flag to 'true' and then report that. This sequence of boxes is 0/1/6/9 on the diagram. If it is not green, then the child can check to see whether it is red. If it is indeed red, the child can set the 'red' flag to 'true' and then report that.

This is sequence 0/1/2/7/9. If it is not red, then the child can check to see whether it is yellow. If it is indeed yellow, the child can set the 'yellow' flag to 'true' and then report that. This sequence is 0/1/2/3/8/9.

If the child has arrived at this point, s/he must not have been able to see the sweet since there are only three colours of sweet in this universe and none of the three possible logical flags have been set. The child must now therefore consider the shape of the bowl from which the sweet was chosen to decide what colour it must be. The next step is to ask whether the bowl was square. If it was indeed square, then the child can again set the 'yellow' flag to true and report that. This sequence is 0/1/2/3/4/8/9.

If the bowl was not square, then the bowl must have been round. The sweets in the round bowl are red and green, so the child should, if performing optimally, set both 'red' and 'green' to true and report both – with the caveat that only one can be correct since the sweet has only one colour. The two dashed 'yes' lines exiting the 'bowl is round' box reflect this optionality. The two sequences are 0/1/2/3/4/5/7/9 and 0/1/2/3/4/5/6/9.

We can represent the child's model or database as follows.

- Query: what colour is the sweet?
- Fact: the sweet was from the round bowl (either it is red or it is green).
- Fact: the sweet was green.

When asked what colour is the sweet, the child can consult its model and read off the answer 'green' to the query.

Adapted modelling process

I will now set out how the flow chart needs to be modified for the situation where the child models an observer lacking some data that the child has. I will do this using a Peterson and Riggs approach. This will show how the child can systematically answer RED when more developed ToM capacities would allow the child to say 'don't know' or 'red or yellow', which resolves Saxe's challenge.

Recall that the key point of the Peterson and Riggs proposal that mind reading in a False Belief Task is to be accomplished by (i) S identifying the thing which O does not know, and then (ii) implementing this as an 'ignore' instruction in S's own system. What does O not know? O does not know that the sweet is green. This gives us the following simulation database – or adapted model:

- Query: what colour is the sweet?
- Fact: the sweet was from the round bowl.
- Fact: the sweet was green.
- Ignore (Fact: the sweet was green).

There will be two consequences of implementing this Ignore instruction. The first consequence is that the child will not exit the flow chart at the first opportunity, by answering the question 'sweet is green?' in the affirmative and immediately exiting to report 'green' – i.e. it will not pass through the sequence 0/1/6/9. It will instead exercise the remainder of the flow chart. Note that none of this need be explicit. The child will then fall through the next two colours because it has not seen the sweet and so there is no reason to say that it is red or it is yellow. The question as to whether the bowl was square will also be answered in the negative. This means that the child arrives at the bottom box, indicating that the bowl was round. Thus far, the child has run through the sequence 0/1/2/3/4/5.

There are now two options for progress, either 'red' or 'green'. But here is where the second consequence of the Ignore instruction comes into play, and it does so deleteriously from the perspective of ToM capacities. The child is ignoring for simulation purposes the fact that the sweet is green. The child is therefore inhibited from moving to box 6. So the child can only exit the bottom box by setting 'red' and reporting that. This means that with this inhibition in place, the child will run the sequence 0/1/2/3/4/5/7/9.

Note that ignoring 'green' played two roles here. One was as a flow chart switch toggle meaning that the bottom of the flow chart was exercised. The second role was to inhibit one of two possible channels before 'report'. We can then hypothesise that what happens as ToM abilities become mature is that the Ignore instruction can be imposed selectively. It should be used as a flow chart toggle: it is correct to inhibit the sequence 0/1/6/9. It should not be used as an output inhibitor: it is wrong to inhibit the sequence 0/1/2/3/4/5/6/9. Since this is the inhibition of an inhibition, which is a difficult task, at a meta-level, it is unsurprising that children do not gain this ability in the first instance.[1] German and Leslie provide a related example of children in a false belief assessment scenario involving 'a very difficult interaction in which the brain has to return to a previously inhibited target' (Mitchell and Riggs 2001, p. 243) so we can see that there is independent empirical confirmation that children find disinhibition after inhibition difficult. We have thus explained why the child wrongly answers 'red' without appealing to the theoretical axiom 'ignorance means you get it wrong'.

This answers the challenge of Saxe (2005a, p. 178):

> The 'incorrect inputs' defence does not work, though, for the systematic errors described above, such as young children's conflation of ignorance and 'being wrong' (Ruffman 1996). . . . If the child were simulating [O], she might accurately express [O]'s ignorance, or else she might assimilate [O] to the self and judge that [O] thinks the bead is green. Simulation Theory offers no account of children's actual, systematic error. It is not enough to say that they used incorrect inputs: the theory must explain why the inputs were wrong in just this way.

As we can now see, the child has in fact simulated O with partial success. They have been successful in simulating O to the extent that they follow O's reasoning through the flow chart, as outlined above. Where they have failed is in simulating O's input that the sweet is not known to be green: they used the wrong input that the sweet was known not to be green – on at least their second use of this datum. If we changed our question in box 1 from 'is the sweet green?' to 'is the sweet known to be green?' then ignorance would suffice to exit the first box towards box 2 whereas currently only denying that the sweet is green – i.e. asserting that it is not green – does so. This is a type of quantifier shift error which has been made by adult expert philosophers more than once and so children falling prey to it should be unsurprising.

It might be thought that the employment of a database metaphor commits this defence to aspects of TT, or forces my position to become a Hybridist account. I dispute this, since it is another species of setting the bar too low for TT. The database might be a temporary register reflecting the current state of a multiple-stage simulation process. That would not constitute the fixed body of knowledge postulated by TT as being consulted by ToM users. There would not be any of the laws that make up TT knowledge either. In this connection note how Pratt (1993, p. 72) provides a form of database operation that is congenial to ST. The idea is that S must 'copy into . . . pretend belief- and desire-boxes the data-structures corresponding to those of his background beliefs and desires which he assumes to be shared' by O. Beliefs would be 'tagged' to indicate whether they were S's own beliefs or those of O being entertained for the purpose of simulation of O. Simulation by S would proceed as follows: '[h]aving cloned a suitable set of pretend beliefs and desires, [S] then lets those data-structures interact with each other and with his standard inferential machinery to yield new data-structures (corresponding to new 'pretend' beliefs and desires) which he can then observe using his usual introspective powers' (Pratt 1993, p. 72). Pratt (1993, p. 72) concludes that 'the suggested encoding scheme fares well when it comes to such simulations' on computing grounds, being simple, flexible, efficient and not postulating anything which appears unparsimonious when compared with what must in any case be available for S's own non-simulation cognitive processing. It is encouraging for simulationists that a promising database ToM model can be constructed which does not commit to TT.[2]

The defence put forward in this section can but need not be seen as a variant of the Wrong Inputs Defence. The fact that the sweet was green was an input into the model, which was then handled incorrectly. It may also be seen as a 'wrong processing' defence, in that one might regard the ToM error as resulting from the input being correct, but being incorrectly processed. The proposition that the sweet was green was ignored correctly at an early stage, in that it led to simulation of a process of reasoning that the child itself did not need to conduct. It was then processed incorrectly at a later stage, when the Ignore instruction should have been relaxed. There is developmental data supporting this type of mechanism elsewhere. As Birch and Bloom (2004, p. 258) comment, 'age-related changes in inhibitory mechanisms . . . have been found across the preschool years'. Similarly, they note that 'inhibition has been found to play an important role in false-belief reasoning' (Birch and Bloom 2004, p. 258). Whether one sees this as a Wrong Inputs Defence is to some extent dependent on a somewhat arbitrary decision on the location of the boundaries of the simulation process. In any case, it is a defence, and therefore valuable, whether it is a Wrong Inputs Defence or not.

Discussion

Application to desires and beliefs

We are now in a position to resolve one problem for ST that is noted regretfully by Harris, a supporter of the view. He criticises TT for not having a cogent explanation of why there is in children a 'lag between desire and belief understanding' (Carruthers and Smith 1996, p. 206) with the former appearing before the latter. Harris wonders how ST can account for this lag whereby children understand belief later than desire. I suggest that ST can do this because, as Astington points out, on 'the simulation view, concepts come from introspection' (Carruthers and Smith 1996, p. 187). This means that mental state concepts like BELIEF and DESIRE are acquired by introspection. By contrast, alongside TT, there is also a theory theory of concepts, whereby, according to Margolis and Laurence (2012, §2.3) 'concepts stand in relation to one another in the same way as the terms of a scientific theory [do] and . . . categorization is a process that strongly resembles scientific theorizing'. So proponents of TT see similarities between how children acquire concepts and how they acquire ToM abilities.

Children are able to introspect in such a way as to acquire DESIRE before they can do so to acquire BELIEF because introspection is essentially inner-directed. DESIRE can be acquired solely from the internal perspective. By internal perspective, I refer to the introspective view that the child has of its own internal states, excluding any reference to the world external to the child. For example, if a child is thirsty, he may desire that that status changes. To be sure, a change in that status may involve a change in the external world – viz. that a drink be produced and consumed – but the central point from the child's perspective is that the child's own introspection-accessible state changes. Were it possible to assuage the child's thirst by some method not involving obvious changes in the world, like for example by using some science fiction mechanism changing various neural weights in the brain of the child such that it no longer experiences thirst, the child will be just as happy as if a drink had been produced.

By contrast, beliefs are essentially outer-directed. Naturally, some of them will have inner components. One example of that will be when the child has a belief about himself that he is thirsty. But the key point about beliefs is their intentionality. They must be about something. That something will almost always be outside. One might argue that no child really has the concept BELIEF until it has the concept FALSE BELIEF; this is suggested by data cited by Harris showing that children 'start to talk more-or-less concurrently about false beliefs, true beliefs and ignorance' (Carruthers and Smith 1996, p. 203). No belief can be false unless there is something external about which it could be false.

We need therefore only make the plausible postulation that the child is more easily and therefore earlier able to introspect to acquire concepts that are inner-directed than outer-directed. In other words, introspection is more suitable for the acquisition of inner-directed concepts like DESIRE than outer-directed ones like BELIEF.

This view, that BELIEF is acquired by introspection, comports well with the solution I have offered here to the problem as to why children assimilate ignorance to error. The outer-directedness of BELIEF is what makes it harder for them to acquire BELIEF; and it is the outer-directed element that is the hard part which takes time. This is why, as I argue, it is changes in handling the outer-directed elements of BELIEF in others which develops as the child's ToM abilities progress. Initially, children are completely unable to simulate false belief at all. In an intermediate stage, they are able to simulate it partially by taking account of the early stages of reasoning someone else would have to conduct in a circumstance where they do not know something that the child does know. But they cannot complete the reasoning by then simulating the other person as not knowing X rather than knowing not X – they appear to assimilate ignorance to error.

When children finally reach full competence, they are able to say that the person who does not know X is ignorant of X rather than wrong about X. To do this, they must add back in consideration of facts about the world rather than just facts about the person, as with desire. Someone can desire something, and a child can understand that desire by introspection, without any consideration of external elements being needed.

Salience of deception defence

Ruffman (1996, p. 407) also examines one possible defence of ST, which asks 'whether it was deception per se that accounted for children's better performance on the False Belief Inference task'. The idea is that defenders of ST could claim that the deception made the important information more salient and more likely to be input into simulation. Ruffman initially denies this possibility by noting the results from a two colour version of the test. Recall that the round bowl contains two sorts of sweet: red ones and green ones. One correct answer is to say that O is ignorant of the colour: the best answer is that O thinks it is red or green. The children tend to make the error of saying that O believes falsely that the sweet is red, if they themselves know it is green i.e. that assimilate ignorance in O to error by O.

Ruffman continues in experiment three to test whether deception can explain better performance in the False Belief Tasks. This is done by introducing a deceptive version of the true belief test. A new bowl is introduced which also contains red sweets, like the round bowl. O is falsely told that the sweet has come from the round bowl, when in fact it has come from the new bowl. Since however the new bowl also contains red sweets, O will despite the deception have a true belief about the colour of the sweet. If deception helped children on the false belief inference test, then it should also help them here. Ruffman (1996, p. 407) found that 'children did not do better on the deceptive version of the True Belief Inference task. In fact, children did slightly though not significantly worse on the deceptive version with a greater proportion assigning a false belief to [O]'. The claim now is that this is a problem for ST because deception cannot be making inputs more salient and more likely to be input into the model; the assumption is that defenders of ST will have recourse to the Wrong Inputs Defence as discussed in Chapter 5. I have now provided a new Partial Simulation Defence in this chapter as an alternative to the Wrong Inputs Defence.

The Ruffman study also makes a point on inputs which is helpful for my case. It brings out some reasons for thinking that my Partial Simulation Defence is not a Wrong Inputs Defence, but a wrong processing defence. My claim is that children improve in processing ability, not the ability to process the right inputs. Ruffman (1996, p. 388) claims that that the observation that children assimilate error to ignorance is more congenial to TT than ST because 'children were generally good at "inputting" or taking account of the relevant information (i.e. the . . . knowledge of the sweets' colours)'. This exposes a useful ambiguity in what is meant by an 'input'. By 'input', Ruffman means raw data gathered from the senses, such as might be expressed in the proposition 'the sweet is green'. In contrast, by 'input', I understand 'input to the simulation', which is what matters for understanding the results of simulation. My view allows that simulation takes place by changing the inputs, changing the processing on those inputs, changing the outputs, or some combination of those three factors.

Both TT and ST allow, as they must, for improving ToM abilities as development progresses. They predict different sorts of development however. As Bolton puts it, '[TT] emphasises increasing theoretical sophistication, while [ST] emphasises increasing understanding of the role of perspective' (Stone and Davies 1995, p. 219). We have seen Saxe's outline of the increased theoretical sophistication that she thinks is illustrated by this experiment: the development would consist in abandoning the mistaken assimilation of ignorance to error. On the ST view by contrast, the change would be due to an improved ability to take the perspective of O, including the ability to ascribe 'ignorance' to O. Note how difficult this might be for the child. It can more easily initially deal with true belief and false belief because it has beliefs derived from its own perspectives, some of which later turn out to be false. It thus has first-hand experience of its own false beliefs. To ascribe ignorance, it needs to become aware, in a meta-belief, that there are propositions about which it does not have a true belief or a false belief – it has no view on them. In other words, it is ignorant of some data which would give warrant to asserting or denying some proposition. This is much more complex, taking place at the meta-belief level, than the assessment of truth or falsity. We can therefore understand why the developing ability to simulate will handle ascription of true belief and false belief before it can handle ascription of ignorance.

Notes

1 Mitchell, Currie, and Ziegler (2009b, p. 527) report a study which found 'a strong and stable link between inhibitory control and false belief task performance in children'.

2 In a similar computing architecture domain, Garson (2003) discusses interesting argument for and against the claim that connectionism supports simulationism. See also the database aspects of Peterson and Riggs (1999), as discussed in Chapter 9.

10 Simulationism and schizophrenia

Introduction

In this chapter, I will give arguments to support three ST claims about ToM in schizophrenia. There is substantial evidence for ToM deficits in patients with schizophrenia (Koelkebeck *et al.* 2010, p. 115; Bora and Pantelis 2012, p. S142). However, many clinical groups exhibit ToM deficiencies. The reason for focussing here solely on schizophrenic subjects is that the pattern of deficits is particularly supportive of the ST account, as augmented by the three claims I outlined above. This support for ST arises because the deficits in schizophrenic subjects are not explained by general cognitive deficiencies, and also correlate with the presence of their symptoms. TT accounts would gain support if the ToM deficits were explained by general cognitive impairments. TT accounts also appear to lack resources to explain why the affective symptoms of schizophrenia are correlated with ToM deficits. ST by contrast predicts exactly this, because if the schizophrenic subject experiences flattened affect, ST predicts that their ToM will project such flattened affect on others, which will constitute systematic ToM error.

The three claims, which can only be made by ST and not by TT, explain the data showing ToM deficits in schizophrenia, thus supporting the ST over the TT account of ToM more generally:

1. One source of ToM deficits in schizophrenic subjects is due to their reduced abilities to introspect their own mental states, with this in turn a result of their impaired sense of being a unified self, or impaired 'ipseity'. This explanation of impaired ToM is only available to simulationist accounts of ToM. There is no obvious reason why impaired ipseity should impair theoretical abilities.
2. A second source of ToM deficits in schizophrenic subjects is their own emotional disturbances. They will project these onto others on the ST account. They do not do this on TT, so TT does not predict the observed relation between flattened affect and impaired ToM in schizophrenic subjects.
3. Schizophrenic subjects exhibit paired deficits in the experiencing and recognition of an emotion, which is predicted by ST and not predicted by TT,

because the simulationist account links experiencing an emotion and ascribing that emotion to others.

The importance of understanding ToM in schizophrenia is underlined by many authors. ToM has been found to be the 'best direct predictor of functioning' (Achim *et al.* 2014, p. S289) in schizophrenic subjects. ToM deficits predict 'poorer clinical and functional outcomes' (Pousa *et al.* 2008, p. 126) for schizophrenic subjects. Balzan *et al.* (2013) aim to treat schizophrenics by addressing their unhelpful application of biases such as Confirmation Bias and the Representativeness Heuristic. The application of biases on the line I have been proposing in this book will also explain impaired ToM in schizophrenic subjects. Konstantakopoulos *et al.* (2014, p. 217) find that ToM deficits predict lack of insight of schizophrenic subjects into their condition. This lack of insight has unhelpful consequences including 'medication adherence . . . and social functioning'. So understanding the causes of the ToM deficits with a view to finding ways of addressing them, or showing how existing ways of addressing them work, would be beneficial to the schizophrenic subjects. For example, Garety *et al.* improve the delusional symptoms of schizophrenic subjects by addressing their 'jumping-to-conclusions' bias. See David, Kapur, and McGuffin (2012, p. 242) for an example of the removal of such a bias resulting in beneficial improved ToM performance. This illustrates my general claim that bias can result in ToM error, and shows it applying in schizophrenic subjects.

In the next section, I will very briefly outline the symptoms of schizophrenia that I will be employing, examine the ToM performance of schizophrenic subjects and provide an initial sketch of implications for the ST vs TT debate. In the final three sections, I will argue in turn for each of the three simulationist claims I listed above that explain the ToM deficits and discuss what these claims mean for the ST vs TT debate.

Symptoms of schizophrenia

There are many subtypes of schizophrenia with different characteristics and complex causation: as Butcher, Mineka, and Hooley (2010, p. 468) remark, 'no one factor can fully explain why schizophrenia develops'. Risk factors include genetic predispositions, a stressful family environment involving overly emotionally expressive family members, brain abnormalities related to dopamine, adolescent cannabis use, and complex interactions between all of the above. Because of this complexity, it is unlikely that any one theoretical approach will be useful across the board.

Schizophrenic subjects may exhibit positive or negative symptoms. Positive symptoms include hallucinations, delusions, thought disorder and active behavioural changes. Cockburn and Cockburn (2011) give examples. A hallucination might be the apparent hearing of 'voices that came from bushes or trees' (Cockburn and Cockburn 2011, p. 23). A delusion might be 'the suspicion that Brighton sits on a network of tunnels concealing dark forces' (Cockburn and

Cockburn 2011, p. 23). Thought disorder means just that, a disruption of the normal somewhat sequential ordering of thoughts, which might manifest itself in a tendency to 'change topics at random' (Cockburn and Cockburn 2011, p. 23). An active behavioural change might be engaging in a new, striking and difficult to comprehend activity, such as 'climbing a viaduct [barefoot] to get a better view of Brighton' (Cockburn and Cockburn 2011, p. 9). Negative symptoms are privative; they represent an absence of previous behaviours rather than positive actions. They might include 'apathy . . . inability to respond to other people . . . and distaste for washing' (Cockburn and Cockburn 2011, p. 23), and flattened affect. We might immediately suspect that an inability to respond to others has some connection to ToM; to the extent that one washes in order to remain inoffensive to others, a reduction in insight into others could conceivably reduce interest in washing and maintaining appearance.

Ipseity is 'selfness' or the sense of being a unified self. Impaired ipseity is widely observed in schizophrenic subjects. Sass *et al.* (2013, pp. 430–431) define ipseity as being 'a crucial sense of existing as a vital and self-identical subject of experience, with an automatic "mineness" of experience'. The impaired ipseity in schizophrenia manifests itself in various symptoms. One example is the phenomenon of 'alien control', in which the patient attributes his own actions to another agent (Salvatore, Dimaggio, and Lysaker 2007, p. 158). Another example would be a failure 'to recognise activities such as speech as self-initiated' (Irani *et al.* 2006, p. 153). Roth describes 'the experience that actions . . . are generated by an outside agency' (Burrows, Norman, and Rubinstein 1986, p. 171) as a primary symptom of schizophrenia.

ToM performance in schizophrenia

Many experiments show ToM deficits in patients with schizophrenia diagnoses. I will in this section briefly describe data supporting four points about these deficits, as follows. Schizophrenic subjects are less accurate than controls when they perform ToM tasks. They are also slower to complete ToM tasks. ToM deficits seem to be primarily associated with schizophrenic subjects who exhibit negative symptoms such as flat affect. The ToM deficits are not explained by general cognitive impairment since they persist even when such factors are controlled for.

In comparison with controls, schizophrenic subjects perform less accurately on a range of ToM tasks. The meta-analysis of Sprong *et al.* (2007, p. 10) concluded that on 'average the theory of mind performance of participants with schizophrenia is more than one standard deviation below that of healthy controls'. Pedersen *et al.* (2012, p. 226) found that 'patients with schizophrenia were less accurate at classifying ToM animations compared with controls (69% vs. 88%) respectively'. Scherzer *et al.* (2012, p. 2) report that the 'ToM deficit was more marked in the disorganized type of schizophrenia and significantly greater than that of schizophrenic subjects presenting a negative or paranoid symptomatology or in remission'. The fact that remitted patients showed reduced ToM deficits may indicate that ToM improvements assist recovery – though the direction of causation could also be inverted.

Clinical groups are also slower to perform ToM tasks. Anselmetti *et al.* (2009, p. 282) found that schizophrenic subjects needed an average of 47s to carry out a picture sorting ToM task as compared with 25s for controls. Brüne and Bodenstein (2005, p. 236) found that schizophrenic subjects needed 213s to sequence ToM pictures as against 83s for controls; these effects were not explained by general cognitive impairments. The brain scanning data show that the schizophrenic subjects were exercising the brain areas associated with ToM only in the second half of the 24 second duration of the animation while the control subjects were doing that only in the first half. All of these data together confirm that exercise of ToM capacities is a more difficult task for schizophrenic subjects than for control subjects. It seems that the slowness relates to engaging the ToM capacities in the first place rather than solely to impaired performance of ToM once engaged.

There are mixed results as to whether we may associate ToM deficits more strongly with subjects exhibiting different subgroups of symptoms, though it does appear that patients with negative symptoms such as flattened affect show the most ToM impairment.[1]

The deficits in ToM appear to be independent of any impairments in general executive functioning or intelligence, although the data in this area are unclear. Some of these ToM deficits are quite dramatic. For instance, experiments have been run in which irony comprehension is measured. This is a ToM task since one cannot appreciate the true meaning of an ironic utterance without understanding the mental state of the speaker; schizophrenic subjects tend to interpret ironic statements literally. Harrington, Siegert, and McClure (2005, p. 262) note a study in which '[o]ne member of the schizophrenia group with an IQ estimate of 125 still misinterpreted 8 of 9 of the ironic statements'.[2]

Implications for ST and schizophrenia

In general, the data are more congenial to ST than to TT. We can see this by considering the perspective taking element of ToM. This, as outlined earlier is the two-stage process of S taking O's perspective by anchoring on S's perspective and then finding O's perspective by adjustment. We saw that perspective taking was at least founded on simulation, as conceded by Epley *et al.* (2004), because that is how S's own perspective enters the picture. Epley *et al.* (2004) attempted to maintain a role for theory in perspective-taking by allotting it responsibility for the adjustments needed to move from S's perspective to O's perspective. This I argued was unmotivated and unparsimonious, since the adjustment could be understood to be further simulation with shifted inputs. Epley *et al.* (2004) gave no framework for deciding how and when simulation and theory were to be used and how they would interact. With this understanding of perspective-taking as entirely simulational in hand, we can agree with Brüne and Bodenstein

(2005, p. 237) that in schizophrenic subjects, 'poor understanding of figurative speech is associated with impaired mental perspective taking, i.e. ToM'.

A further study also looked at ToM in schizophrenic subjects using a picture sequencing task. Similarly to the other studies, Langdon *et al.* (2001, p. 81) found that 'false-belief picture sequencing ability significantly predicted the odds of being a patient' even after any cognitive impairments were controlled for. Langdon *et al.* (2001) discuss briefly some potential implications of simulationist accounts of ToM in schizophrenia. They contrast ST with their favoured account, being ToMM or TT(Innate) as I termed it earlier. They distinguish between the two by asserting that ToM impairments have different causes on the two competing accounts. On TT(Innate), ToM deficits are caused by 'selective damage to a domain-specific mentalising module' (Langdon *et al.* 2001, p. 86). On ST, ToM deficits are caused by 'general difficulty entertaining any state of affairs that runs counter to current reality' (Langdon *et al.* 2001, p. 86). They give two examples of the counterfactuals in question. One is the false belief of O, which is counterfactual in virtue of being false. The second is a future hypothetical state. This would cause problems for S in predicting S's own future behaviour under counterfactual conditions, which is essential for useful action planning.

This account of Langdon *et al.* (2001) assumes that the only defence available to ST to account for ToM errors is the Wrong Inputs Defence. We can see that because both of the difficulties outlined above would be solved by the inputs being correct, or in other words by S being able to handle counterfactual reasoning correctly. However, as I have argued at length in this book, there is also a Bias Mismatch Defence available to ST. It is difficult to expand on this by giving the exact Bias Mismatches involved without a more precise specification of the false beliefs or hypothetical future scenarios involved. However, we can easily imagine that there will be Affect Mismatch between S and O in both of those scenarios, thus motivating the claim that Bias Mismatch would arise. We can also easily imagine that false beliefs of O will have variable salience or Vividness. This would allow a mismatch in terms of Availability to arise between S and O and explain the systematic ToM errors in exactly the same way as I have been proposing throughout.[3]

Langdon *et al.* (2001, p. 86) also discuss two hypotheses they think can be 'derived from simulation theory'. These are as follows. First, 'poor mentalising might reflect an impaired ability to reason consequentially on the basis of hypothetical states' (Langdon *et al.* 2001, p. 86). Second, 'poor mentalising occurs because an individual is "captured" by more salient concrete information' (Langdon *et al.* 2001, p. 86). They conclude eventually that TT(Innate) is a better explanation of their data than ST on the basis that their data do not support these two hypotheses. It is unclear whether Langdon *et al.* (2001, p. 86) intend the claim that these two hypotheses 'can be derived from simulation theory' to be understood as meaning that ST is committed to the two hypotheses or merely that they are possible consequences of some versions of ST. The second hypothesis, they say, is 'consistent with a simulation view' (Langdon *et al.* 2001, p. 86), which leaves open the possibility of simulationist views which are not committed to the second hypothesis. Arguments that ST entails the two hypotheses are not given and it does not appear obvious what they might be. Absent such arguments, I maintain that ST is not committed to the two hypotheses and therefore may survive data tending to disconfirm them.

Impaired ipseity impairs ToM

I argue for the claim that impaired ipseity in schizophrenic subjects causes their ToM deficits. This explanation is natural on the ST account because the starting point for S to explain O's behaviour is S himself, and so S needs a good view of who S is. Exactly that is what is impaired when ipseity is impaired. Further, the data support ST in its Introspectionist strain, because they show that the reason for the occasions when schizophrenic subjects perform badly on ToM tasks is that they lack insight into themselves and their own emotions. Such an explanation is not available to TT accounts, since they deny Introspectionism.

Why do schizophrenic subjects have ToM deficits? I propose that it is because they are impaired in their ability to introspect their own mental states and emotions, and that this impairment could be due to their impaired ipseity, as mentioned above. This means that patients are no longer sure of the boundaries of the self, so they do not know whose emotions it is they are supposed to be introspecting. It seems plausible that S will be impaired and slowed in ToM if S is not sure whether S or O has just spoken. An example of one way this may manifest itself is given by Cockburn and Cockburn (2011, p. 104), who note scanning data suggesting that 'inner speech is received by the part of the brain handling the reception of external speech, so it appears to come from a separate entity'. Impaired ipseity is also noted by Carpenter and Hanlon who write that issues arise for the schizophrenic patient 'from the disruption of his (her) sense of identity [so such] questions as: "Who am I?" become urgent' (Burrows, Norman, and Rubinstein 1986, p. 127).[4]

This is consistent with the views of Campbell (1999, p. 609), who argues that only in schizophrenic subjects, there is the possibility of error in relation to who it is that is in a psychological state. He writes that if you are not schizophrenic, you 'can get it wrong about which psychological state you are in, but you cannot get it right about the psychological state but wrong about whose psychological state it is'. This contrasts with the schizophrenic subjects who have it seems an additional task to perform when exercising ToM in relation to themselves: they observe events and actions taking place 'in the world' and they have to decide which of them are actions performed by them.

The impaired ipseity view of schizophrenia I propose is linked to but distinct from the impaired agency view proposed by Frith (Campbell 1999, p. 611). On the impaired agency view, schizophrenia is 'fundamentally a deficiency in the sense of agency'. Impaired ipseity and an impaired sense of agency are not identical, since the former could be a cause of the latter: if I do not know who I am, I may also not know that I am acting. I could potentially retain a fully agential view of a reduced self, so again we can see that impaired ipseity and impaired agency are linked but separate.

The impaired agency view is not committed to the impaired ipseity view; though Campbell (1999, pp. 621–622) discusses both. By extension, the impaired agency view is not committed to the proposal I am making, that impaired ipseity in schizophrenic subjects causes their ToM deficits. Indeed, Frith and Corcoran (1996) do not mention these possible underlying causes of ToM deficits when they might; instead they focus on the link between paranoid symptoms and ToM deficits. Also, Corcoran, Mercer, and Frith (1995, p. 6) suggest that the 'blunted affect seen in patients with negative features reflects an impairment in social inference or "theory of mind"'; so their idea is that the impaired ToM causes the blunted affect while my simulationist idea is that the blunted affect causes the impaired ToM.

On ST, the additional task of identifying the self, or failing to do so fully and accurately, would cause delays in ToM, as are observed in schizophrenic subjects. Even if S can run the simulations correctly, S has to identify the simulation outputs that are actions of S and are thus to be attributed to O and also avoid attributing non-actions of S to O. That could be quite time-consuming, especially if multiple simulations are needed. Some support for this line may be garnered from the remark of Sarfati *et al.* (1999, p. 184) that schizophrenic subjects show an 'impoverished ability both to comment on internal states and to describe interpersonal cues'. The objection that this could also reflect verbalisation deficits is blocked by Sprong *et al.* (2007, pp. 10–11) observing that 'impairment of theory of mind does not appear to be affected by verbalisation deficits that have been reported in people with schizophrenia'.

Some writers see the typical ToM deficits in schizophrenic subjects as supportive of the ST account; we can agree with them that introspection abilities are key. Dimaggio *et al.* (2008, p. 778) argue that 'the more individuals are able to reflect on and retrieve episodes from their life narratives, the more they are likely to grasp others' thoughts and emotions'. This idea fits very naturally with the simulationist perspective, for two reasons. First, Dimaggio *et al.* (2008) suggest that capacities in ToM applied by S to O when S and O are the same person will benefits S's ToM capacities when O is a different person. When individuals reflect on their life narratives, they will in effect be simulating themselves and obtaining access to their emotional and mental states at prior times. And then it will be relevant, as Dimaggio *et al.* (2008, p. 780) also point out, that 'people able to recognise and express their emotions tend to have good mind-reading skills'. This will feed into their ability to explain their own behaviour which will then enhance their ability to explain and predict the behaviour of others. Second, the approach is in accord with Introspectionism, which is the claim that we have direct and privileged access to our own mental states. As we have seen, TT tends to set its face against Introspectionism while ST can accommodate both Introspectionism and its denial.

Another implication of this view that schizophrenics have ToM impairments deriving from their impaired ipseity plays out in how often they will use their

ToM. Since they have to spend time working out which of the events they perceive in the world are in fact actions of theirs, we might expect that they will sometimes also over-activate their ToM when simulating others. They may apply ToM whenever they see a character in a situation where non-schizophrenic subjects would not. Non-schizophrenic subjects would only activate their ToM when there is not just the presence of a character but in addition the requirement to predict or explain his behaviour. Applying this implication, ST predicts the results of Brazo *et al.* (2012, p. S142) who found that in schizophrenics 'a character could trigger ToM processes even if not necessary'. ToM is activated in the schizophrenics by the mere presence of the character because it is not obvious to them when the character is acting intentionally and needs ToM interpretation and when there are merely events occurring in the vicinity of the character and these events are not his actions.

Also intriguing in this context are the results of Lysaker *et al.* (2012, p. 293), who found that what we might term a poor or incoherent story of the self or weak 'narrative development' was 'strongly associated with social withdrawal'. One would expect both that loss of ipseity impairs narrative development and impaired ToM causes social withdrawal. So on the ST and impaired ipseity explanation of the ToM deficits I am proposing, we predict the observed association between weak narrative development and social withdrawal. The link between ToM and social withdrawal has been widely held by investigators; Lagodka *et al.* (2010, p. 325) note it 'has been assumed that Theory of Mind (ToM) is the most predictive factor of social functioning in schizophrenia'.

This impaired ipseity account predicts that schizophrenic subjects will exhibit impaired ToM only when they are experiencing symptoms and not when they are in remission. That would distinguish them from autistic subjects, whose condition does not remit significantly; for schizophrenic subjects, between '20% and 25% will have one episode with full remission' (Birchwood and Jackson 2001, p. 23). This is what is observed; Sarfati and Hardy-Baylé (1999, p. 618) note that 'autistic subjects never develop the capacity to attribute mental states to others whereas schizophrenic subjects "try to use lost abilities"'.[5] Consistently with this claim, Shin *et al.* (2008, p. 113) note that '[d]eficits in ToM capability may be modest at the prodromal stage of schizophrenia' and Sarfati and Hardy-Baylé (1999, p. 618) suggest that the 'theory of mind deficit seems to disappear in patients who are [in] remission' – of which, more below.[6]

I will note finally that there is a radical Nietzschean line available here which suggests that the schizophrenic subjects are correct and non-schizophrenic subjects are incorrect about ipseity. Nietzsche sees the self as an artificial unity constructed over what is in fact a competing assembly of drives. The automatic assumption that everything my body does is 'down to me' or represents actions I have chosen would similarly be mistaken. I may be able to choose what to eat, but I cannot decide when to be hungry, or what type of person interests me sexually, or when that occurs. These 'actions' seem to be selected by another part of my self. As Nietzsche (2003, pp. 43–44) suggests, 'such conceptions as "soul as multiplicity of the subject" and "soul as social structure of the drives and emotions" want henceforth to possess civic rights in science'.[7]

Our belief in our own ipseity and our ownership of all our 'own' actions would fall into the category of what Nietzsche terms 'necessary errors'; falsehoods without which we cannot function. The mechanism by which the illusion of ipseity is maintained is unclear, but whatever it is, it may have ceased to function in schizophrenia. This is suggested by an example of remission given by Birchwood and Spencer who write of a patient that 'Margaret believed that she could not act or make a decision without reference to her voice; however, she described periods when she was relaxed and the voices quiescent where she would be making decisions' (Gelder *et al.* 2012, §6.3.2.4). What this could mean is that Margaret has 'taken ownership' of the voice, which is at other times a manifestation of the multiplicity of the subject, and that explains why she now feels that she is making the decisions, and is hence no longer distressed by the situation. It might be that our abilities to understand and assist schizophrenic subjects might be improved if we realised the possibility that the delusions may not be held solely by schizophrenic subjects.

Emotional disturbance impairs ToM

I will now move on to considering a further linked claim. I will argue that even if the schizophrenic subjects can overcome their impaired ipseity sufficiently well to introspect their own mental states, if they introspect unusual affective states, that could still cause them to exhibit impaired ToM. So the observed ToM deficits could be caused by either or both impaired ipseity or flattened affect in schizophrenic subjects.

Schizophrenic subjects exhibit emotional markers including flat affect; as Birchwood and Jackson (2001, p. 18) note '[n]egative symptoms primarily concern losses or diminution in emotion'. And as Shamay-Tsoory *et al.* (2007, p. 11) show, 'individuals with high level of negative symptoms of schizophrenia may demonstrate selective impairment in their ability to attribute affective mental states'. These proposals are readily understood on a simulationist line, on which the affective flattening of a schizophrenic S will impair the ability of S to empathise or recognise emotional states of O.

The impaired empathy results from the fact that S's starting point for recognising the emotions of O in a particular scenario will be S's own projected emotional state in that scenario. If S has had flattened affect or any emotional disturbances for some time, these may influence S's predictions for O, leading S to ascribe flattened affect also to O. This will not occur on a per se basis, i.e. S will not explicitly endorse a TT axiom of the form 'I have flattened affect therefore so will O'. Rather, S will apply flattened emotional inputs to his simulation by starting from his own emotions. This will lead to systematic ToM error via affective mismatch, a central theme of this book.

On the ST line, S uses his own mental and emotional systems to simulate O and predict his behaviour. As argued above, if schizophrenics are impaired in terms of introspection, their simulation of O will be similarly deficient. They cannot access themselves as accurately or quickly as control subjects. The other requirement is that what they introspect be relevantly similar between S and O. This suggests a further potential explanation for the ToM deficits in schizophrenic subjects: even if the process of introspection proceeds undisturbed, it may be directed upon atypical affective states, whether flattened, anxious, hostile or depressed. This second explanation, which may operate in parallel with the first, suggests that if schizophrenic S's accurately introspect their own disturbed state, they may then exhibit impaired ToM performance in that they project some of their disturbed states on to O. Such projection is what is found by Cassetta and Goghari (2014, p. S303) who note on a sarcasm comprehension test – a practical ToM task – that 'schizophrenia patients endorsed responses associated with personality pathology (e.g. high levels of affective lability [and] anxiousness)' and that 'ToM abilities were negatively related to affective lability [and] anxiousness'. Also, as Carpenter and Hanlon observe, 'impairment in [empathy and rapport] is considered crucial to the diagnosis of schizophrenia' (Burrows, Norman, and Rubinstein 1986, p. 124). The link between empathy and ToM impairment is clear on ST and obscure on TT, so ST has a ready explanation for impaired ToM in schizophrenics and TT does not.

An account suggesting that flattened or negative affect causes ToM impairments also predicts that depressed subjects will show similar deficits to schizophrenic subjects. There is some evidence for this; Zobel *et al.* (2010, p. 821) found that '[c]hronically depressed patients were markedly impaired in all ToM . . . tasks'. It must be noted in this connection that Möller and von Zerssen report that 'depressive syndromes can be regarded as extremely prevalent in acutely ill schizophrenic patients' (Burrows, Norman, and Rubinstein 1986, p. 184). This opens the possibility that ToM deficits in schizophrenic subjects are explained by their depression.[8] That is still consistent with the line I am proposing that flattened affect impairs ToM, but further empirical work would clearly be useful here.

The causation may also run in the opposite direction. Placing schizophrenic subjects in non-threatening social situations such as may ideally be done in the therapeutic setting will give them an opportunity to improve their ToM abilities, which will give them better insights into their own emotional states, which will address the flattened affect. For these reasons then, we may agree with Birchwood and Jackson (2001, p. 28) when they suggest that 'social resolution and reintegration are essential to the recovery process' and that better social reintegration in developing countries explains the relatively improved outcomes seen in those countries. There is evidence that 'compromised ToM abilities in schizophrenia significantly contribute to correctly predicting patients' poor social functioning' (Brüne 2005, p. 36). TT proponents here will presumably explain the positive ToM outcomes from social reintegration as stemming from the opportunities arising to confirm/disconfirm hypotheses and axioms. The process of recovery of ToM would then be similar to the process of acquiring ToM undergone by pre-five-year-old children. However, if there is a pattern of declining ToM with flat affect during severe schizophrenic episodes which declines are reversed in remission, then TT proponents are left proposing cycles of theory acquisition and loss. That seems less parsimonious and less plausible than the natural ST explanation, which is simply that the ToM deficits are caused by the affective flattening in episodes and come and go with it.

TT proponents may not appeal to general cognitive impairment in schizophrenic subjects to explain impaired ToM. Bozikas *et al.* (2011, p. 130) found that schizophrenic subjects 'performed poorly on ToM tasks even after controlling for their cognitive deficits'. Similarly, Pickup and Frith (2001, p. 216) found that schizophrenic subjects 'showed a ToM deficit even when memory and IQ were controlled'. Harrington, Siegert, and McClure (2005, p. 267) conclude from their literature review that the evidence 'stands strongly in support of there being a ToM deficit associated with schizophrenia that cannot be accounted for by either executive functioning or more general cognitive impairments'. Moreover, if making theoretical inferences from mental states is an exercise which benefits from IQ, one might expect that the highly intelligent schizophrenic patient referred to above would be in a position to use his intelligence to perform well on the irony comprehension task; the opposite was observed. So there is a great deal of evidence confirming that cognitive impairment does not explain the ToM deficits of schizophrenic subjects and TT proponents must provide an alternative explanation of them. ST accounts may use either or both of the impaired ipseity or flattened affect explanations I have provided.

Given the importance – on the ST account as augmented with the Bias Mismatch defence line I have been proposing – of the idea of Affect Mismatch between S and O causing ToM error – we would expect disturbed affective states in schizophrenic subjects to result in ToM deficits.[9] That idea is central to the defence of ST I have given that seeks to explain systematic ToM error. By contrast, on the TT account, there is little more to ToM than theoretically inferring the beliefs and desires of others, so there is no particular reason to think that Affect Mismatch between S and O will lead to ToM errors. Gordon divides accounts of ToM into 'hot' and 'cold' approaches, with ST being hot and TT being cold. As he explains, TT 'chiefly engages our intellectual processes [and] makes no essential use of our own capacities for emotion' whereas ST 'exploits one's own motivational and emotional resources' (Carruthers and Smith 1996, p. 11). Thus TT has no resources to explain impaired ToM in subjects like the schizophrenic patients who exhibit atypical affect, while such an explanation is almost automatic on ST. Similarly, it is unclear what the TT explanation would be of the recent results of Leonhardt *et al.* (2014, S338) who found that schizophrenic subjects with impaired self-reflective abilities were also less able to grasp the emotional states of others. On TT, no self-reflectivity is needed to recognise the emotions of others because no self-reflection is needed to employ theoretical axioms.

The account I am proposing here holds that flattened affect explains the ToM deficits of schizophrenic subjects. Naturally then, it predicts that schizophrenic subjects will only exhibit impaired ToM when also exhibiting flat affect and not when that symptom is in remission. One objection here, which might also be brought against the claim for which I argued in the previous section, would rely on the suggestion of Sprong *et al.* (2007, p. 9) that schizophrenic 'patients in remission also showed a significantly worse performance than controls'. However, on detailed inspection, this appears not to conflict with my claim that remission of symptoms will be correlated with improved ToM capacities. Sprong *et al.* (2007, p. 6) give five sources of data to back their claim. I will briefly discuss each of them.

Herold *et al.* (2002) studied a sample of remitted schizophrenic patients and found no statistically significant difference in ToM performance on three out of four tasks between the patients and controls. The one task where there was a significant difference was on irony comprehension. The second study, Randall *et al.* (2003) is also described by the authors as 'preliminary'. Randall *et al.* (2003, pp. 292–293) write that their findings in relation to a remitted medicated group 'suggest that residual cognitive abnormalities may be found in remitted paranoid patients but, because of the relatively small number involved . . . this inference must be treated with caution'. Corcoran, Mercer, and Frith (1995, p. 10) found that patients 'who were symptom free at the time of testing showed normal performance on the hinting task' i.e. these remitted patients showed no ToM deficits. Corcoran, Cahill, and Frith (1997) compared the abilities of schizophrenic subjects with controls on understanding two types of visual jokes: with and without mental state components. Corcoran, Cahill, and Frith (1997, pp. 325–326) found that the 'performance of the patients in the remitted/other symptom subgroup did not differ from that of the normal control group for either type of joke'. Pickup and Frith (2001, p. 216) 'predicted that schizophrenic patients with behavioural signs would have impaired ToM relative to controls [and] that remitted schizophrenics, and those with only passivity symptoms, would have intact ToM' and these predictions were confirmed. Pickup and Frith (2001, pp. 215–216) also note that 'a 1-point increase in neg[ative] beh[aviour] multiplied the odds of intact ToM by . . . 0.25'. This means that a minor increase on a ten-point scale of negative behaviour, including 'blunt affect', caused a dramatic decrease in the probability of intact ToM; see also Sprong *et al.* (2007, p. 6) for results to the effect that subjects showing 'behavioural signs of negative symptoms and/or incoherence [were] most impaired'. Langdon *et al.* (2001, p. 98) find that both 'picture-sequencing errors . . . predicted higher ratings of flat affect . . . and general negative symptoms' and that 'false-belief errors (indexing poor mentalising) predicted higher ratings of flat affect'. They also find no correlation between ToM deficits and positive symptoms.[10]

Analysis of all of these data lead Sprong *et al.* (2007, pp. 7–9) to the conclusion that there were effect sizes[11] of $d = -2.231$ for disorganised patients; $d = -1.278$ for non-disorganised patients; $d = -1.241$ for paranoid patients and $d = -0.692$ for remitted patients, all in relation to controls. Since -0.692 is 31 per cent of -2.231, this means that remitted patients have moved most of the way back in terms of the distance between disorganised patients and controls. There could be a continuity model linking ipseity, psychotic symptoms and impaired ToM with remission in the first two categories correlated with recovery in the latter. It is also possible that the persistence over months or longer of psychotic experiences has lasting effects on the ToM of patients even when in remission from florid symptoms. That idea gains support from measurements showing 'ToM performance negatively correlated . . . with length of illness' (Harrington, Siegert, and McClure 2005, p. 257).

In any case, given the severe social and behavioural impairments that result from ToM deficits, the reversal of those deficits will almost be definitional of remission. I conclude that these data are not sufficient to support convincingly any objection to the effect that remitted patients also show ToM deficits; they do not challenge the claim that symptoms such as flattened affect result in impaired ToM. This is what is confirmed by Pickup and Frith (2001), predicted by ST and not predicted by TT.

Paired deficits in experiencing and ascribing emotions

I will now discuss a third related argument for ST which relies on the distinction mentioned above between the hotness of ST and the coldness of TT. ST is hot since it uses our emotions whereas TT is cold; it employs inferences rather than emotions. Thus, ST and not TT predicts that persons who experience an emotion less often or less intensely will also ascribe it less often or less intensely.

Goldman and Sripada (2005, p. 193) argue that there are data to support the claim that 'for three emotions, fear, disgust, and anger, deficits in face-based recognition are paired with deficits in the experiencing of the same emotion' and that only the simulationist account can explain this. The data they cite include for example a woman with amygdala damage who had paired deficits: she did not experience fear nor did she accurately attribute it to others. Similarly, Lysaker *et al.* (2012, p. 290) introduce evidence to the effect that 'negative symptom severity is linked to concurrent impairments in ToM . . . and emotional recognition'. I agree with the first claim which supports my arguments above. I also agree with the latter claim that links emotion experience and ascription in schizophrenic subjects, since it supports the argument I will make now. This paired deficit in schizophrenic subjects is also confirmed by Lincoln *et al.* (2011, S26) who found that '[n]egative symptoms were significantly associated with difficulties in the abilities to infer emotions'. Thus, flattened affect in schizophrenic subjects was associated with impaired ToM capacities in the area of ascribing emotions to O, as was discussed previously.

To support their claim of a paired deficit in anger experiencing and recognition, Goldman and Sripada (2005, p. 197) offer some interesting data. They note an experiment in which dopamine antagonists were administered, inhibiting the normal effects of dopamine. It is known that dopamine is 'involved in the processing of aggression'. The results were that following suppression of dopamine by the antagonist, 'subjects were significantly worse at recognising angry faces' (Goldman and Sripada 2005, p. 197) but unimpaired at ascribing other facially expressed emotions. So suppression of dopamine leads to paired deficits in experiencing and ascribing anger. The related claim I have been urging is that schizophrenic subjects by contrast produce more anger and over-attribute it to others. Therefore, we might predict just from this ToM data that schizophrenic subjects would have elevated dopaminergic activity. This is exactly what is observed. Evans *et al.* (2005, Chapter 5) point out that studies of the dopamine system of schizophrenic subjects 'have found evidence of overactivity'. Moreover, Evans *et al.* (2005, Chapter 5) note that medication for schizophrenia 'targets principally the dopamine system'. We might then surmise that on the ST line that there are two reasons for the efficacy of the medication: it both reduces anger in the schizophrenic S's and that then reduces the frequency with which schizophrenic S's wrongly attribute anger to O.

These face-based emotion recognition abilities together with paired deficits in experiencing and ascription of emotions present difficulties for the TT account. There does not seem to be a TT explanation of faced-based emotional recognition in non-schizophrenic subjects; Goldman and Sripada (2005, p. 198) write that they are 'not aware of any *specific* TT-based proposal in the literature' so they attempt to provide one. It would presumably be a set of theoretical axioms linking particular emotions to particular faces. The competing ST account would be that recognition is achieved by experiencing, presumably in an attenuated form. Damage to the system that produces an emotion would produce the paired deficit in recognising it that we have been discussing. By contrast, 'there is no reason to expect a paired deficit under TT. Why should conceptual representations of fear occur in the same region that underlies fear experience?' (Goldman and Sripada 2005, p. 199).

Goldman and Sripada are here making a neurological argument when they discuss 'regions'; the idea is that a brain lesion in the region responsible for fear would result in a paired deficit in fear experiencing and ascription. While this argument may well be correct, the ST account need not commit itself to a 'same region' neurological explanation of the paired deficits. Since on ST ascription of an emotion requires the ability to produce that emotion, impairment of the former would impair the latter whether or not they are co-located. Goldman and Sripada also note here that the TT proponent might say that the capacity to experience fear and to recognise it might be coincidentally co-located or coincidentally related, but then the ST proponent can suggest that this is unlikely to be the case for all three of the emotions for which Goldman and Sripada show paired deficits. Moreover, the same scenario is seen more widely in non-schizophrenic subjects as well. Dimaggio *et al.* (2008, p. 780) cite studies showing that 'people without psychiatric conditions who have a limited ability to recognise their own thoughts and feelings, sometimes called alexithymia, also have difficulty recognising, understanding and empathizing with the feelings of other[s]'. So it is more plausible that there are systematic paired deficits of experiencing and ascription for all emotions; and systematic paired over-ascription of emotions in subjects who over-produce that emotion. Again, this is consistent with the ST as augmented by the Affect Mismatch ideas I have proposed.

Notes

1 See Harrington, Siegert, and McClure (2005, p. 257) and Lincoln *et al.* (2011, S26).
2 Scherzer *et al.* (2012, pp. 1–2) provide a comprehensive series of references further describing ToM performance in schizophrenic subjects. See also Brüne (2005), Harrington, Siegert, and McClure (2005) and Sprong *et al.* (2007) for literature reviews.
3 Mitchell, Currie, and Ziegler (2009b) use the salience of S's beliefs to explain systematic ToM error.
4 The results of Bosco *et al.* (2009, p. 312) to the effect that 'first-person ToM is better preserved in schizophrenia than third-person ToM' could potentially be a problem for this line. However, Bosco *et al.* (2009, p. 312) themselves note contradictory evidence and Badgaiyan (2009) suggests known memory deficits in schizophrenic subjects will be problematic if ToM is assessed by asking subjects about the past, as Bosco *et al.* (2009) did.
5 Sarfati and Hardy-Baylé (1999) attribute the term in single quotes to Frith.
6 An objection to this account can arise from results holding that patients with 'subjective symptoms of passivity such as thought insertion or delusions of alien control and patients in remission performed relatively normally on ToM tasks' (Brüne 2005, p. 34). This suggests that it would be useful to have some more data specifically relating to introspection abilities, if a non-ipseity related explanation of ToM slowness can be found.
7 See Parkes (1995) for more on Nietzsche's 'revisioning of the I in terms of drives'; see also Gardner (Gemes and May 2009, Chapter 1).
8 Against this, Kettle, O'Brien-Simpson, and Allen (2008) find ToM deficits in first-episode schizophrenic subjects but not in depressed subjects.
9 Also note the finding of Brazo *et al.* (2012, p. S142) that schizophrenic subjects exhibit 'impaired performances in facial emotion recognition and ToM processes'.
10 Harrington, Siegert, and McClure (2005, p. 275) disagree with the conclusion that ToM impairments are predominantly associated with negative symptoms.
11 The 'effect size statistic is computed as the difference between the mean of the schizophrenia group and the mean of the control group, divided by the pooled standard deviation' (Sprong *et al.* 2007, p. 7).

11 Conclusions

We began by setting out our central task. This was to defend ST against a serious challenge from TT and hybrid theorists. The challenge was that ST alone could not account for the observed systematic errors in ToM performance of different kinds under different types of scenario. No response had been provided by the ST side to this challenge, and therefore it could be seen that there was an urgent need for ST proponents to provide a response. Such a response is now in place, and we may now see that the response is comprehensive, parsimonious and convincing. We may therefore conclude that ST alone is in a stronger position than had been thought, and the TT and especially the mainstream hybrid positions are to the same extent weakened.

The story began with a consideration of the possible logical variety of accounts of ToM. We examined both the scientific and modular versions of TT, and the transformation and replication variants of ST. We spent some time considering further possible variants of ST, all of which appeared worthy of further consideration. We did not select a champion; the purpose of this book was to defend all versions of ST. The debate as to which version if any is superior may be deferred. The more serious problem of whether ST was in fact separate from TT was considered; we saw that the 'collapse risk' of ST entailing TT was in fact manageable. Avoiding the error of 'setting the bar too low' was crucial here. With that in hand, we could be confident that there was a version of ST which could be separate from TT and could succeed without needing to decide which exact one it was.

We then gave the TT opposition, ably represented by Saxe, their best case. We agreed that there was a serious problem for ST in explaining the systematic errors in ToM. We did not attempt to deny that these errors occurred or that they were systematic. We agreed that TT could explain them parsimoniously by assuming the employment of a false ToM axiom. We agreed that ST needed a response. We conceded that the difficulty for ST was sharpened by Saxe's astute observation that the errors were systematically different in different scenarios. Why would ToM errors be like that if ST were correct? After all, one of the ST claims is that we use our own minds to simulate our own minds in different circumstances, so how could we be wrong? We considered four different types of data introduced by Saxe: the 'too rosy' ToM error cases; the 'too cynical' cases; the charge of suspicious congruency where our false beliefs about minds seem to corrupt our ToM and some developmental data where it looks like children use a false ToM axiom. The conclusion at this stage was that the TT opposition to ST had a very strong case which needed answering.

We then moved on to consider whether the mainstream hybrid approach could deal with these problems, and decided that it could not. The idea was that hybrid approaches must be the right answer because the challenge set out above to ST must mean that some TT is needed to respond to the challenge. We saw though that there were two sorts of difficulty for hybrid positions. One sort was that such hybrid positions involve TT and therefore inherit all of the objections to TT. But a further, unique and really quite severe sort of difficulty arises from trying to make TT and ST work together. These severe problems around resolving questions such as whether and how TT and ST interact and how that works led us to dismiss the mainstream hybrid position.

The stage was then set for a new approach. We introduced the Bias Mismatch Defence, suggesting that there were new resources available to ST to allow it to respond to the various forms of the systematic error challenge by allowing that S and O may apply different cognitive biases. Moreover, they may do so systematically because either they are differently involved affectively speaking in the particular scenario, or because they use different systems of reasoning. We outlined the various biases that we would later employ to explain a large array of data that TT proponents use to show systematic ToM error.

The next four chapters, from Chapter 6 to Chapter 9, represented the data-driven heart of the argument. We saw how different biases being applied by S and O could explain dozens of experiments in both the 'too rosy' and 'too cynical' directions of ToM error. We also dealt with the suspicious congruency challenge by using bias mismatches. Naturally, if some commentators suggest different combinations of biases to explain the data, that would constitute a 'friendly amendment', remaining entirely consistent with the Bias Mismatch Defence.

We further demanded that all positions take coherent stances according to whether they assert or deny introspectionism, behaviourism and all such claims: no reasonable position may simultaneously assert or deny *any* claim. We saw also how a hitherto unremarked complexity in the task for children performing the False Belief Task could explain the data without resorting to the assumption that they employed a false ToM axiom, as TT proponents claim. The new ST idea here was that they must disinhibit a previously inhibited response in order to succeed on the False Belief Task. Since we know independently that children find such disinhibition difficult, we have a new ST explanation of the data. Here, as elsewhere in this book, we have seen how elements of psychology may be applied in other novel areas of psychology to explain the data.

We closed this book with some more speculative remarks on the topic of ToM deficits in schizophrenia. Perhaps these remarks may be of some use to those researching schizophrenia; we may certainly hope so. But what they clearly did was introduce new arguments for ST as against TT: it looks as though the observed ToM deficits in schizophrenic subjects are easily explained on ST. By contrast, it is not clear what explanations are available to TT proponents. If they provide some, we may consider them. TT proponents must also explain why schizophrenic subjects exhibit paired deficits in experiencing and ascribing certain emotions, while such an explanation is automatic on ST.

In sum: we have shown that ST can not only respond to the systematic error challenge but it may do so more parsimoniously than the alternatives. We may therefore conclude that the current mainstream hybrid/TT consensus is in error so ST is the correct account of ToM.

Bibliography

Achim, A. M. *et al.* (2014). 'Poster #T3 Predictors Of Theory Of Mind And Social Functioning Impairments In Patients With Recent-Onset Of Psychosis'. In: *Schizophrenia Research* 153, Supplement 1.0. Abstracts Of The 4th Biennial Schizophrenia International Research Conference, S289–S290. DOI: 10.1016/S0920-9964(14)70820-5.

Andrews, K. (2008). 'It's In Your Nature: A Pluralistic Folk Psychology'. In: *Synthese* 165.1, pp. 13–29. DOI: 10.1007/S11229-007-9230-5.

Anselmetti, S. *et al.* (2009). '"Theory" Of Mind Impairment In Patients Affected By Schizophrenia And In Their Parents'. In: *Schizophrenia Research* 115.2–3, pp. 278–285. DOI: 10.1016/J.Schres.2009.09.018.

Apperly, I. A. (2008). 'Beyond Simulation-Theory And Theory-Theory: Why Social Cognitive Neuroscience Should Use Its Own Concepts To Study "Theory Of Mind"'. In: *Cognition* 107.1, pp. 266–283. DOI: 10.1016/J.Cognition.2007.07.019.

Apperly, I. A. (2009). 'Alternative Routes To Perspective-Taking: Imagination And Rule-Use May Be Better Than Simulation And Theorising'. In: *British Journal Of Developmental Psychology* 27.3, pp. 545–553. DOI: 10.1348/026151008X400841.

Arkway, A. (2000). 'The Simulation Theory, The Theory Theory And Folk Psychological Explanation'. In: *Philosophical Studies* 98.2, pp. 115–137. DOI: 10.1023/A%3A1018331121169.

Asch, S. E. (1952). *Social Psychology*. Prentice-Hall. URL: http://www.worldcat.org/title/social-psychology/oclc/254969

Bach, T. (2011). 'Structure-Mapping: Directions From Simulation To Theory'. In: *Philosophical Psychology* 24.1, p. 23. DOI: 10.1080/09515089.2010.533261.

Badgaiyan, R. D. (2009). 'Theory Of Mind And Schizophrenia'. In: *Consciousness And Cognition* 18.1, pp. 320–322. DOI: 10.1016/j.concog.2008.10.008.

Balzan, R. P. *et al.* (2013). 'Metacognitive Training For Patients With Schizophrenia: Preliminary Evidence For A Targeted, Single-Module Programme'. In: *The Australian And New Zealand Journal Of Psychiatry*. DOI: 10.1177/0004867413508451.

Baron-Cohen, S. (1993). 'The Concept Of Intentionality: Invented Or Innate?' In: *Behavioral And Brain Sciences* 16.1, pp. 29–30. DOI: 10.1017/S0140525X00028661.

Baron-Cohen, S. (2001). 'Theory Of Mind In Normal Development And Autism'. In: *Prisme* 34, pp. 174–183. URL: http://www.autism-community.com/wp-content/uploads/2010/11/TOM-in-TD-and-ASD.pdf

Bellugi, U. *et al.* (2007). 'Affect, Social Behavior, And The Brain In Williams Syndrome'. In: *Current Directions In Psychological Science* 16.2, pp. 99–104. DOI: 10.1111/j.1467-8721.2007.00484.x.

Bem, D. J. (1967). 'Serf-Perception: An Alternative Interpretation Of Cognitive Dissonance Phenomena'. In: *Psychological Review* 74.3, pp. 183–200. URL: http://www.ncbi.nlm.nih.gov/pubmed/5342882

Bem, D. J. (1972). 'Self-Perception Theory'. In: *Advances in Experimental Social Psychology*, ed. by L. Berkowitz. Vol. 6. Academic Press, pp. 1–62. DOI: 10.1016/S0065-2601(08)60024-6.

Biggs, S. (2007). 'The Phenomenal Mindreader: A Case For Phenomenal Simulation'. In: *Philosophical Psychology* 20.1, p. 29. DOI: 10.1080/09515080601108013.

Birch, S. A. J. and P. Bloom (2004). 'Understanding Children's And Adults' Limitations In Mental State Reasoning'. In: *Trends In Cognitive Sciences* 8.6, pp. 255–260. DOI: 10.1016/J.Tics.2004.04.011.

Birchwood, M. J. and C. Jackson (2001). *Schizophrenia–Clinical Psychology A Modular Course*. Psychology Press. ISBN: 9780863775536. URL: https://www.worldcat.org/title/schizophrenia/oclc/48239865

Bishop, M. A. and S. M. Downes (2002). 'The Theory Theory Thrice Over: The Child As Scientist, Superscientist, Or Social Institution?' In: *Studies In History And Philosophy Of Science* 33.1, pp. 117–132. DOI: 10.1016/S0039-3681(01)00029-2.

Blackburn, S. W (1992). 'Theory, Observation, And Drama'. In: *Mind And Language* 7.1–2, pp. 187–203. DOI: 10.1111/J.1468-0017.1992.Tb00204.X.

Bora, E. and C. Pantelis (2012). 'Poster #141 Theory Of Mind Impairment At Risk Conditions To Psychosis And In First-Degree Relatives Of Schizophrenia: Systematic Review And Meta-Analysis'. In: *Schizophrenia Research* 136, Supplement 1.0. Abstracts Of The 3rd Biennial Schizophrenia International Research Conference, S142. DOI: 10.1016/S0920-9964(12)70455-3.

Bosco, F. M. *et al.* (2009). 'Th.O.M.A.S.: An Exploratory Assessment Of Theory Of Mind In Schizophrenic Subjects'. In: *Cogprints* 18.1, pp. 306–319. DOI: 10.1016/j.concog.2008.06.006.

Botterill, G. and P. Carruthers (1999). *The Philosophy Of Psychology*. Cambridge University Press. ISBN: 9780521559157. URL: http://www.worldcat.org/title/philosophy-of-psychology/oclc/51037082

Bozikas, V P. *et al.* (2011). 'Insights Into Theory Of Mind In Schizophrenia: The Impact Of Cognitive Impairment'. In: *Schizophrenia Research* 130.1–3, pp. 130–136. DOI: 10.1016/J.Schres.2011.04.025.

Bramel, D. (1962). 'A Dissonance Theory Approach To Defensive Projection'. In: *Journal of Abnormal and Social Psychology* 64, pp. 121–129. URL: http://www.ncbi.nlm.nih.gov/pubmed/13872441

Brazo, P. *et al.* (2012). 'Poster #142 Social Cognition In Schizophrenic Patients: Which Role For Facial Emotion Recognition And Theory Of Mind?' In: *Schizophrenia Research* 136, Supplement 1.0. Abstracts Of The 3rd Biennial Schizophrenia International Research Conference, S142. DOI: 10.1016/S0920-9964(12)70456-5.

Brüne, M. (2005). '"Theory Of Mind" In Schizophrenia: A Review Of The Literature'. In: *Schizophrenia Bulletin* 31.1, pp. 21–42. DOI: 10.1093/Schbul/Sbi002.

Brüne, M. and L. Bodenstein (2005). 'Proverb Comprehension Reconsidered – "Theory Of Mind" And The Pragmatic Use Of Language In Schizophrenia'.

In: *Schizophrenia Research* 75.2–3, pp. 233–239. DOI: 10.1016/j.schres.2004.11.006.

Burrows, G., T. Norman, and G. Rubinstein (1986). *Handbook Of Studies On Schizophrenia: Epidemiology, Aetiology And Clinical Features.* Elsevier. URL: http://www.worldcat.org/title/handbook-of-studies-on-schizophrenia/oclc/13092404

Butcher, J. N., S. Mineka, and J. M. Hooley (2010). *Abnormal Psychology.* Allyn & Bacon. ISBN: 9780205594955. URL: http://www.worldcat.org/title/abnormal-psychology/oclc/298325737

Butterfill, S. A. and I. A. Apperly (2013). 'How To Construct A Minimal Theory Of Mind'. In: *Mind And Language* 28.5, pp. 606–637. DOI: 10.1111/Mila.12036.

Campbell, J. (1999). 'Schizophrenia, The Space Of Reasons, And Thinking As A Motor Process'. In: *The Monist* 82.4, pp. 609–625. DOI: 10.5840/Monist199982426.

Carruthers, P. (2009). 'Simulation And The First-Person'. In: *Philosophical Studies* 144.3, pp. 467–475. DOI: 10.1007/S11098-009-9357-Y.

Carruthers, P. and P. K. Smith (1996). *Theories Of Theories Of Mind.* Cambridge University Press. ISBN: 9780521559164. URL: http://www.worldcat.org/title/theories-of-theories-of-mind/oclc/807599472

Cassetta, B. D. and V. Goghari (2014). 'Poster #T40 Theory Of Mind And Personality Pathology In Schizophrenia Patients And First-Degree Relatives'. In: *Schizophrenia Research* 153, Supplement 1.0. Abstracts Of The 4th Biennial Schizophrenia International Research Conference, S303. DOI: 10.1016/S0920-9964(14)70857–6.

Chalmers, D. J. (1997). *The Conscious Mind: In Search Of A Fundamental Theory.* Oxford University Press. ISBN: 9780195117899. URL: http://www.worldcat.org/title/conscious-mind/oclc/439674143

Cherlin, A. (1990). 'A Review: The Strange Career Of The "Harvard-Yale Study"'. In: *The Public Opinion Quarterly* 54.1, pp. 117–124. URL: http://www.jstor.org/stable/2749395

Cherniak, C. (1983). 'Rationality And The Structure Of Human Memory'. In: *Synthese* 57.2, pp. 163–186. DOI: 10.1007/BF01064000.

Cockburn, P. and H. Cockburn (2011). *Henry's Demons: Living With Schizophrenia, A Father And Son's Story.* Simon & Schuster UK. ISBN: 9781847377111. URL: https://www.worldcat.org/title/henrys-demons-living-with-schizophrenia-a-father-and-sons-story/oclc/611964981

Cohan, J. A. (2002). '"I Didn't Know" And "I Was Only Doing My Job": Has Corporate Governance Careened Out Of Control? A Case Study Of Enron's Information Myopia'. In: *Journal Of Business Ethics* 40.3, pp. 275–299. URL: http://www.jstor.org/stable/25074887

Corcoran, R., C. Cahill, and C. Frith (1997). 'The Appreciation Of Visual Jokes In People With Schizophrenia: A Study Of "Mentalising" Ability'. In: *Schizophrenia Research* 24.3, pp. 319–327. DOI: 10.1016/S0920-9964(96)00117-X.

Corcoran, R., G. Mercer, and C. Frith (1995). 'Schizophrenia, Symptomatology And Social Inference: Investigating "Theory Of Mind" In People With Schizophrenia'. In: *Schizophrenia Research* 17.1, pp. 5–13. DOI: 10.1016/0920-9964(95)00024–G.

Crane, T. (2003). *The Mechanical Mind: A Philosophical Introduction To Minds, Machines And Mental Representation.* Taylor & Francis. ISBN: 9780203426319.

URL: http://www.worldcat.org/title/mechanical-mind-a-philosophical-introduction-to-minds-machines-and-mental/oclc/437079517
Daniel, S. (1993). 'The Anthropology Of Folk Psychology'. In: *Behavioral And Brain Sciences* 16.1, pp. 38–39. DOI: 10.1017/S0140525X00028752.
Darley, J. M. and C. D. Batson (1973). '"From Jerusalem To Jericho": A Study Of Situational And Dispositional Variables In Helping Behavior'. In: *Journal Of Personality And Social Psychology* 27.1, pp. 100–108. DOI: 10.1037/H0034449.
D'Ausilio, A. *et al.* (2009). 'The Motor Somatotopy Of Speech Perception'. In: *Current Biology* 19.5, pp. 381–385. DOI: 10.1016/J.Cub.2009.01.017.
David, A. S., S. Kapur, and P. McGuffin (2012). *Schizophrenia: The Final Frontier – A Festschrift For Robin M. Murray.* Taylor & Francis. ISBN: 9781136670879. URL: http://www.worldcat.org/title/schizophrenia-the-final-frontier-a-festschrift-for-robin-m-murray/oclc/671465387
Davidson, D. (1963). 'Actions, Reasons, And Causes'. In: *Journal Of Philosophy* 60, pp. 685–700. DOI: 10.1093/0199246270.003.0001.
Davidson, D. (2001). *Inquiries Into Truth And Interpretation.* Vol. 11. Oxford University Press, pp. 27–40. DOI: 10.1093/0199246297.001.0001.
Davies, M. and T. Stone (1995). *Folk Psychology: The Theory Of Mind Debate.* Wiley. ISBN: 9780631195153. URL: http://www.worldcat.org/title/folk-psychology-theory-of-mind-debate/oclc/301528886
Davies, M. and T. Stone (2001). 'Mental Simulation, Tacit Theory, And The Threat Of Collapse'. In: *Philosophical Topics* 29, pp. 127–173. DOI: 10.5840/philtopics2001291/212.
Dennett, D. C. (1979). *Brainstorms: Philosophical Essays On Mind And Psychology.* Harvester. ISBN: 9780855275853. URL: http://www.worldcat.org/title/brainstorms-philosophical-essays-on-mind-and-psychology/oclc/5329396
Dennett, D. C. (1993). *Consciousness Explained.* Penguin Adult. ISBN: 9780140128673. URL: http://www.worldcat.org/title/consciousness-explained/oclc/28709065
Dennett, D. C. (2007). *Breaking The Spell: Religion As A Natural Phenomenon.* Penguin Adult. ISBN: 9780141017778. URL: http://www.worldcat.org/title/breaking-the-spell-religion-as-a-natural-phenomenon/oclc/470564789
Dimaggio, G. *et al.* (2008). 'Know Yourself And You Shall Know The Other . . . To A Certain Extent: Multiple Paths Of Influence Of Self-Reflection On Mindreading'. In: *Consciousness And Cognition* 17.3, pp. 778–789. DOI: 10.1016/J.Concog.2008.02.005.
Dreyfus, H. L. (2006). 'Overcoming The Myth Of The Mental'. In: *Topoi* 25.1–2, pp. 43–49. DOI: 10.1007/S11245-006-0006-1.
Edwards, K. and E. E Smith (1996). 'A Disconfirmation Bias In The Evaluation Of Arguments'. In: *Journal Of Personality And Social Psychology* 71.1, pp. 5–24. DOI: 10.1037//0022-3514.71.1.5.
Epley, N. *et al.* (2004). 'Perspective Taking As Egocentric Anchoring And Adjustment'. In: *Journal Of Personality And Social Psychology* 87, pp. 327–339. DOI: 10.1037/0022-3514.87.3.327.
Evans, D. L. *et al.* (2005). *Treating And Preventing Adolescent Mental Health Disorders: What We Know And What We Don't Know: A Research Agenda For Improving The Mental Health Of Our Youth.* Oxford University Press. ISBN: 9780195173642. DOI: 10.1093/9780195173642.001.0001.

Evans, J. S. B. T. (1990). *Bias In Human Reasoning: Causes And Consequences*. Lawrence Erlbaum Associates, Incorporated. ISBN: 9780863771569. URL: http://www.worldcat.org/title/bias-in-human-reasoning-causes-and-consequences/oclc/35142289

Fadiga, L. *et al.* (2002). 'Speech Listening Specifically Modulates The Excitability Of Tongue Muscles'. In: *European Journal Of Neuroscience* 15.2, pp. 399–402. DOI: 10.1046/J.0953-816X.2001.01874.X.

Farrant, B. M., J. Fletcher, and M. T. Maybery (2006). 'Specific Language Impairment, Theory Of Mind, And Visual Perspective Taking: Evidence For Simulation Theory And The Developmental Role Of Language'. In: *Child Development* 77.6, pp. 1842–1853. DOI: 10.1111/J.1467-8624.2006.00977.X.

Fodor, J. A. (1974). 'Special Sciences (Or: The Disunity Of Science As A Working Hypothesis)'. In: *Synthese* 28.2, pp. 97–115. DOI: 10.1007/Bf00485230.

Fodor, J. A. (1987). *Psychosemantics: The Problem Of Meaning In The Philosophy Of Mind*. MIT Press. ISBN: 0262560526. URL: http://www.worldcat.org/ISBN/0262560526

Fodor, J. A. (1994). 'Concepts: A Potboiler'. In: *Cognition* 50.1–3, pp. 95–113. DOI: 10.1016/0010-0277(94)90023-X.

Fodor, J. A. (2008). *LOT 2: The Language Of Thought Revisited*. Oxford University Press. ISBN: 9780191563478. URL: http://www.worldcat.org/title/lot-2-the-language-of-thought-revisited/oclc/299380071

Fodor, J. A. and E. Lepore (1996). 'The Red Herring And The Pet Fish: Why Concepts Still Can't Be Prototypes'. In: *Cognition* 58.2, pp. 253–270. DOI: 10.1016/0010-0277(95)00694-X.

Friedman, O. and A. R. Petrashek (2009). 'Children Do Not Follow The Rule "Ignorance Means Getting It Wrong"'. In: *Journal Of Experimental Child Psychology* 102.1, pp. 114–121. DOI: 10.1016/J.Jecp.2008.07.009.

Frith, C. and R. Corcoran (1996). 'Exploring "Theory Of Mind" In People With Schizophrenia'. In: *Psychological Medicine* 26.3, pp. 521–30. DOI: 10.1017/S0033291700035601.

Fuller, T (2013). 'Is Scientific Theory Change Similar To Early Cognitive Development? Gopnik On Science And Childhood'. In: *Philosophical Psychology* 26.1, p. 109. DOI: 10.1080/09515089.2011.625114.

Gallese, V. and A. I. Goldman (1998). 'Mirror Neurons And The Simulation Theory Of Mind-Reading'. In: *Trends In Cognitive Sciences* 2.12, pp. 493–501. DOI: 10.1016/S1364-6613(98)01262-5.

Garson, J. W. (2003). 'Simulation And Connectionism: What Is The Connection?' In: *Philosophical Psychology* 16.4, pp. 499–514. DOI: 10.1080/0951508032000121805.

Gelder, M. G. *et al.* (2012). *New Oxford Textbook Of Psychiatry*. Oxford University Press. ISBN: 9780199696758. DOI: 10.1093/med/9780199696758.001.0001.

Gemes, K. and S. May (2009). *Nietzsche On Freedom And Autonomy*. Oxford University Press. ISBN: 9780199231560. URL: http://www.worldcat.org/title/nietzsche-on-freedom-and-autonomy/oclc/803955501

Gilovich, T. (1993). *How We Know What Isn't So*. Free Press. ISBN: 9780029117064. URL: http://www.worldcat.org/title/how-we-know-what-isnt-so-the-fallibility-of-human-reason-in-everyday-life/oclc/832440458

Gilovich, T., D. Griffin, and D. Kahneman (2002). *Heuristics And Biases: The Psychology Of Intuitive Judgment*. Cambridge University Press. ISBN:

9780521796798. URL: http://www.worldcat.org/title/heuristics-and-biases-the-psychology-of-intuitive-judgement/oclc/47364085
Glymour, C. (2000). 'Android Epistemology For Babies: Reflections On "Words, Thoughts And Theories"'. In: *Synthese* 122.1/2, pp. 53–68. URL: http://www.jstor.org/stable/20118243
Goldie, P. (1999). 'How We Think Of Others' Emotions'. In: *Mind And Language* 14.4, pp. 394–423. DOI: 10.1111/1468-0017.00118.
Goldie, P. (2002). *The Emotions*. Clarendon Press. ISBN: 9780199253043. URL: http://www.worldcat.org/title/emotions-a-philosophical-exploration/oclc/807099376
Goldie, P. (2011). 'Grief: A Narrative Account'. In: *Ratio* 24.2, pp. 119–137. DOI: 10.1111/J.1467-9329.2011.00488.X.
Goldman, A. I. (1989). 'Interpretation Psychologized'. In: *Mind And Language* 4.3, pp. 161–185. DOI: 10.1111/J.1468-0017.1989.Tb00249.X.
Goldman, A. I. (1992). 'In Defense Of The Simulation Theory'. *In: Mind And Language* 7.1–2, pp. 104–119. DOI: 10.1111/J.1468-0017.1992.Tb00200.X.
Goldman, A. I. (1993a). 'Functionalism, The Theory-Theory And Phenomenology'. In: *Behavioral And Brain Sciences* 16.1, pp. 101–113. DOI: 10.1017/S0140525X00029265.
Goldman, A. I. (1993b). 'The Psychology Of Folk Psychology'. In: *Behavioral And Brain Sciences* 16.1, pp. 15–28. DOI: 10.1017/S0140525X00028648.
Goldman, A. I. (2004). 'Epistemology And The Evidential Status Of Introspective Reports I'. In: *Journal Of Consciousness Studies* 11.7–8, pp. 1–16. URL: http://philpapers.org/rec/GOLEAT-2
Goldman, A. I. (2006). *Simulating Minds: The Philosophy, Psychology, And Neuroscience Of Mindreading*. Oxford University Press, USA. ISBN: 9780198031765. URL: https://www.worldcat.org/title/simulating-minds-the-philosophy-psychology-and-neuroscience-of-mindreading/oclc/63390792
Goldman, A. I. (2009). 'Replies To Perner And Brandl, Saxe, Vignemont, And Carruthers'. In: *Philosophical Studies* 144.3, pp. 477–491. DOI: 10.1007/S11098-009-9358-X.
Goldman, A. I. and N. Sebanz (2005). 'Simulation, Mirroring, And A Different Argument From Error'. In: *Trends In Cognitive Sciences* 9.7, p. 320. DOI: 10.1016/J.Tics.2005.05.008.
Goldman, A. I. and C. S. Sripada (2005). 'Simulationist Models Of Face-Based Emotion Recognition'. In: *Cognition* 94.3, pp. 193–213. DOI. 10.1016/J.Cognition.2004.01.005.
Gopnik, A. (1993a). 'How We Know Our Minds: The Illusion Of First-Person Knowledge Of Intentionality'. In: *Behavioral And Brain Sciences* 16.1, pp. 1–14. DOI: 10.1017/S0140525X00028636.
Gopnik, A. (1993b). 'Theories And Illusions'. In: *Behavioral And Brain Sciences* 16.1, pp. 90–100. DOI: 10.1017/S0140525X00029253.
Gopnik, A. and H. M. Wellman (1992). 'Why The Child's Theory Of Mind Really Is A Theory'. In: *Mind And Language* 7.1–2, pp. 145–171. DOI: 10.1111/J.1468-0017.1992.Tb00202.X.
Gordon, R. M. (1986). 'Folk Psychology As Simulation'. In: *Mind And Language* 1.2, pp. 158–171. DOI: 10.1111/J.1468-0017.1986.Tb00324.X.
Gordon, R. M. (1992). 'The Simulation Theory: Objections And Misconceptions'. *In: Mind And Language* 7.1–2, pp. 11–34. DOI: 10.1111/J.1468-0017.1992.Tb00195.X.

Gordon, R. M. (1995). 'Sympathy, Simulation, And The Impartial Spectator'. In: *Ethics* 105.4, pp. 727–742. DOI: 10.1086/293750.
Gordon, R. M. (2005). 'Simulation And Systematic Errors In Prediction'. In: *Trends In Cognitive Sciences* 9.8, pp. 361–362. DOI: 10.1016/J.Tics.2005.06.003.
Greenwood, J. D. (1999). 'Simulation, Theory-Theory And Cognitive Penetration: No "Instance Of The Fingerpost"'. In: *Mind And Language* 14.1, pp. 32–56. DOI: 10.1111/1468-0017.00102.
Haney, C., C. Banks, and P. Zimbardo (1973). 'Interpersonal Dynamics In A Simulated Prison'. In: *International Journal Of Criminology And Penology* 1.1, pp. 69–97. URL: http://www.prisonexp.org/pdf/ijcp1973.pdf
Harrington, L., R. J. Siegert, and J. McClure (2005). 'Theory Of Mind In Schizophrenia: A Critical Review'. In: *Cognitive Neuropsychiatry* 10.4, pp. 249–286. DOI: 10.1080/13546800444000056.
Harris, P. L. (1992). 'From Simulation To Folk Psychology: The Case For Development'. In: *Mind And Language* 7.1–2, pp. 120–144. DOI: 10.1111/J.1468-0017.1992.Tb00201.X.
Harris, P. L. (2009). 'Simulation (Mostly) Rules: A Commentary'. In: *British Journal Of Developmental Psychology* 27.3, pp. 555–559. DOI: 10.1348/026151009X415484.
Heal, J. (1998). 'Understanding Other Minds From The Inside'. In: *Royal Institute Of Philosophy Supplement* 43, pp. 83–99. DOI: 10.1017/Cbo9780511615894.005.
Heal, J. (2000). 'The Inaugural Address: Other Minds, Rationality And Analogy'. In: *Aristotelian Society Supplementary Volume* 74.1, pp. 1–19. DOI: 10.1111/1467-8349.T01-1-00060.
Heal, J. (2003). *Mind, Reason And Imagination: Selected Essays In Philosophy Of Mind And Language*. Cambridge University Press. ISBN: 9780521017169. URL: http://www.worldcat.org/title/mind-reason-and-imagination-selected-essays-in-philosophy-of-mind-and-language/oclc/470066271
Herold, R. *et al.* (2002). 'Theory Of Mind Deficit In People With Schizophrenia During Remission'. In: *Psychological Medicine* 32.6, pp. 1125–1129. DOI: 10.1017/S0033291702005433.
Hume, D. (2000). *A Treatise Of Human Nature: Being An Attempt To Introduce The Experimental Method Of Reasoning Into Moral Subjects*. Oxford University Press. ISBN: 9780198751724. URL: http://www.worldcat.org/title/treatise-of-human-nature/oclc/41981924
Igoe, A. R. and H. Sullivan (1993). 'Self-Presentation Bias And Continuing Motivation Among Adolescents'. In: *The Journal Of Educational Research* 87.1, pp. 18–22. DOI: 10.1080/00220671.1993.9941161.
Irani, F. *et al.* (2006). 'Self-Face Recognition And Theory Of Mind In Patients With Schizophrenia And First-Degree Relatives'. In: *Schizophrenia Research* 88.1–3, pp. 151–60. DOI: 10.1016/J.Schres.2006.07.016.
Ivry, R. B. and T. C. Justus (2001). 'A Neural Instantiation Of The Motor Theory Of Speech Perception'. In: *Trends Neurosci* 24.9, pp. 513–515. DOI: 10.1016/S0166-2236(00)01897-X.
Jackson, F. (1999). 'All That Can Be At Issue In The Theory-Theory Simulation Debate'. In: *Philosophical Papers* 28.2, pp. 77–96. DOI: 10.1080/05568649909506593.
Johansson, P. *et al.* (2006). 'How Something Can Be Said About Telling More Than We Can Know: On Choice Blindness And Introspection'. In: *Consciousness And Cognition* 15.4, pp. 673–692. DOI: 10.1016/J.Concog.2006.09.004.

Kahneman, D. (2011). *Thinking, Fast And Slow.* Allen Lane. ISBN: 9781846140556. URL: http://www.worldcat.org/title/thinking-fast-and-slow/oclc/751738755

Kamtekar, R. (2004). 'Situationism And Virtue Ethics On The Content Of Our Character'. In: *Ethics* 114.3, pp. 458–491. DOI: 10.1086/381696.

Kettle, J. W. L., L. O'Brien-Simpson, and N. B. Allen (2008). 'Impaired Theory Of Mind In First-Episode Schizophrenia: Comparison With Community, University And Depressed Controls'. In: *Schizophrenia Research* 99.1–3, pp. 96–102. DOI: 10.1016/J.Schres.2007.11.011.

King, D. B. and M. Wertheimer (1992). 'Review Of The Legacy Of Solomon Asch: Essays In Cognition And Social Psychology By Irvin Rock'. In: *The American Journal Of Psychology* 105.1, pp. 123–130. URL: http://www.jstor.org/stable/1422986

Koelkebeck, K. *et al.* (2010). 'Theory Of Mind In First-Episode Schizophrenia Patients: Correlations With Cognition And Personality Traits'. In: *Schizophrenia Research* 119.1–3, pp. 115 –123. DOI: 10.1016/J.Schres.2009.12.015.

Konstantakopoulos, G. *et al.* (2014). 'The Relationship Between Insight And Theory Of Mind In Schizophrenia'. In: *Schizophrenia Research* 152.1, pp. 217–222. DOI: 10.1016/J.Schres.2013.11.022.

Kopcha, T. J. and H. Sullivan (2006). 'Self-Presentation Bias In Surveys Of Teachers' Educational Technology Practices'. In: *Educational Technology Research And Development* 55.6, pp. 627–646. DOI: 10.1007/S11423-006-9011-8.

Kruger, J. and T. Gilovich (1999). '"Naive Cynicism" In Everyday Theories Of Responsibility Assessment: On Biased Assumptions Of Bias'. In: *Journal Of Personality And Social Psychology* 76.5, pp. 743–753. DOI: 10.1037/0022-3514.76.5.743.

Kühberger, A *et al.* (1995). 'Choice Or No Choice: Is The Langer Effect Evidence Against Simulation?' In: *Mind And Language* 10.4, pp. 423–436. DOI: 10.1111/J.1468-0017.1995.Tb00022.X.

Kunda, Z. (1990). 'The Case For Motivated Reasoning'. In: *Psychological Bulletin* 108.3, pp. 480–498. DOI: 10.1037/0033-2909.108.3.480.

Lagodka, A. *et al.* (2010). 'Is Theory Of Mind Linked To Social Impairment In Elderly Patients With Schizophrenia?' In: *Schizophrenia Research* 117.2–3, pp. 325–325. DOI: 10.1016/J.Schres.2010.02.554.

Langdon, R. *et al.* (2001). 'Mentalising, Exec. Planning And Disengagement In Schizophrenia'. In: *Cognitive Neuropsychiatry* 6.2, pp. 81–108. DOI: 10.1080/135468000042000061.

Leonhardt, B. L. *et al.* (2014). 'Poster #T138 Capacities For Theory Of Mind, Metacognition, And Neurocognitive Function As Independently Related To Performance On A Test Of Emotional Recognition'. In: *Schizophrenia Research* 153, Supplement 1.0. Abstracts Of The 4th Biennial Schizophrenia International Research Conference, S338. DOI: 10.1016/S0920-9964(14)70955-7.

Lewis, M. M. (2004). *Moneyball: The Art Of Winning An Unfair Game.* W. W. Norton. ISBN: 9780393324815. URL: http://www.worldcat.org/title/moneyball/oclc/778974649

Liberman, A. (1985). 'The Motor Theory Of Speech Perception Revised'. In: *Cognition* 21.1, pp. 1–36. DOI: 10.1016/0010-0277(85)90021-6.

Lincoln, T. M. *et al.* (2011). 'Negative Symptoms And Social Cognition: Identifying Targets For Psychological Interventions'. In: *Schizophrenia Bulletin* 37 Suppl 2, S23–32. DOI: 10.1093/Schbul/Sbr066.

Lysaker, P. H. *et al.* (2012). 'Development Of Personal Narratives As A Mediator Of The Impact Of Deficits In Social Cognition And Social Withdrawal On Negative Symptoms In Schizophrenia'. In: *The Journal Of Nervous And Mental Disease* 200.4, pp. 290–295. DOI: 10.1097/Nmd.0B013E31824Cb0F4.

Malle, B. F. and S. D. Hodges (2005). *Other Minds: How Humans Bridge The Divide Between Self And Others.* Guilford Publication. ISBN: 9781593854683. URL: http://www.worldcat.org/title/other-minds-how-humans-bridge-the-divide-between-self-and-others/oclc/141382018

Margolis, E. and S. Laurence (2012). 'Concepts'. In: *The Stanford Encyclopedia Of Philosophy.* Ed. by Edward N. Zalta. Fall 2012. Metaphysics Research Lab, Csli, Stanford University. URL: http://Plato.Stanford.Edu/Archives/Fall2012/Entries/Concepts

Markman, K. D., W. M. P. Klein, and J. A. Suhr (2012). *Handbook Of Imagination And Mental Simulation.* Taylor & Francis. ISBN: 9781136678097. URL: https://www.worldcat.org/title/handbook-of-imagination-and-mental-simulation/oclc/222134918

McKay, R. T. and D. C. Dennett (2009). 'The Evolution Of Misbelief'. In: *Behavioral And Brain Sciences* 32.6, pp. 493–510. DOI: 10.1017/S0140525X09990975.

McKee, M. and R. Diethelm (2010). 'How The Growth Of Denialism Undermines Public Health'. In: *British Medical Journal* 341.7786, pp. 1309–1311. URL: http://www.jstor.org/stable/25766559

Milgram, S. (1963). 'Behavioral Study Of Obedience'. In: *The Journal Of Abnormal And Social Psychology* 67.4, p. 371. DOI: 10.1037/H0040525.

Miller, D. and R. Ratner (1998). 'The Disparity Between The Actual And Assumed Power Of Self-Interest'. In: *Journal Of Personality And Social Psychology* 74.1, pp. 53–62. DOI: 10.1037//0022-3514.74.1.53.

Mind and Language (1992). 'Introduction'. In: *Mind and Language* 7.1–2, pp. 1–10. DOI: 10.1111/J.1468-0017.1992.Tb00194.X.

Mitchell, J. P. (2005). 'The False Dichotomy Between Simulation And Theory-Theory: The Argument's Error'. In: *Trends In Cognitive Sciences* 9.8, pp. 363–364. DOI: 10.1016/J.Tics.2005.06.010.

Mitchell, P., G. Currie, and F. Ziegler (2009a). 'Is There An Alternative To Simulation And Theory In Understanding The Mind?' In: *British Journal Of Developmental Psychology* 27.3, pp. 561–567. DOI: 10.1348/026151009X441935.

Mitchell, P., G. Currie, and F. Ziegler (2009b). 'Two Routes To Perspective: Simulation And Rule-Use As Approaches To Mentalizing'. In: *British Journal Of Developmental Psychology* 27.3, pp. 513–543. DOI: 10.1348/026151008X334737.

Mitchell, P. and K. J. Riggs (2001). *Children's Reasoning And The Mind.* Psychology Press. ISBN: 9780863778551. URL: http://www.worldcat.org/title/childrens-reasoning-and-the-mind/oclc/807892904

Nagel, J. (2011). 'The Psychological Basis Of The Harman-Vogel Paradox'. In: *Philosophers' Imprint* 11.5, pp. 1–28. URL: http://hdl.handle.net/2027/spo.3521354.0011.005.

Nestler, S. (2010). 'Belief Perseverance'. In: *Social Psychology* 41.1, pp. 35–41. DOI: 10.1027/1864-9335/A000006.

Nichols, S. and S. P. Stich (2003). *Mindreading: An Integrated Account Of Pretence, Self-Awareness, And Understanding Other Minds.* Clarendon. ISBN: 9780198236108. DOI: 10.1093/0198236107.001.0001.

Nichols, S., S. P. Stich, and A. Leslie (1995). 'Choice Effects And The Ineffectiveness Of Simulation: Response To Kühberger et al'. In: *Mind And Language* 10.4, pp. 437–445. DOI: 10.1111/J.1468-0017.1995.Tb00023.X.

Nietzsche, F. W. (2003). *Beyond Good And Evil: Prelude To A Philosophy Of The Future*. Penguin. ISBN: 9780140449235. URL: https://www.worldcat.org/title/beyond-good-and-evil-prelude-to-a-philosophy-of-the-future-friedrich-nietzsche/oclc/51108998

Nisbett, R. E. and N. Bellows (1977). 'Verbal Reports About Causal Influences On Social Judgments: Private Access Versus Public Theories'. In: *Journal Of Personality And Social Psychology* 35.9, pp. 613–624. DOI: 10.1037//0022-3514.35.9.613.

Nisbett, R. E. and T. D. Wilson (1977). 'Telling More Than We Can Know: Verbal Reports On Mental Processes'. In: *Psychological Review* 84.3, pp. 231–259. DOI: 10.1037//0033-295X.84.3.231.

Ogden, R. M. (1933). 'Gestalt Psychology And Behaviourism'. In: *The American Journal Of Psychology* 45.1, p. 151. DOI: 10.2307/1414201.

Onishi, K. H. and R. Baillargeon (2005). 'Do 15-Month-Old Infants Understand False Beliefs?' In: *Science* 308.5719, pp. 255–258. DOI: 10.1126/Science.1107621.

O'Shaughnessy, B. (1991). 'The Anatomy Of Consciousness'. In: *Philosophical Issues* 1, pp. 135–177. DOI: 10.2307/1522927.

Parkes, G. (1995). 'Nietzsche On The Fabric(ation) Of Experience'. In: *Journal Of Nietzsche Studies* 9/10, pp. 7–35. URL: http://www.jstor.org/stable/20717622

Pedersen, A. *et al.* (2012). 'Theory Of Mind In Patients With Schizophrenia: Is Mentalizing Delayed?' In: *Schizophrenia Research* 137.1–3, pp. 224–9. DOI: 10.1016/J.Schres.2012.02.022.

Peterson, D. M. and K. J. Riggs (1999). 'Adaptive Modelling And Mindreading'. In: *Mind And Language* 14.1, pp. 80–112. DOI: 10.1111/1468-0017.00104.

Pickup, G. J. and C. Frith (2001). 'Theory Of Mind Impairments In Schizophrenia: Symptomatology, Severity, Specificity'. In: *Psychological Medicine* 31.2, pp. 207–220. DOI: 10.1017/S0033291701003385.

Pousa, E. *et al.* (2008). 'Exploratory Study Of The Association Between Insight And Theory Of Mind (ToM) In Stable Schizophrenia Patients'. In: *Cognitive Neuropsychiatry* 13.3, pp. 210–232. DOI: 10.1080/13546800701849066.

Pratt, I. (1993). 'Matching And Mental-State Ascription'. In: *Behavioral And Brain Sciences* 16.1, pp. 71–72. DOI: 10.1017/S0140525X00029071.

Premack, D. and G. Woodruff (1978). 'Does The Chimpanzee Have A Theory Of Mind?' In: *Behavioral And Brain Sciences* 1.4, pp. 515–526. DOI: 10.1017/S0140525X00076512.

Prentice, R. A. (2007). 'Ethical Decision Making: More Needed Than Good Intentions'. In: *Financial Analysts Journal* 63.6, pp. 17–30. DOI: 10.2469/Faj.V63.N6.4923.

Pronin, E., T. Gilovich, and L. Ross (2004). 'Objectivity In The Eye Of The Beholder: Divergent Perceptions Of Bias In Self Versus Others'. In: *Psychological Review* 111.3, pp. 781–799. DOI: 10.1037/0033-295X.111.3.781.

Quine, W. V. (1951). 'Main Trends In Recent Philosophy: Two Dogmas Of Empiricism'. In: *The Philosophical Review* 60.1, pp. 20–43. URL: http://www.jstor.org/stable/2181906

Randall, F. *et al.* (2003). 'Attention, Theory Of Mind, And Causal Attributions In People With Persecutory Delusions: A Preliminary Investigation'. In: *Cognitive Neuropsychiatry* 8.4, pp. 287–94. DOI: 10.1080/135468000057.

Rey, G. (2013). 'We Are Not All "Self-Blind": A Defense Of A Modest Introspectionism'. In: *Mind And Language* 28.3, pp. 259–285. DOI: 10.1111/Mila.12018.

Ross, L., T. M. Amabile, and J. L. Steinmetz (1977). 'Social Roles, Social Control, And Biases In Social-Perception Processes'. In: *Journal Of Personality And Social Psychology* 35, pp. 485–494. DOI: 10.1037//0022-3514.35.7.485.

Ross, L., D. Greene, and P. House (1977). 'The "False Consensus Effect": An Egocentric Bias In Social Perception And Attribution Processes'. In: *Journal Of Experimental Social Psychology* 13.3, pp. 279 –301. DOI: 10.1016/0022-1031(77)90049-X.

Ross, L., M. R. Lepper, and M. Hubbard (1975). 'Perseverance In Self Perception And Social Perception: Biased Attributional Processes In The Debeliefing Paradigm'. In: *Journal Of Personality And Social Psychology* 32.5, pp. 880–892. DOI: 10.1037//0022-3514.32.5.880.

Ruffman, T. (1996). 'Do Children Understand The Mind By Means Of Simulation Or A Theory? Evidence From Their Understanding Of Inference'. In: *Mind And Language* 11.4, pp. 388–414. DOI: 10.1111/J.1468-0017.1996.Tb00053.X.

Ryle, G. (2009). *The Concept Of Mind*. Routledge. ISBN: 9780415485470. URL: http://www.worldcat.org/title/concept-of-mind/oclc/297405035

Salvatore, G., G. Dimaggio, and P. H. Lysaker (2007). 'An Intersubjective Perspective On Negative Symptoms Of Schizophrenia: Implications Of Simulation Theory'. In: *Cognitive Neuropsychiatry* 12.2, pp. 144–164. DOI: 10.1080/13546800600819921.

Sarfati, Y. and M. C. Hardy-Baylé (1999). 'How Do People With Schizophrenia Explain The Behaviour Of Others? A Study Of Theory Of Mind And Its Relationship To Thought And Speech Disorganization In Schizophrenia'. In: *Psychological Medicine* 29.3, pp. 613–620. URL: http://www.ncbi.nlm.nih.gov/pubmed/10405082

Sarfati, Y. *et al.* (1999). 'Investigating Theory Of Mind In Schizophrenia: Influence Of Verbalisation In Disorganised And Non-Disorganised Patients'. In: *Schizophrenia Research* 37.2, pp. 183–190. URL: http://www.ncbi.nlm.nih.gov/pubmed/10374653

Sass, L. *et al.* (2013). 'Anomalous Self-Experience In Depersonalisation And Schizophrenia: A Comparative Investigation'. In: *Consciousness And Cognition* 22.2, pp. 430–441. DOI: 10.1016/J.Concog.2013.01.009.

Saxe, R. (2005a). 'Against Simulation: The Argument From Error'. In: *Trends In Cognitive Sciences* 9.4, pp. 174–179. DOI: 10.1016/J.Tics.2005.01.012.

Saxe, R. (2005b). 'Hybrid Vigour: Reply To Mitchell'. In: *Trends In Cognitive Sciences* 9.8, p. 364. DOI: 10.1016/J.Tics.2005.06.017.

Saxe, R. (2005c). 'On Ignorance And Being Wrong: Reply To Gordon'. In: *Trends In Cognitive Sciences* 9.8, pp. 362–363. DOI: 10.1016/J.Tics.2005.06.002.

Saxe, R. (2005d). 'Tuning Forks In The Mind: Reply To Goldman And Sebanz'. In: *Trends In Cognitive Sciences* 9.7, p. 321. DOI: 10.1016/J.Tics.2005.05.011.

Scherzer, P. *et al.* (2012). 'A Study Of Theory Of Mind In Paranoid Schizophrenia: A Theory Or Many Theories?' In: *Frontiers In Psychology* 3. DOI: 10.3389/Fpsyg.2012.00432.

Scholl, B. J. and A. M. Leslie (1999). 'Modularity, Development And "Theory Of Mind"'. In: *Mind And Language* 14.1, pp. 131–153.DOI: 10.1111/1468-0017.00106.

Scholl, B. J. and A. M. Leslie (2001). 'Minds, Modules, And Meta-Analysis'. In: *Child Development* 72.3, pp. 696–701. DOI: 10.1111/1467-8624.00308.

Segal, G. M. A. (2014). 'Alcoholism, Disease And Insanity'. In: *Forthcoming In Philosophy, Psychiatry And Psychology.* URL: http://www.gabrielsegal.co.uk/recent-work/

Shamay-Tsoory, S. G. *et al.* (2007). 'Dissociation Of Cognitive From Affective Components Of Theory Of Mind In Schizophrenia'. In: *Psychiatry Research* 149.1–3, pp. 11–23. DOI: 10.1016/J.Psychres.2005.10.018.

Shin, N.-Y. *et al.* (2008). 'Deficit Of Theory Of Mind In Individuals At Ultra High Risk For Schizophrenia: Relationship With Executive Dysfunction And Its Implication For Treatment Strategy'. In: *Schizophrenia Research* 98.2008, pp. 112–113. DOI: 10.1016/J.Schres.2007.12.260.

Shoemaker, S. (1975). 'Functionalism And Qualia'. In: *Philosophical Studies* 27.5, pp. 291–315. DOI: 10.1007/BF01225748.

Short, T. L. (1992). 'The Design Of The ZEUS Regional First Level Trigger Box And Associated Trigger Studies'. PhD Thesis. University of Bristol. URL: http://discovery.ucl.ac.uk/1354624/.

Short, T. L. (2012). 'Nietzsche On Memory'. MPhilStud Thesis. UCL. URL: http://discovery.ucl.ac.uk/1421265/.

Short, T. L. (2014). 'How Can We Reconcile The Following Apparent Truths: "Sherlock Holmes Doesn't Exist" And "Sherlock Holmes Was Created By Conan Doyle"?' In: *Opticon1826* 16.8, pp. 1–9. DOI: 10.5334/Opt.Bs.

Sloman, S. A. (1996). 'The Empirical Case For Two Systems Of Reasoning'. In: *Psychological Bulletin* 119, pp. 3–22. DOI: 10.1037//0033-2909.119.1.3.

Soteriou, M. (2013). *The Mind's Construction: The Ontology Of Mind And Mental Action.* OUP Oxford. ISBN: 9780199678457. URL: http://www.worldcat.org/title/minds-construction-the-ontology-of-mind-and-mental-action/oclc/829743933

Sperling, G. (1960). 'The Information Available In Visual Presentations'. In: *Psychological Monographs* 74, pp. 1–29. DOI: 10.1037/H0093759.

Sprong, M. *et al.* (2007). 'Theory Of Mind In Schizophrenia: Meta-Analysis'. In: *The British Journal Of Psychiatry: The Journal Of Mental Science* 191, pp. 5–13. DOI: 10.1192/Bjp.Bp.107.035899.

Stanley, J. (2011). *Know How.* OUP Oxford. ISBN: 9780199695362. URL: http://www.worldcat.org/title/know-how/oclc/706025101

Stich, S. P. and S. Nichols (1992). 'Folk Psychology: Simulation Or Tacit Theory?' In: *Mind And Language* 7.1–2, pp. 35–71. DOI: 10.1111/J.1468-0017.1992.Tb00196.X.

Stich, S. P. and S. Nichols (1998). 'Theory Theory To The Max'. In: *Mind And Language* 13.3, pp. 421–449. DOI: 10.1111/1468-0017.00085.

Stich, S. P. and S. Nichols (2002). 'Folk Psychology'. In: *Blackwell Guide To Philosophy Of Mind* 7.1–2, pp. 35–71. ISBN: 9780470998762. DOI: 10.1002/9780470998762.Ch10.

Stone, T. and M. Davies (1995). *Mental Simulation: Evaluations And Applications – Reading In Mind And Language.* Wiley. ISBN: 9780631198734. URL: http://www.worldcat.org/title/mental-simulation-evaluations-and-applications/oclc/495403648

Strijbos, D. W. and L. C. De Bruin (2013). 'Universal Belief-Desire Psychology? A Dilemma For Theory Theory And Simulation Theory'. In: *Philosophical Psychology* 26.5, p. 744. DOI: 10.1080/09515089.2012.711034.

Taleb, N. N. (2007). *Fooled By Randomness: The Hidden Role Of Chance In Life And In The Markets*. Penguin Books Limited. ISBN: 9780141930237. URL: http://www.worldcat.org/title/fooled-by-randomness-the-hidden-role-of-chance-in-life-and-in-the-markets/oclc/827950242

Taleb, N. N. (2008). *The Black Swan: The Impact Of The Highly Improbable*. Penguin Books Limited. ISBN: 9780141034591. URL: http://www.worldcat.org/title/black-swan-the-impact-of-the-highly-improbable/oclc/175283761

Tversky, A. and D. Kahneman (1973). 'Availability: A Heuristic For Judging Frequency And Probability'. In: *Cognitive Psychology* 5.2, pp. 207–232. DOI: 10.1016/0010-0285(73)90033-9.

Tversky, A. and D. Kahneman (1974). 'Judgment Under Uncertainty: Heuristics And Biases'. In: *Science* 185.4157, pp. 1124–1131. DOI: 10.1126/Science.185.4157.1124.

Tversky, A. and D. Kahneman (1983). 'Extensional Versus Intuitive Reasoning: The Conjunction Fallacy In Probability Judgment'. In: *Psychological Review* 90.4, pp. 293–315. DOI: 10.1037/0033-295X.90.4.293.

Webber, J. (2010). *Reading Sartre: On Phenomenology And Existentialism*. Taylor & Francis. ISBN: 9780203844144. URL: http://www.worldcat.org/title/reading-sartre-on-phenomenology-and-existentialism/oclc/551722193

White, P. A. (1988). 'Knowing More About What We Can Tell: "Introspective Access" And Causal Report Accuracy 10 Years Later'. In: *British Journal Of Psychology* 79.1, pp. 13–45. DOI: 10.1111/J.2044-8295.1988.Tb02271.X.

Wimmer, H. and J. Perner (1983). 'Beliefs About Beliefs: Representation And Constraining Function Of Wrong Beliefs In Young Children's Understanding Of Deception'. In: *Cognition* 13.1, pp. 103–128. DOI: 10.1016/0010-0277(83)90004-5.

Wittgenstein, L. (2001). *Philosophical Investigations: The German Text, With A Revised English Translation*. Wiley. ISBN: 9780631231271. URL: http://www.worldcat.org/title/philosophical-investigations/oclc/496575871

Zobel, I. *et al.* (2010). 'Theory Of Mind Deficits In Chronically Depressed Patients'. In: *Depression And Anxiety* 27.9, pp. 821–828. DOI: 10.1002/Da.20713.

Index

For Product Safety Concerns and Information please contact our EU
representative GPSR@taylorandfrancis.com
Taylor & Francis Verlag GmbH, Kaufingerstraße 24, 80331 München, Germany

www.ingramcontent.com/pod-product-compliance
Ingram Content Group UK Ltd.
Pitfield, Milton Keynes, MK11 3LW, UK
UKHW022125190926
475702UK00013B/1650

* 9 7 8 1 1 3 8 2 9 4 3 4 9 *